Amazon Redshift Cookbook

Recipes for building modern data
warehousing solutions

Shruti Worlikar

Thiyagarajan Arumugam

Harshida Patel

BIRMINGHAM—MUMBAI

Amazon Redshift Cookbook

Group Product Manager: Kunal Parikh

Publishing Product Manager: Ali Abidi

Senior Editor: Mohammed Yusuf Imaratwale

Content Development Editor: Nazia Shaikh

Technical Editor: Arjun Varma

Copy Editor: Safis Editing

Project Coordinator: Aparna Ravikumar Nair

Proofreader: Safis Editing

Indexer: Vinayak Purushotham

Production Designer: Vijay Kamble

First published: July 2021

Production reference: 2270721

Published by Packt Publishing Ltd.
Livery Place
35 Livery Street
Birmingham
B3 2PB, UK.

ISBN 978-1-80056-968-3

www.packt.com

Foreword

Amazon Redshift is a fully managed cloud data warehouse house service that enables you to analyze all your data. Tens of thousands of customers use Amazon Redshift today to analyze exabytes of structured and semi-structured data across their data warehouse, operational databases, and data lake using standard SQL.

Our Analytics Specialist Solutions Architecture team at AWS work closely with customers to help use Amazon Redshift to meet their unique analytics needs. In particular, the authors of this book, **Shruti**, **Thiyagu**, and **Harshida** have worked hands-on with hundreds of customers of all types, from startups to multinational enterprises. They've helped projects ranging from migrations from other data warehouses to Amazon Redshift, to delivering new analytics use cases such as building a predictive analytics solution using Redshift ML. They've also helped our Amazon Redshift service team to better understand customer needs and prioritize new feature development.

I am super excited that **Shruti**, **Thiyagu**, and **Harshida** have authored this book, based on their deep expertise and knowledge of Amazon Redshift, to help customers quickly perform the most common tasks. This book is designed as a cookbook to provide step-by-step instructions across these different tasks. It has clear instructions on prerequisites and steps required to meet different objectives such as creating an Amazon Redshift cluster, loading data in Amazon Redshift from Amazon S3, or querying data across OLTP sources like Amazon Aurora directly from Amazon Redshift.

I recommend this book to any new or existing Amazon Redshift customer who wants to learn not only what features Amazon Redshift provides, but also how to quickly take advantage of them.

Eugene Kawamoto

Director, Product Management

Amazon Redshift, AWS

Contributors

About the authors

Shruti Worlikar is a cloud professional with technical expertise in data lakes and analytics across cloud platforms. Her background has led her to become an expert in on-premises-to-cloud migrations and building cloud-based scalable analytics applications. Shruti earned her bachelor's degree in electronics and telecommunications from Mumbai University in 2009 and later earned her masters' degree in telecommunications and network management from Syracuse University in 2011. Her work history includes work at J.P. Morgan Chase, MicroStrategy, and **Amazon Web Services (AWS)**. She is currently working in the role of Manager, Analytics Specialist SA at AWS, helping customers to solve real-world analytics business challenges with cloud solutions and working with service teams to deliver real value. Shruti is the DC Chapter Director for the non-profit **Women in Big Data (WiBD)** and engages with chapter members to build technical and business skills to support their career advancements. Originally from Mumbai, India, Shruti currently resides in Aldie, VA, with her husband and two kids.

Thiyagarajan Arumugam (Thiyagu) is a principal big data solution architect at AWS, architecting and building solutions at scale using big data to enable data-driven decisions. Prior to AWS, Thiyagu as a data engineer built big data solutions at Amazon, operating some of the largest data warehouses and migrating to and managing them. He has worked on automated data pipelines and built data lake-based platforms to manage data at scale for the customers of his data science and business analyst teams. Thiyagu is a certified AWS Solution Architect (Professional), earned his master's degree in mechanical engineering at the Indian Institute of Technology, Delhi, and is the author of several blog posts at AWS on big data. Thiyagu enjoys everything outdoors – running, cycling, ultimate frisbee – and is currently learning to play the Indian classical drum the mrudangam. Thiyagu currently resides in Austin, TX, with his wife and two kids.

Harshida Patel is a senior analytics specialist solution architect at AWS, enabling customers to build scalable data lake and data warehousing applications using AWS analytical services. She has presented Amazon Redshift deep-dive sessions at re:Invent. Harshida has a bachelor's degree in electronics engineering and a master's in electrical and telecommunication engineering. She has over 15 years of experience architecting and building end-to-end data pipelines in the data management space. In the past, Harshida has worked in the insurance and telecommunication industries. She enjoys traveling and spending quality time with friends and family, and she lives in Virginia with her husband and son.

About the reviewers

Anusha Challa is a senior analytics specialist solution architect at AWS with over 10 years of experience in data warehousing both on-premises and in the cloud. She has worked on multiple large-scale data projects throughout her career at **Tata Consultancy Services (TCS)**, EY, and AWS. She has worked with hundreds of Amazon Redshift customers and has built end-to-end scalable, reliable, and robust data pipelines.

Vaidy Krishnan leads business development for AWS, helping customers successfully adopt and be successful with AWS analytics services. Prior to AWS, Vaidy spent close to 15 years building, marketing, and launching analytics products to customers in market-leading companies such as Tableau and GE across industries ranging from healthcare to manufacturing. When not at work, Vaidy likes to travel and golf.

Table of Contents

2

Data Management

3

Loading and Unloading Data

4

Data Pipelines

5

Scalable Data Orchestration for Automation

6

Data Authorization and Security

7

Performance Optimization

8
Cost Optimization

9

Lake House Architecture

10

Extending Redshift's Capabilities

Appendix

Other Books You May Enjoy

Index

Preface

Amazon Redshift is a fully managed, petabyte-scale AWS cloud data warehousing service. It enables you to build new data warehouse workloads on AWS and migrate on-premises traditional data warehousing platforms to Redshift.

This book on Amazon Redshift starts by focusing on the Redshift architecture, showing you how to perform database administration tasks on Redshift. You'll then learn how to optimize your data warehouse to quickly execute complex analytic queries against very large datasets. Because of the massive amount of data involved in data warehousing, designing your database for analytical processing lets you take full advantage of Redshift's columnar architecture and managed services. As you advance, you'll discover how to deploy fully automated and highly scalable **extract, transform, and load** (ETL) processes, which help minimize the operational efforts that you have to invest in managing regular ETL pipelines and ensure the timely and accurate refreshing of your data warehouse. Finally, you'll gain a clear understanding of Redshift use cases, data ingestion, data management, security, and scaling so that you can build a scalable data warehouse platform.

By the end of this Redshift book, you'll be able to implement a Redshift-based data analytics solution and will have understood the best practice solutions to commonly faced problems.

Who this book is for

This book is for anyone involved in architecting, implementing, and optimizing an Amazon Redshift data warehouse, such as data warehouse developers, data analysts, database administrators, data engineers, and data scientists. Basic knowledge of data warehousing, database systems, and cloud concepts and familiarity with Redshift would be beneficial.

What this book covers

Chapter 1, Getting Started with Amazon Redshift, discusses how Amazon Redshift is a fully managed, petabyte-scale data warehouse service in the cloud. An Amazon Redshift data warehouse is a collection of computing resources called nodes, which are organized into a group called a cluster. Each cluster runs an Amazon Redshift engine and contains one or more databases. This chapter walks you through the process of creating a sample Amazon Redshift cluster to set up the necessary access and security controls to easily get started with a data warehouse on AWS. Most operations are click-of-a-button operations; you should be able to launch a cluster in under 15 minutes.

Chapter 2, Data Management, discusses how a data warehouse system has very different design goals compared to a typical transaction-oriented relational database system for **online transaction processing (OLTP)**. Amazon Redshift is optimized for the very fast execution of complex analytic queries against very large datasets. Because of the massive amounts of data involved in data warehousing, designing your database for analytical processing lets you take full advantage of the columnar architecture and managed service. This chapter delves into the different data structure options to set up an analytical schema for the easy querying of your end users.

Chapter 3, Loading and Unloading Data, looks at how Amazon Redshift has in-built integrations with data lakes and other analytical services and how it is easy to move and analyze data across different services. This chapter discusses scalable options to move large datasets from a data lake based out of Amazon S3 storage as well as AWS analytical services such as Amazon EMR and Amazon DynamoDB.

Chapter 4, Data Pipelines, discusses how modern data warehouses depend on ETL operations to convert bulk information into usable data. An ETL process refreshes your data warehouse from source systems, organizing the raw data into a format you can more readily use. Most organizations run ETL as a batch or as part of a real-time ingest process to keep the data warehouse current and provide timely analytics. A fully automated and highly scalable ETL process helps minimize the operational effort that you must invest in managing regular ETL pipelines. It also ensures the timely and accurate refresh of your data warehouse. Here we will discuss recipes to implement real-time and batch-based AWS native options to implement data pipelines for orchestrating data workflows.

Chapter 5, Scalable Data Orchestration for Automation, looks at how for large-scale production pipelines, a common use case is to read complex data originating from a variety of sources. This data must be transformed to make it useful to downstream applications such as machine learning pipelines, analytics dashboards, and business reports. This chapter discusses building scalable data orchestration for automation using native AWS services.

Chapter 6, Data Authorization and Security, discusses how Amazon Redshift security is one of the key pillars of a modern data warehouse for data at rest as well as in transit. In this chapter, we will discuss the industry-leading security controls provided in the form of built-in AWS IAM integration, identity federation for **single sign-on (SSO)**, multi-factor authentication, column-level access control, Amazon **Virtual Private Cloud (VPC)**, and AWS KMS integration to protect your data. Amazon Redshift encrypts and keeps your data secure in transit and at rest using industry-standard encryption techniques. We will also elaborate on how you can authorize data access through fine-grained access controls for the underlying data structures in Amazon Redshift.

Chapter 7, Performance Optimization, examines how Amazon Redshift being a fully managed service provides great performance out of the box for most workloads. Amazon Redshift also provides you with levers that help you maximize the throughputs when data access patterns are already established. Performance tuning on Amazon Redshift helps you manage critical SLAs for workloads and easily scale up your data warehouse to meet/exceed business needs.

Chapter 8, Cost Optimization, discusses how Amazon Redshift is one of the best price-performant data warehouse platforms on the cloud. Amazon Redshift also provides you with scalability and different options to optimize the pricing, such as elastic resizing, pause and resume, reserved instances, and using cost controls. These options allow you to create the best price-performant data warehouse solution.

Chapter 9, Lake House Architecture, looks at how AWS provides purpose-built solutions to meet the scalability and agility needs of the data architecture. With its in-built integration and governance, it is possible to easily move data across the data stores. You might have all the data centralized in a data lake, but use Amazon Redshift to get quick results for complex queries on structured data for business intelligence queries. The curated data can now be exported into an Amazon S3 data lake and classified to build a machine learning algorithm. In this chapter, we will discuss in-built integrations that allow easy data movement to integrate a data lake, data warehouse, and purpose-built data stores and enable unified governance.

Chapter 10, Extending Redshift Capabilities, looks at how Amazon Redshift allows you to analyze all your data using standard SQL, using your existing business intelligence tools. Organizations are looking for more ways to extract valuable insights from data, such as big data analytics, machine learning applications, and a range of analytical tools to drive new use cases and business processes. Building an entire solution from data sourcing, transforming data, reporting, and machine learning can be easily accomplished by taking advantage of the capabilities provided by AWS's analytical services. Amazon Redshift natively integrates with other AWS services, such as Amazon QuickSight, AWS Glue DataBrew, Amazon AppFlow, Amazon ElastiCache, Amazon Data Exchange, and Amazon SageMaker, to meet your varying business needs.

To get the most out of this book

You will need access to an AWS account to perform all the recipes in this book. You will need either administrator access to the AWS account or to work with an administrator to help create the IAM user, roles, and policies as listed in the different chapters. All the data needed in the setup is provided as steps in recipes, and the Amazon S3 bucket is hosted in the Europe (Ireland) (eu-west-1) AWS region. It is preferable to use the Europe (Ireland) AWS region to execute all the recipes. If you need to run the recipes in a different region, you will need to copy the data from the source bucket (s3://packt-redshift-cookbook/) to an Amazon S3 bucket in the desired AWS region, and use that in your recipes instead.

Software/hardware covered in the book	OS requirements
SQL Workbench/J	Windows, macOS, or Linux
An IDE	Windows, macOS, or Linux
A command-line tool	Windows, macOS, or Linux
The AWS CLI	Windows, macOS, or Linux
Python 3.x	Windows, macOS, or Linux
Java 8	Windows, macOS, or Linux
Psql 8.x	Windows, macOS, or Linux

If you are using the digital version of this book, we advise you to type the code yourself or access the code via the GitHub repository (link available in the next section). Doing so will help you avoid any potential errors related to the copying and pasting of code.

Download the example code files

You can download the example code files for this book from GitHub at `https://github.com/PacktPublishing/Amazon-Redshift-Cookbook`. In case there's an update to the code, it will be updated on the existing GitHub repository.

We also have other code bundles from our rich catalog of books and videos available at `https://github.com/PacktPublishing/`. Check them out!

Download the color images

We also provide a PDF file that has color images of the screenshots/diagrams used in this book. You can download it here: `https://static.packt-cdn.com/downloads/9781800569683_ColorImages.pdf`.

Conventions used

There are a number of text conventions used throughout this book.

`Code in text`: Indicates code words in text, database table names, folder names, filenames, file extensions, pathnames, dummy URLs, user input, and Twitter handles. Here is an example: "To create the Amazon Redshift cluster, we used the `redshift` command and the `create-cluster` subcommand."

A block of code is set as follows:

```
SELECT 'hello world';
```

When we wish to draw your attention to a particular part of a code block, the relevant lines or items are set in bold:

```
        "NodeType": "dc2.large",
        "ElasticResizeNumberOfNodeOptions": "[4]",
    ...
        "ClusterStatus": "available"
```

Any command-line input or output is written as follows:

```
!pip install psycopg2-binary
### boto3 is optional, but recommended to leverage the AWS
Secrets Manager storing the credentials  Establishing a
Redshift Connection
!pip install boto3
```

Bold: Indicates a new term, an important word, or words that you see onscreen. For example, words in menus or dialog boxes appear in the text like this. Here is an example: "Navigate to your notebook instance and open **JupyterLab**."

> **Tips or important notes**
> Appear like this.

Get in touch

Feedback from our readers is always welcome.

General feedback: If you have questions about any aspect of this book, mention the book title in the subject of your message and email us at `customercare@packtpub.com`.

Errata: Although we have taken every care to ensure the accuracy of our content, mistakes do happen. If you have found a mistake in this book, we would be grateful if you would report this to us. Please visit www.packtpub.com/support/errata, selecting your book, clicking on the Errata Submission Form link, and entering the details.

Piracy: If you come across any illegal copies of our works in any form on the Internet, we would be grateful if you would provide us with the location address or website name. Please contact us at copyright@packt.com with a link to the material.

If you are interested in becoming an author: If there is a topic that you have expertise in and you are interested in either writing or contributing to a book, please visit authors. packtpub.com.

Share Your Thoughts

Once you've read *Amazon Redshift Cookbook*, we'd love to hear your thoughts! Scan the QR code below to go straight to the Amazon review page for this book and share your feedback.

https://packt.link/r/1800569688

Your review is important to us and the tech community and will help us make sure we're delivering excellent quality content.

1
Getting Started with Amazon Redshift

Amazon Redshift is a fully managed data warehouse service in **Amazon Web Services** (**AWS**). You can query all your data, which can scale from gigabytes to petabytes, using SQL. Amazon Redshift integrates into the data lake solution though the lake house architecture, allowing you access all the structured and semi-structured data in one place. Each Amazon Redshift data warehouse is hosted as a cluster (a group of servers or nodes) that consists of one leader node and a collection of one or more compute nodes. Each cluster is a single tenant environment (which can be scaled to a multi-tenant architecture using data sharing), and every node has its own dedicated CPU, memory, and attached disk storage that varies based on the node's type.

This chapter will walk you through the process of creating a sample Amazon Redshift cluster and connecting to it from different clients.

The following recipes will be discussed in this chapter:

- Creating an Amazon Redshift cluster using the AWS console
- Creating an Amazon Redshift cluster using the AWS CLI
- Creating an Amazon Redshift cluster using an AWS CloudFormation template
- Connecting to an Amazon Redshift cluster using the Query Editor
- Connecting to an Amazon Redshift cluster using the SQL Workbench/J client

- Connecting to an Amazon Redshift cluster using a Jupyter Notebook
- Connecting to an Amazon Redshift cluster programmatically using Python
- Connecting to an Amazon Redshift cluster programmatically using Java
- Connecting to an Amazon Redshift cluster programmatically using .NET
- Connecting to an Amazon Redshift cluster using the command line (psql)

Technical requirements

The following are the technical requirements for this chapter:

- An AWS account.
- An AWS administrator should create an IAM user by following *Recipe 1 – Creating an IAM user* in the *Appendix*. This IAM user will be used to execute all the recipes in this chapter.
- An AWS administrator should deploy the AWS CloudFormation template to attach the IAM policy to the IAM user, which will give them access to Amazon Redshift, Amazon SageMaker, Amazon EC2, AWS CloudFormation, and AWS Secrets Manager. The template is available here: `https://github.com/ PacktPublishing/Amazon-Redshift-Cookbook/blob/master/ Chapter01/chapter_1_CFN.yaml`.
- Client tools such as SQL Workbench/J, an IDE, and a command-line tool.
- You will need to authorize network access from servers or clients to access the Amazon Redshift cluster: `https://docs.aws.amazon.com/redshift/ latest/gsg/rs-gsg-authorize-cluster-access.html`.
- The code files for this chapter can be found here: `https://github.com/ PacktPublishing/Amazon-Redshift-Cookbook/tree/master/ Chapter01`.

Creating an Amazon Redshift cluster using the AWS Console

The AWS Management Console allows you to interactively create an Amazon Redshift cluster via a browser-based user interface. It also recommends the right cluster configuration based on the size of your workload. Once the cluster has been created, you can use the Console to monitor the health of the cluster and diagnose query performance issues from a unified dashboard.

Getting ready

To complete this recipe, you will need the following:

- A new or existing AWS Account. If new AWS accounts need to be created, go to https://portal.aws.amazon.com/billing/signup, enter the necessary information, and follow the steps on the site.

- An IAM user with access to Amazon Redshift.

How to do it...

Follow these steps to create a cluster with minimal parameters:

1. Navigate to the AWS Management Console and select Amazon Redshift: https://console.aws.amazon.com/redshiftv2/.

2. Choose the AWS region (eu-west-1) or corresponding region from the top-right of the screen. Then, click **Next**.

3. On the Amazon Redshift Dashboard, select **CLUSTERS**, and then click **Create cluster**.

4. In the **Cluster configuration** section, type in any meaningful **Cluster identifier**, such as myredshiftcluster.

5. Choose either **Production** or **Free trial**, depending on what you plan to use this cluster for.

6. Select the **Help me choose** option for sizing your cluster for the steady state workload. Alternatively, if you know the required size of your cluster (that is, the node type and number of nodes), select **I'll choose**. For example, you can choose **Node type: dc2.large** with **Nodes: 2**.

7. In the **Database configurations** section, specify values for **Database name** (optional), **Database port** (optional), **Master user name**, and **Master user password**; for example:

- **Database name** (optional): Enter dev
- **Database port** (optional): Enter 5439
- **Master user name**: Enter awsuser
- **Master user password**: Enter a value for the password

8. Optionally, configure the **Cluster permissions** and **Additional configurations** sections when you want to pick a specific network and security configurations. The console defaults to the preset configuration otherwise.

9. Choose **Create cluster**.

10. The cluster creation takes a few minutes to complete. Once this has happened, navigate to **Amazon Redshift | Clusters | myredshiftcluster | General information** to find the JDBC/ODBC URL to connect to the Amazon Redshift cluster.

Creating an Amazon Redshift cluster using the AWS CLI

The AWS **command-line interface (CLI)** is a unified tool for managing your AWS services. You can use this tool on the command-line Terminal to invoke the creation of an Amazon Redshift cluster.

The command-line tool automates cluster creation and modification. For example, you can create a shell script that can create manual point in time snapshots for the cluster.

Getting ready

To complete this recipe, you will need to do the following:

- Install and configure the AWS CLI based on your specific operating system at `https://docs.aws.amazon.com/cli/latest/userguide/install-cliv2.html` and use the `aws configure` command to set up your AWS CLI installation, as explained here: `https://docs.aws.amazon.com/cli/latest/userguide/cli-configure-quickstart.html`.

- Verify that the AWS CLI has been configured using the following command, which will list the configured values:

```
$ aws configure list
```

Name	Value	Type	Location
access_key	****************PA4J	iam-role	
secret_key	****************928H	iam-role	
region	eu-west-1	config-file	

- Create an IAM user with access to Amazon Redshift.

How to do it...

Follow these steps to create an Amazon Redshift cluster using the command-line tool:

1. Depending on the operation system the AWS CLI has been installed on, open a shell program such as bash or zsh in Linux-based systems or the Windows command line.

2. Use the following command to create a two-node `dc2.large` cluster with the minimal set of parameters of cluster-identifier (any unique identifier for the cluster), node-type/number-of-nodes and the master user credentials. Replace `<MasterUserPassword>` in the following command with a password of your choice. The password must be 8-64 characters long and must contain at least one uppercase letter, one lowercase letter, and one number. You can use any printable ASCII character except /, " ", or, or @:

```
$ aws redshift create-cluster --node-type dc2.large --number-
of-nodes 2 --master-username adminuser --master-user-password
<MasterUserPassword> --cluster-identifier myredshiftcluster
```

Here is the expected sample output:

```
{
    "Cluster": {
        "PubliclyAccessible": true,
        "MasterUsername": "adminuser",
        "VpcSecurityGroups": [
            {
                "Status": "active",
                "VpcSecurityGroupId": "sg-abcdef7"
            }
        ],
        "NumberOfNodes": 2,
        "PendingModifiedValues": {
            "MasterUserPassword": "****"
        },
        "VpcId": "vpc-abcdef99",
        "ClusterParameterGroups": [
            {
                "ParameterGroupName": "default.redshift-1.0",
```

```
            "ParameterApplyStatus": "in-sync"
        }
    ],
    "DBName": "dev",
    "ClusterSubnetGroupName": "default",
    "EnhancedVpcRouting": false,
"ClusterIdentifier": "myredshiftcluster",
    "NodeType": "dc2.large",
    "Encrypted": false,
    "ClusterStatus": "creating"
  }
}
```

3. It will take a few minutes to create the cluster. You can monitor the status of the cluster creation process using the following command:

```
$ aws redshift describe-clusters --cluster-identifier
myredshiftcluster
```

Here is the expected sample output:

```
myredshiftcluster
{
    "Clusters": [
            "NumberOfNodes": 2,
            "DBName": "dev",
            "Endpoint": {
                "Port": 5439,
                "Address": "myredshiftcluster.abcdefghijk.eu-
west-1.redshift.amazonaws.com"
            },
            "NodeType": "dc2.large",
            "ElasticResizeNumberOfNodeOptions": "[4]",
...
            "ClusterStatus": "available"
        }
    ]
```

```
}
```

Note that `"ClusterStatus":  "available"` indicates that the cluster is ready for use and that you can connect to it using the `"Address":  "myredshiftcluster.abcdefghijk.eu-west-1.redshift.amazonaws.com"` endpoint.

The cluster is now ready. Now, you use an ODBC/JDBC to connect to the Amazon Redshift cluster.

How it works...

The AWS CLI uses a hierarchical structure in the command line that is specified in the following order:

```
$aws <command> <subcommand> [options and parameters]
```

These parameters can take different types of input values, such as strings, numbers, maps, lists, and JSON structures. What is supported depends on the command and subcommand that you specify. The AWS CLI also support help text for conveniently scripting the command. To see the help text, you can run any of the following commands:

```
$aws help
$aws <command> help
$aws <command> <subcommand> help
```

To create the Amazon Redshift cluster, we used the `redshift` command and the `create-cluster` subcommand.

You can refer to `https://docs.aws.amazon.com/cli/latest/reference/redshift/create-cluster.html` for the full set of parameters we used or by using the following command on the AWS CLI:

```
$aws redshift create-cluster help
```

Creating an Amazon Redshift cluster using an AWS CloudFormation template

With an AWS CloudFormation template, you treat your infrastructure as code, which enables you to create an Amazon Redshift cluster using a json/yaml file. The declarative code in the file contains the steps to create the AWS resources, and it also enables easy automation and distribution. This template allows you to standardize the Amazon Redshift Cluster's creation to meet your organizational infrastructure and security standards. Furthermore, you can distribute them to different teams within your organization using the AWS service catalog for easy setup.

Getting ready

To complete this recipe, you will need to do the following:

- Create an IAM user with access to AWS CloudFormation, Amazon EC2, and Amazon Redshift.

How to do it...

We will create a CloudFormation template to author the Amazon Redshift cluster infrastructure as code using the JSON-based template. Follow these steps to create an Amazon Redshift cluster using the CloudFormation template:

1. Download the AWS CloudFormation template from https://github.com/PacktPublishing/Amazon-Redshift-Cookbook/blob/master/Chapter01/Creating_Amazon_Redshift_Cluster.json.

2. Navigate to the AWS Console, choose **CloudFormation**, and then choose **Create stack**, as shown in the following screenshot:

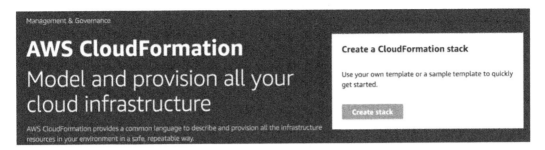

Figure 1.1 – Create stack

3. Click on the **Template is ready** and **Upload a template file** options and choose the file that was downloaded (Creating_Amazon_Redshift_Cluster.json) from your local computer. Then, click **Next.**

4. Enter the following input parameters:

    a. **Stack name**: Enter a name for the stack; for example, myredshiftcluster.

    b. **ClusterType**: A single-node or a multi-node cluster.

    c. **DatabaseName**: Enter a database name; for example, dev.

    d. **InboundTraffic**: Restrict the CIDR ranges of IPs that can access the cluster. 0.0.0.0/0 opens the cluster so that it's globally accessible.

    e. **MasterUserName**: Enter a database master username; for example, awsuser.

    f. **MasterUserPassword**: Enter a master user password. The password must be 8-64 characters long and must contain at least one uppercase letter, one lowercase letter, and one number. It can contain any printable ASCII character except /, " ", or, or @.

    g. **NodeType**: Enter the node type; for example, dc2.large.

    h. **NumberofNodes**: Enter the number of compute nodes; for example, 2.

    i. **Redshift cluster port**: Choose any TCP/IP port; for example, 5439.

5. Click **Next** and **Create Stack**.

6. The AWS `CloudFormation` template has deployed all the infrastructure and configuration listed in the template. It will wait until the status changes to **CREATE_COMPLETE**.

7. Now, you can check the output section of the `CloudFormation` stack and look for the cluster endpoint or navigate to **Amazon Redshift | Clusters | myredshiftcluster | General information** to find the JDBC/ODBC URL to connect to the Amazon Redshift cluster.

How it works...

Let's see how this `CloudFormation` template works. The `CloudFormation` template is organized into three broad sections; that is, input parameters, resources, and outputs. Let's discuss them one by one.

The `Parameters` section is used to allow user input choices and can also be used to apply constraints against its value. To create the Amazon Redshift resource, we must collect parameters such as database name, master username/password, and cluster type. These parameters will later be substituted when you create the necessary resources. Here is an illustration of the `Parameters` section from the template:

```
"Parameters": {
        "DatabaseName": {
            "Description": "The name of the first database to
be created when the cluster is created",
            "Type": "String",
            "Default": "dev",
            "AllowedPattern": "([a-z]|[0-9])+"
        },
        "NodeType": {
            "Description": "The type of node to be
provisioned",
            "Type": "String",
            "Default": "dc2.large",
            "AllowedValues": [
                "ra3.16xlarge",
                "ra3.4xlarge",
                "ra3.xlplus",
                "dc2.large",
```

```
            "dc2.8xlarge"
        ]
    }
```

In the preceding input section, `DatabaseName` is a string value that defaults to `dev` and also enforces alphanumeric validation when specified using the `AllowedPattern:` `"([a-z]|[0-9])+` condition check. Similarly, `NodeType` defaults to `dc2.large` and is allowed a valid `NodeType` from a list of values.

The `Resources` section contains a list of resource objects, and the Amazon Resource is invoked using `AWS::Redshift::Cluster`, along with references to the input parameters, such as `DatabaseName`, `ClusterType`, `NumberOfNodes`, `NodeType`, `MasterUsername`, `MasterUserPassword`, and so on:

```
"Resources": {
        "RedshiftCluster": {
            "Type": "AWS::Redshift::Cluster",
            "DependsOn": "AttachGateway",
            "Properties": {
                "ClusterType": {
                    "Ref": "ClusterType"
                },
                "NumberOfNodes": {
...
                },
                "NodeType": {
                    "Ref": "NodeType"
                },
                "DBName": {
                    "Ref": "DatabaseName"
                },
..
```

The `Resources` section references the input section for values such as `NumberOfNodes`, `NodeType`, and `DatabaseName`, all of which will be used when the resource is created.

The output section is a handy way to capture essential information about the resources or input parameters that you want to be available once the stack has been created. This allows you to easily identify the resource object names that have been created. For example, you can capture an output such as `ClusterEndpoint`, which will be used to connect to the cluster, as follows:

```
"Outputs": {
        "ClusterEndpoint": {
            "Description": "Cluster endpoint",
            "Value": {
                "Fn::Join": [
                    ":",
                    [
                        {
                            "Fn::GetAtt": [
                                "RedshiftCluster",
                                "Endpoint.Address"
                            ]
                        },
                        {
                            "Fn::GetAtt": [
                                "RedshiftCluster",
                                "Endpoint.Port"
                            ]
                        }
                    ]
                ]
            }
        }
```

When authoring the template from scratch, you can take advantage of the AWS `CloudFormation` Designer – an integrated development environment for authoring and validating code. Once the template is ready, you can launch the resources by creating a stack (collection of resources) using the AWS CloudFormation console, API, or AWS CLI. You can also update or delete it afterward.

Connecting to an Amazon Redshift cluster using the Query Editor

The Query Editor is a thin client browser-based interface available on the AWS Management Console for running SQL queries on Amazon Redshift clusters directly. Once you have created the cluster, you can use the Query Editor to jumpstart querying the cluster without needing to set up the JDBC/ODBC driver. This recipe will show you how get started with the Query Editor so that you can access your Redshift clusters.

The Query Editor allows you to do the following:

- Explore the schema
- Run multiple DDL and DML SQL commands
- Run single/multiple select statements
- View query execution details
- Save a query
- Download a query result set that's up to 100 MB in size in a .CSV, text, or HTML file

Getting ready

To complete this recipe, you will need do the following:

- Create an IAM user with access to Amazon Redshift and AWS Secrets Manager.
- Store the database credentials in Amazon Secrets Manager using *Recipe 2 – Storing database credentials using Amazon Secrets Manager* in the *Appendix*.

How to do it...

Follow these steps to query an Amazon Redshift cluster using the Amazon Redshift Query Editor:

1. Connect to the Amazon Redshift cluster using the secrets that you've stored. Navigate to the Amazon Redshift console and choose **Editor**.

2. Choose **Connect to database** and select the **AWS secrets Manager** option. Choose the secret we created earlier and click **Connect**:

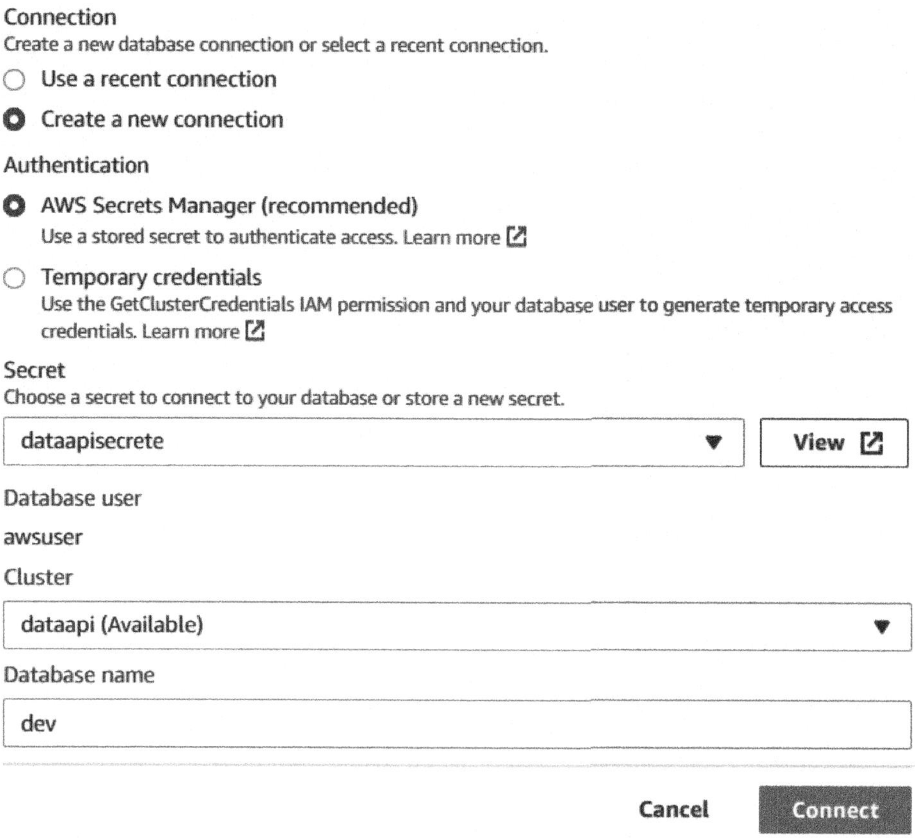

Connection
Create a new database connection or select a recent connection.

○ Use a recent connection

◉ Create a new connection

Authentication

◉ AWS Secrets Manager (recommended)
Use a stored secret to authenticate access. Learn more ↗

○ Temporary credentials
Use the GetClusterCredentials IAM permission and your database user to generate temporary access credentials. Learn more ↗

Secret
Choose a secret to connect to your database or store a new secret.

| dataapisecrete ▼ | View ↗ |

Database user

awsuser

Cluster

| dataapi (Available) ▼ |

Database name

| dev |

Cancel   **Connect**

Figure 1.2 – Setting up Amazon Redshift credentials using Amazon Secrets Manager

3. Now that you have successfully connected to the Redshift database, type the following query into the Query Editor:

```
SELECT 'hello world';
```

4. Then, you can click on **Run** to execute the query:

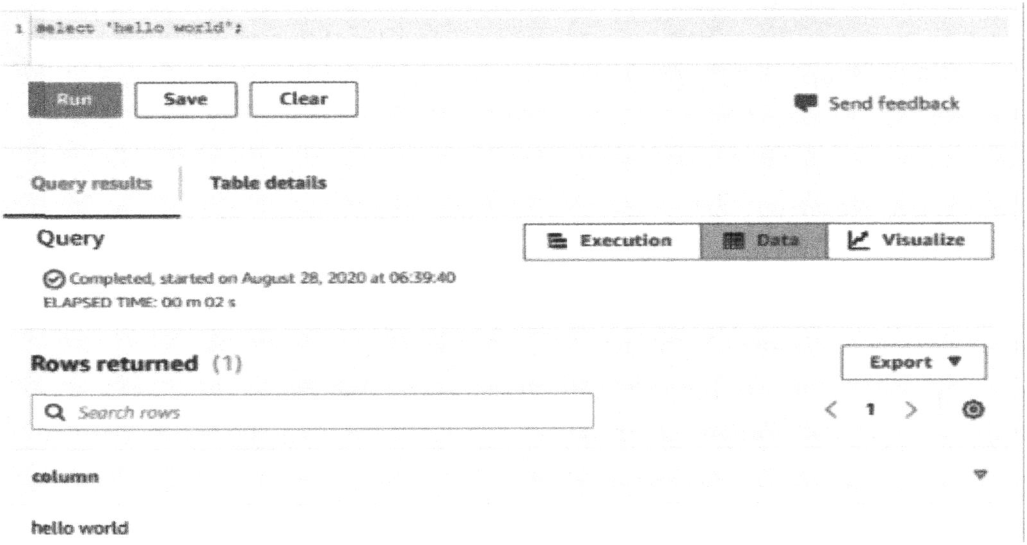

Figure 1.3 – Amazon Redshift Query Editor for a sample query

The results of the query will appear in the **Query Results** section. You are now connected to the Amazon Redshift cluster and ready to execute more queries.

Connecting to an Amazon Redshift cluster using the SQL Workbench/J client

There are multiple ways to connect to an Amazon Redshift cluster, but one of the most popular options is to connect using a UI-based tool. SQL Workbench/J is a free cross-platform SQL query tool that you can use to connect to your own local client.

Getting ready

To complete this recipe, you will need to do the following:

- Create an Amazon Redshift cluster and the necessary login credentials (username and password).

- Install SQL Workbench/J (`https://www.sql-workbench.eu/manual/install.html`).

- Download Amazon Redshift `Driver`. Please check out `Configuring a JDBC connection` to download the latest driver version.

- Modify the security group attached to the Amazon Redshift cluster to allow a connection from a local client.

- Navigate to **Amazon Redshift | Clusters | myredshiftcluster | General information** to find the JDBC/ODBC URL for connecting to the Amazon Redshift cluster.

How to do it...

Follow these steps to connect to your cluster using the SQL Workbench/J client tool from your computer:

1. Open SQL Workbench/J by double-clicking on the `SQLWorkbench.exe` file (on Windows) or the **SQLWorkbenchJ** application (on Mac).

2. From the **SQL Workbench**/J menu, select **File**, and then select **Connect window**.

3. Select **Create a new connection profile**.

4. In the **New profile** box, enter any profile name; for example, `examplecluster_ jdbc`.

5. Select **Manage Drivers**. The **Manage Drivers** dialog will open. Select **Amazon Redshift**:

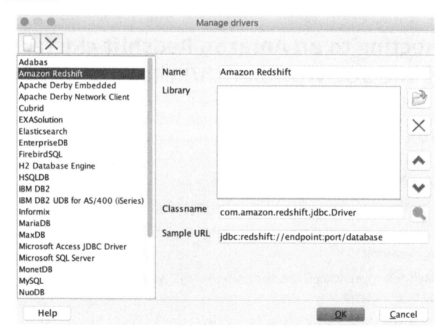

Figure 1.4 – SQL Workbench/J – Manage drivers

6. Select the folder icon adjacent to the Library box, browse and point it to the Amazon Redshift driver location, and then select **Choose**:

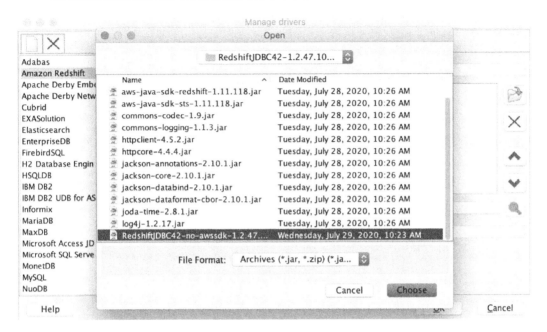

Figure 1.5 – SQL Workbench/J – selecting your Amazon Redshift driver

7. To set up the profile for the Amazon Redshift connection, enter the following details:

- In the **Driver** box, select the Amazon Redshift drive.

- For **URL**, copy and paste the Amazon Redshift cluster JDBC URL you obtained previously.

- For **Username**, enter the username (or the master username) associated with the cluster.

- For **Password**, provide the password associated with the username.

- Checkmark the **Autocommit** box.

8. Select the **Save profile list** icon, as shown in the following screenshot:

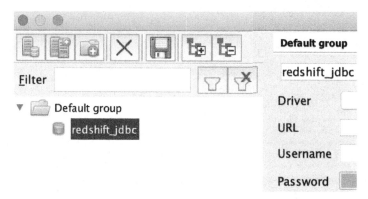

Figure 1.6 – Choosing an Amazon Redshift connection profile

9. Select **OK**:

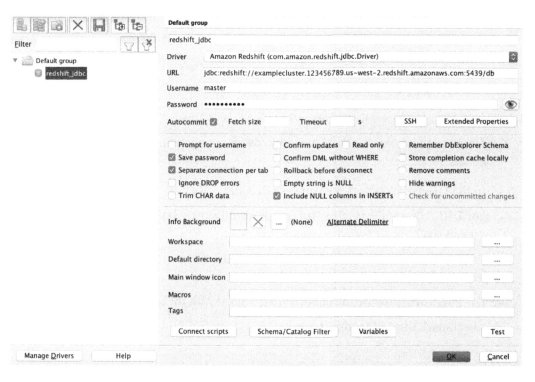

Figure 1.7 – Amazon Redshift connection profile

10. After setting up the JDBC connection, you can use the query to ensure you are connected to the Amazon Redshift cluster:

```
select * from information_schema.tables;
```

A list of records will appear in the **Results** tab if the connection is successful:

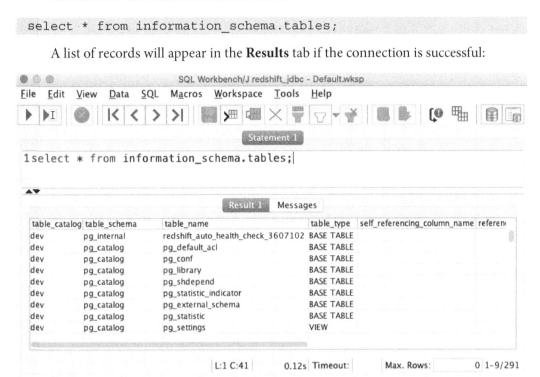

Figure 1.8 – Sample query output from SQL Workbench/J

Connecting to an Amazon Redshift Cluster using a Jupyter Notebook

Jupyter Notebooks is an interactive web application that enables you to analyze clusters interactively. Jupyter Notebooks applications are widely used by users such as business analysts, data scientists, and so on to perform data wrangling and exploration. Using a Jupyter Notebook, you can access all the historical data available in Amazon Redshift and combine it with the data that's available in the other sources, such as Amazon S3-based data lake. For example, you might want to build a forecasting model based on the historical sales data in Amazon Redshift, which will be combined with the clickstream data available in the data lake. Jupyter Notebooks are the tool of choice here due to the versatility they provide in terms of exploration tasks and the strong support from the open source community.

Getting ready

To complete this recipe, you will need to do the following:

- Create an IAM user with access to Amazon Redshift, Amazon EC2, and Amazon Secrets Manager.

- Create an Amazon Redshift cluster in a VPC. For more information, see `Creating a Cluster in a VPC`.

- Create a notebook instance (such as Amazon SageMaker) running the Jupyter Notebook in the same VPC as Amazon Redshift (`https://docs.aws.amazon.com/sagemaker/latest/dg/howitworks-create-ws.html`).

- Modify the security group attached to the Amazon Redshift cluster to allow connections from the Amazon SageMaker notebook instance.

- Store the database credentials in Amazon Secrets Manager using *Recipe 2 – Storing database credentials using Amazon Secrets Manger* in the *Appendix*.

How to do it...

Follow these steps to connect to the Amazon Redshift cluster using a Jupyter Notebook:

1. Open the AWS Console and navigate to the Amazon SageMaker Service.

2. Navigate to your notebook instance and open **JupyterLab**. When using the Amazon SageMaker notebook, find the notebook instance that was launched and click on the **Open JupyterLab** link, as shown in the following screenshot:

1.9 – Navigating to JupyterLab using the AWS Console

3. Now, let's install the Python driver libraries to connect to Amazon Redshift by using the following code in the Jupyter Notebook. Then, set the kernel to `conda_python3`:

```
!pip install psycopg2-binary
### boto3 is optional, but recommended to leverage the AWS
```

```
Secrets Manager storing the credentials  Establishing a
Redshift Connection
!pip install boto3
```

> **Important Note**
>
> You can connect to the Amazon Redshift cluster using Python libraries such as Psycopg (`https://pypi.org/project/psycopg2-binary/`) or use pg (`https://www.postgresql.org/docs/7.3/pygresql.html`) to connect to the Jupyter Notebook. Alternatively, you can also use a JDBC, but for the ease of scripting with Python, the following illustrations will use either of the preceding libraries.

4. Grant the Amazon SageMaker instance permission to use the stored secret. In the AWS Secrets Manager console, click on your secret and find the Secret ARN. Replace the ARN information in the resource section with the following JSON code:

```
{
    "Version": "2012-10-17",
    "Statement": [
        {
            "Effect": "Allow",
            "Action": [
                "secretsmanager:GetResourcePolicy",
                "secretsmanager:GetSecretValue",
                "secretsmanager:DescribeSecret",
                "secretsmanager:ListSecretVersionIds"
            ],
            "Resource": [
                "arn:aws:secretsmanager:eu-west-
1:123456789012:secret:aes128-1a2b3c"
            ]
        }
    ]
}
```

5. Now, you must attach this policy as an inline policy to the execution role for your SageMaker notebook instance. To do so, follow these steps:

a) Navigate to the Amazon SageMaker console.

b) Select **Notebook Instances**.

c) Click on your notebook instance (the one running this notebook, most likely).

d) Under **Permissions and Encryption**, click on the IAM role link.

e) You should now be on an IAM console, where you can select **Add inline policy**. Click on the link that appears.

f) On the **Create Policy** page that appears, click **JSON** and replace the JSON lines that appear with the preceding code block.

g) Click **Review Policy**.

h) On the next page, select a human-friendly name for the policy and click **Create policy**.

6. Finally, paste the ARN for your secret into the following code block of your Jupyter Notebook to connect to the Amazon Redshift cluster:

```
# Put the ARN of your AWS Secrets Manager secret for your
redshift cluster here:
secret_arn="arn:aws:secretsmanager:eu-west-
1:123456789012:secret:aes128-1a2b3c"
# This will get the secret from AWS Secrets Manager.
import boto3
import json
session = boto3.session.Session()
client = session.client(
    service_name='secretsmanager'
)
get_secret_value_response = client.get_secret_value(
    SecretId=secret_arn
)


if 'SecretString' in get_secret_value_response:
    connection_info = json.loads(get_secret_value_
response['SecretString'])
else:
```

```
    print("ERROR: no secret data found")
# Sanity check for credentials
expected_keys = set(['user', 'password', 'host', 'database',
'port'])
if not expected_keys.issubset(connection_info.keys()):
    print("Expected values for ",expected_keys)
    print("Received values for ",set(connection_info.keys()))
    print("Please adjust query or assignment as required!")


# jdbc:redshift://HOST:PORT/DBNAME
import time
import psycopg2
database = "dev"
con=psycopg2.connect(
    dbname    = database,
    host      = connection_info["host"],
    port      = connection_info["port"],
    user      = connection_info["username"],
    password = connection_info["password"]
)
```

7. Run basic queries against the database. These queries make use of the `cursor` class to execute a basic query in Amazon Redshift:

```
cur = con.cursor()
cur.execute("SELECT sysdate")
res = cur.fetchall()
print(res)
cur.close()
```

8. Optionally, you can use the following code to connect to Amazon Redshift using your Amazon SageMaker notebook: `https://github.com/PacktPublishing/Amazon-Redshift-Cookbook/blob/master/Chapter01/Connecting_to_AmazonRedshift_using_JupyterNotebook.ipynb`.

Connecting to an Amazon Redshift cluster using Python

Python is widely used for data analytics due to its simplicity and ease of use. In this recipe, we will use Python programming to connect using the Amazon Redshift Data API.

The Data API allows you to access Amazon Redshift without the need to use the JDBC or ODBC drivers. You can execute SQL commands on an Amazon Redshift cluster by invoking a secure API endpoint provided by the Data API. The Data API ensures that your SQL queries will be submitted asynchronously. You can now monitor the status of the query and retrieve your results later. The Data API is supported on all major programming languages, including Python, Go, Java, Node.js, PHP, Ruby, and C++, along with the AWS SDK.

Getting ready

To complete this recipe, you will need to do the following:

- Create an IAM user with access to Amazon Redshift, Amazon Secrets Manager, and Amazon EC2.

- Store the database credentials in Amazon Secrets Manager using *Recipe 2 – Storing database credentials using Amazon Secrets Manager* in the *Appendix*.

- Open a Linux machine Terminal such as Amazon EC2, deployed in the same VPC as the Amazon Redshift cluster.

- Install Python 3.6 or higher on the Linux instance where you will write and execute the code. If you have not installed Python, you can download it from `https://www.python.org/downloads/`.

- Install the AWS SDK for Python (Boto3) on the Linux instance. You can reference the getting started guide at `https://aws.amazon.com/sdk-for-python/`.

- Modify the security group attached to the Amazon Redshift cluster to allow connections from the Amazon EC2 Linux instance, which will allow access to execute the Python code.

- Create a VPC endpoint for Amazon Secrets Manager and allow security groups to allow the Linux instance to access the Secrets Manager VPC endpoint.

How to do it...

Follow these steps to use a Linux Terminal to connect to Amazon Redshift using Python:

1. Open the Linux Terminal and install the latest AWS SDK for Python (Boto3) using the following command:

```
pip install boto3
```

2. Next, we will write the Python code. Type `python` on the Linux Terminal and start typing the following code. First, we will import the `boto3` package and establish a session:

```
import boto3
import json

redshift_cluster_id = "myredshiftcluster"
redshift_database = "dev"
aws_region_name = "eu-west-1"
secret_arn="arn:aws:secretsmanager:eu-west-
1:123456789012:secret:aes128-1a2b3c"
def get_client(service, aws_region_name):
    import botocore.session as bc
    session = bc.get_session()
    s = boto3.Session(botocore_session=session, region_
name=region)
    return s.client(service)
```

3. Now, you can create a client object from the `boto3.Session` object using `RedshiftData`:

```
rsd = get_client('redshift-data')
```

4. Next, we will execute a SQL statement. We will use the secrets ARN key to run a statement. You can execute DDL or DML statements here. The query's execution is asynchronous in nature. When the statement is executed, it returns `ExecuteStatementOutput`, which includes the statement ID:

```
resp = rsd.execute_statement(
    SecretArn= secret_arn
    ClusterIdentifier=redshift_cluster_id,
```

```
        Database= redshift_database,
        Sql="SELECT sysdate;"
)
queryId = resp['Id']
print(f"asynchronous query execution: query id {queryId}")
```

5. Check the status of the query using `describe_statement`, as well as the number of records that have been retrieved:

```
stmt = rsd.describe_statement(Id=queryId)
desc = None
while True:
        desc = rsd.describe_statement(Id=queryId)
        if desc["Status"] == "FINISHED":
            break
            print(desc["ResultRows"])
```

6. Now, you can retrieve the results of the preceding query using `get_statement_result`. This returns JSON-based metadata and results that can be verified using the following statement:

```
if desc and desc["ResultRows"]  > 0:
    result = rsd.get_statement_result(Id=queryId)
    print("results JSON" + "\n")
    print(json.dumps(result, indent = 3))
```

> **Note**
> The query results can only be retrieved for 24 hours.

The complete script for the preceding Python code is also available at `https://github.com/PacktPublishing/Amazon-Redshift-Cookbook/blob/master/Chapter01/Python_Connect_to_AmazonRedshift.py`. It can be executed as `python Python_Connect_to_AmazonRedshift.py`.

Connecting to an Amazon Redshift cluster programmatically using Java

Java has been used for decades to build and orchestrate data pipeline tasks, ranging from cleaning and processing to data analysis. Java can programmatically access Amazon Redshift to build automated applications. In this recipe, we will use an AWS-provided Redshift JDBC driver in Java to connect to an Amazon Redshift cluster.

Getting ready

To complete this recipe, you will need to do the following:

- Create an Amazon Redshift cluster and login credentials.
- Install Java 8 and have an IDE to develop and run the code in. Alternatively, you can use AWS Cloud9. The AWS Cloud9 IDE offers a rich code editing experience and a runtime debugger with support for several programming languages. It also provides a built-in terminal. You can set up AWS Cloud9 for Java using the instructions provided at https://docs.aws.amazon.com/cloud9/latest/user-guide/sample-java.html.
- Modify the security group that's attached to the Amazon Redshift cluster to allow a connection from the server or client running the Java application, which will allow you to execute the Java code.
- Navigate to **Amazon Redshift | Clusters | myredshiftcluster | General information** and capture the JDBC/ODBC URL to connect to the Amazon Redshift cluster.

How to do it...

Follow these steps to connect to Amazon Redshift using Java:

1. Let's get started by downloading the Amazon Redshift JDBC driver:

```
wget https://s3.amazonaws.com/redshift-downloads/drivers/
jdbc/1.2.47.1071/RedshiftJDBC42-no-awssdk-1.2.47.1071.jar --no-
check-certificate
```

2. Include java home in your path:

```
PATH=$PATH:$HOME/.local/bin:$HOME/bin:/usr/lib/jvm/java
```

3. Set a `classpath` for the driver:

```
export CLASSPATH=.:/home/ec2-user/environment/RedshiftJDBC42-
no-awssdk-1.2.47.1071.jar
```

4. We will use the following Java code to connect to our Amazon Redshift database and query the tables. The entire code, which is available in `java_connect_toRedshift.java`, can be referenced on GitHub.

5. First, we must import the Java `sql` package, which provides an API for connecting to and accessing the datastore:

```
import java.sql.*;
import java.util.Properties;
```

6. Let's construct the JDBC URL string and store the database user and credentials in variables. Replace the variable values in `<>` with the appropriate values for your Amazon Redshift cluster:

```
 static final String dbURL = "<Amazon Redshift Cluster JDBC
URL>";
    static final String MasterUsername = "<dbuser>";
    static final String MasterUserPassword = "<yourPassword>"
```

Refer to `https://docs.aws.amazon.com/redshift/latest/mgmt/jdbc20-obtain-url.html` for instructions on how to construct the JDBC URL.

7. To dynamically load the driver at runtime, you must specify the driver class. This will be used by the driver manager to load the driver:

```
Class.forName("com.amazon.redshift.jdbc.Driver");
```

8. Use the driver manager's `getConnection` property to establish a connection to your Amazon Redshift database using the JDBC driver:

```
Connection conn = null;
Class.forName("com.amazon.redshift.jdbc.Driver");
Properties props = new Properties();
props.setProperty("user", MasterUsername);
props.setProperty("password", MasterUserPassword);
conn = DriverManager.getConnection(dbURL, props);
```

9. We are now ready to execute the query and retrieve results from the database. For this, we will use the `Statement` class. The query we will be using will retrieve the `pg_catalog` tables and views. The `executeQuery` property will execute the query against the Redshift database and return `resultset`:

```
    stmt = conn.createStatement();
    String sql = "select * from information_schema.tables
where table_schema = 'pg_catalog';";
      ResultSet rs = stmt.executeQuery(sql);
```

10. To retrieve the result set, we will loop through using `rs.next()` to progress the cursor until the end of the returned records:

```
      while(rs.next()){
        //Retrieve two columns.
        String catalog = rs.getString("table_catalog");
        String name = rs.getString("table_name");
      //Display values.
        System.out.print("Catalog: " + catalog);
        System.out.println(", Name: " + name);
        }
```

11. Remember to close the connection:

```
  conn.close();
```

Optionally, you can download the code for connecting to the Amazon Redshift cluster using Java directly from `https://github.com/PacktPublishing/Amazon-Redshift-Cookbook/blob/master/Chapter01/ConnectToCluster.java`.

Connecting to an Amazon Redshift cluster programmatically using .NET

.NET can connect to Amazon Redshift programmatically to build data-enabled applications such as business intelligence portals, share the data through an application interface, and more. In this recipe, we will install an AWS provided Amazon Redshift ODBC driver and connect to the database using .NET.

Getting ready

To complete this recipe, you will need to do the following:

- Download and configure an Amazon Redshift ODBC driver for Windows using the details provided here: https://docs.aws.amazon.com/redshift/latest/mgmt/configure-odbc-connection.html#install-odbc-driver-windows.

- Utilize Visual Studio IDE for .NET. You can do this from the AWS Cloud9 IDE, which offers a rich code editing experience and a runtime debugger that supports several programming languages. It also provides a built-in terminal. You can set up AWS Cloud9 for .NET core at https://docs.aws.amazon.com/cloud9/latest/user-guide/sample-dotnetcore.html.

- Modify the security group attached to the Amazon Redshift cluster to allow connections from the server or client running the .NET application, which will allow to execute the .NET code.

- Capture your Amazon Redshift cluster's hostname and login credentials.

How to do it...

Follow these steps to learn how to use Visual Studio Code to create an application that can connect to Amazon Redshift:

1. Open Visual Studio Code and create a Windows console project called ConnectToRedshift.

2. The following is some sample .NET code for connecting to your Amazon Redshift cluster and executing a query to list the pg_catalog tables. The entire code in dotNet_connect_toRedshift.cs can be found on GitHub.

3. We will import the System.Data collection of classes to connect to the Redshift database using the ODBC driver and retrieve results:

```
using System;
using System.Data;
using System.Data.Odbc;
```

4. Capture the cluster's endpoint, port, dbuser, and password in variables. The database is dev. Replace the variable values in <> with the appropriate values for your Amazon Redshift cluster:

```
 string server = "<Amazon Redshift Cluster HostName>"; // Eg:
cookbookcluster-2ee55abd.cvqfeilxsadl.eu-west-1.redshift.
```

```
amazonaws.com
 string port = "5439";
 string masterUsername = "<dbuser>";
 string masterUserPassword = "<yourPassword>";
 string DBName = "dev";
```

5. Construct the ODBC connection string for your Amazon Redshift database. For 64-bit and 32-bit systems, the connection string is as follows. Use the connection string that's specific to your driver. Here, we will use the 32-bit driver connection string:

```
/*     string connString = "Driver={Amazon Redshift (x64)};" +
                   String.Format("Server={0};Database={1};" +
"UID={2};PWD={3};Port={4};SSL=true;Sslmode=Require",
                   server, DBName, masterUsername,
                   masterUserPassword, port);
          */
          //Redshift ODBC Driver - 32 bits
       string connString = "Driver={Amazon Redshift (x86)};" +
                   String.Format("Server={0};Database={1};" +
"UID={2};PWD={3};Port={4};SSL=true;Sslmode=Require",
server, DBName, masterUsername,
                   masterUserPassword, port);
```

6. Frame the SQL to get the list of pg_catalog tables and views:

```
   string query = "select * from information_schema.tables where
table_schema = 'pg_catalog';";
```

7. Now, connect to the Redshift database using the ODBC provider:

```
   OdbcConnection conn = new OdbcConnection(connString);
          conn.Open();
```

8. Execute the query and retrieve the results using your data provider
    `OdbcDataApapter` object. The results will be displayed on `system.out`:

```
string sql = query;
OdbcDataAdapter da = new OdbcDataAdapter(sql, conn);
da.Fill(ds);
dt = ds.Tables[0];
foreach (DataRow row in dt.Rows)
{
    Console.WriteLine(row["table_catalog"] + ",
" + row["table_name"]);
}
```

9. Remember to close the connection:

```
conn.Close();
```

10. Build and then run the solution. The console output will display the `pg_catalog`
    objects, as follows (tables, views, and so on):

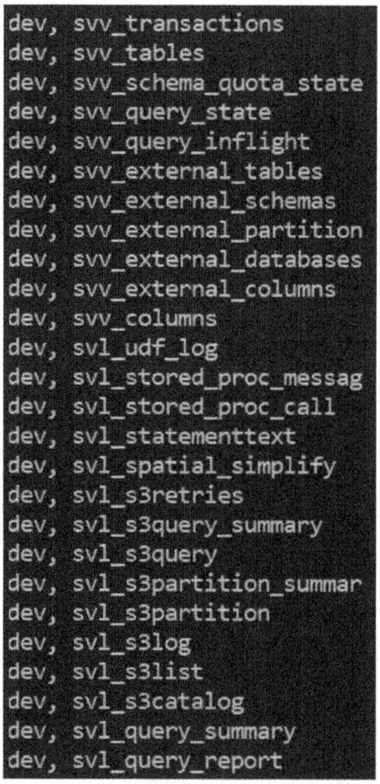

```
dev, svv_transactions
dev, svv_tables
dev, svv_schema_quota_state
dev, svv_query_state
dev, svv_query_inflight
dev, svv_external_tables
dev, svv_external_schemas
dev, svv_external_partition
dev, svv_external_databases
dev, svv_external_columns
dev, svv_columns
dev, svl_udf_log
dev, svl_stored_proc_messag
dev, svl_stored_proc_call
dev, svl_statementtext
dev, svl_spatial_simplify
dev, svl_s3retries
dev, svl_s3query_summary
dev, svl_s3query
dev, svl_s3partition_summar
dev, svl_s3partition
dev, svl_s3log
dev, svl_s3list
dev, svl_s3catalog
dev, svl_query_summary
dev, svl_query_report
```

Figure 1.10 – .NET code output after execution

11. Optionally, you can use this code to allow Visual Studio Code to access your Amazon Redshift cluster (`https://github.com/PacktPublishing/Amazon-Redshift-Cookbook/blob/master/Chapter01/DotNet_connect_toRedshift.cs`).

Connecting to an Amazon Redshift cluster using the command line

PSQL is a command-line frontend to PostgreSQL. It allows you to query the data interactively. In this recipe, we will learn how to install psql and run interactive queries.

Getting ready

To complete this recipe, you will need to do the following:

- Install psql (this comes with PostgreSQL). To learn more about using psql, you can refer to `https://www.postgresql.org/docs/8.4/static/app-psql.html`. Based on your operating system, you can download the corresponding PostgreSQL binary from `https://www.postgresql.org/download/`.

- If you are using a Windows OS, before running psql, you must set the `PGCLIENTENCODING` environment variable to UTF-8:

```
set PGCLIENTENCODING=UTF8
```

- Capture your Amazon Redshift cluster and login credentials.

- Modify the security group attached to the Amazon Redshift cluster to allow connections from the server or client running the psql application, which will allow you to execute the psql code.

How to do it...

Follow these steps to connect to Amazon Redshift through a command-line interface:

1. Open the command-line interface and type in `psql` to make sure it is installed.

2. Provide the connection credentials shown in the following command line to connect to Amazon Redshift:

```
C:\Program Files\PostgreSQL\10\bin> .\psql -h cookbookcluster-
2ee55abd.cvqfeilxsadl.eu-west-1.redshift.amazonaws.com -d dev
-p 5439 -U dbuser
```

```
Password for user dbuser:
Type "help" for help.


dev=# help
You are using psql, the command-line interface to PostgreSQL.
Type:   \copyright for distribution terms
        \h for help with SQL commands
        \? for help with psql commands
        \g or terminate with semicolon to execute query
        \q to quit
```

To connect to Amazon Redshift using the psql command line, you will need the cluster's endpoint, the database's username, and the necessary port. You can use the following command to connect to the Redshift cluster:

```
psql -h <clusterendpoint> -U <dbuser> -d <databasename> -p
<port>
```

3. To check the database connection, you can use a sample query, as shown in the following command:

```
dev=# select sysdate;
```

With that, you have successfully connected to the Amazon Redshift cluster and are ready to run SQL queries!

2
Data Management

Amazon Redshift is a data warehousing service optimized for **online analytical processing (OLAP)** applications. You can start with just a few hundred **gigabytes (GB)** of data and scale to a **petabyte (PB)** or more. Designing your database for analytical processing lets you take full advantage of Amazon Redshift's columnar architecture.

An analytical schema forms the foundation of your data model. This chapter explores how you can set up this schema, thus enabling convenient querying using standard **Structured Query Language (SQL)** and easy administration of access controls.

The following recipes are discussed in this chapter:

- Managing a database in an Amazon Redshift cluster
- Managing a schema in a database
- Managing tables
- Managing views
- Managing materialized views
- Managing stored procedures
- Managing **user-defined functions (UDFs)**

Technical requirements

In order to complete the recipes in this chapter, you will need a SQL client of your choice to access the Amazon Redshift cluster (for example, MySQL Workbench).

Managing a database in an Amazon Redshift cluster

Amazon Redshift consists of at least one database, and it is the highest level in the namespace hierarchy for the objects in the cluster. This recipe will guide you through the steps needed to create and manage a database in Amazon Redshift.

Getting ready

To complete this recipe, you will need the following:

- Access to any SQL interface such as a SQL client or query editor
- An Amazon Redshift cluster endpoint

How to do it...

Let's now set up and configure a database on the Amazon Redshift cluster. Use the SQL client to connect to the cluster and execute the following commands:

1. We will create a new database called qa in the Amazon Redshift cluster. To do this, use the following code:

```
CREATE DATABASE qa
WITH
OWNER awsuser
CONNECTION LIMIT 50;
```

2. To view the details of the database, you will query the PG_DATABASE_INFO, as shown in the following code snippet:

```
SELECT datname, datdba, datconnlimit
FROM pg_database_info
WHERE datdba > 1;
```

This is the expected output:

```
datname datdba  datconnlimit
qa 100 UNLIMITED
```

This query will list the databases that exist in the cluster. If a database is successfully created, it will show up in the query result.

3. To make changes to the database—such as **database name**, **owner**, and **connection limit**—use the following command, replacing `<qauser>` with the respective Amazon Redshift username:

```
/* Change database owner */
ALTER DATABASE qa owner to <qauser>;


/* Change database connection limit */
ALTER DATABASE qa CONNECTION LIMIT 100;


/* Change database name */
ALTER DATABASE qa RENAME TO prod;
```

4. To verify that the changes have been successfully completed, you will query the system table `pg_database_info`, as shown in the following code snippet, to list all the databases in the cluster:

```
SELECT datname, datdba, datconnlimit
FROM pg_database_info
WHERE datdba > 1;
```

This is the expected output:

```
datname datdba datconnlimit
prod 100 100
```

5. You can connect to the `prod` database using the connection endpoint, as follows:

```
<RedshiftClusterHostname>:<Port>/prod
```

Here, `prod` refers to the database you would like to connect to.

6. To delete the previously created database, execute the following query:

```
DROP DATABASE prod;
```

> **Important note**
>
> It is best practice to have only one database in production per Amazon Redshift cluster. Multiple databases could be created in a development environment to enable separation of functions such a development/unit testing/**quality assurance (QA)**. Within the same session, it is not possible to access objects across multiple databases, even though they are present in the same cluster. The only exception to this rule is database users and groups that are available across the databases.

Managing a schema in a database

In Amazon Redshift, a schema is a namespace that groups database objects such as **tables**, **views**, **stored procedures**, and so on. Organizing database objects in a schema is good for security monitoring and also logically groups the objects within a cluster. In this recipe, we will create a sample schema that will be used to hold all the database objects.

Getting ready

To complete this recipe, you will need access to any SQL interface such as a SQL client or query editor.

How to do it...

1. Users can create a schema using the CREATE SCHEMA command. The following steps will enable you to set up a schema with the name finance and add the necessary access to the groups.

2. Create finance_grp, audit_grp, and finance_admin_user groups using the following command:

```
create group finance_grp;
create group audit_grp;
create user finance_admin_usr with password
'<PasswordOfYourChoice>';
```

3. Create a schema named finance with a space quota of 2 terabytes (TB), with a finance_admin_usr schema owner:

```
CREATE schema finance authorization finance_admin_usr
QUOTA 2 TB;
```

You can also modify an existing schema using ALTER SCHEMA or DROP SCHEMA.

4. For the `finance` schema, grant access privileges of USAGE and ALL to the `finance_grp` group. Further, grant read access to the tables in the schema using a SELECT privilege for the `audit_grp` group:

```
GRANT USAGE on SCHEMA finance TO GROUP finance_grp;
GRANT USAGE on SCHEMA finance TO GROUP audit_grp;
GRANT ALL ON schema finance to GROUP finance_grp;
GRANT SELECT ON ALL TABLES IN SCHEMA finance TO GROUP
audit_grp;
```

5. You can verify that the schema and owner group have been created by using the following code:

```
select nspname as schema, usename as owner
from pg_namespace, pg_user
where pg_namespace.nspowner = pg_user.usesysid
and pg_namespace.nspname ='finance';
```

6. Create a `foo` table (or `view/database object`) within the schema by prefixing the schema name along with the table name, as shown in the following command:

```
CREATE TABLE finance.foo (bar int);
```

7. Now, in order to select the `foo` table from the `finance` schema, you will have to prefix the schema name along with the table name, as shown in the following command:

```
select * from finance.foo;
```

The preceding SQL code will not return any rows.

8. Assign a search path to conveniently reference the database objects directly, without requiring the complete namespace of the schema qualifier. The following command sets the search path as `finance` so that you don't need to qualify the schema name every time when working with database objects:

```
set search_path to '$user', finance, public;
```

> **Important note**
>
> The search path allows a convenient way to access the database objects without having to specify the target schema in the namespace when authoring the SQL code. The search path can be configured using the `search_path` parameter with a comma-separated list of schema names. When referencing the database object in a SQL when no target schema is provided, the database object that is in the first available schema list is picked up. You can configure the search path by using the `SET search_path` command at the current session level or at the user level.

9. Now, executing the following `SELECT` query without the schema qualifier automatically locates the `foo` table in the `finance` schema:

```
select * from foo;
```

The preceding SQL code will not return any rows.

Now, the new `finance` schema is ready for use and you can keep creating new database objects in this schema.

> **Important note**
>
> A database is automatically created by default with a `PUBLIC` schema. Identical database object names can be used in different schemas of the database. For example, `finance.customer` and `marketing.customer` are valid table definitions that can be created without any conflict, where `finance` and `marketing` are schema names and `customer` is the table name. Schemas serve the key purpose of easy management through this logical grouping—for example, you can grant `SELECT` access to all the objects at a schema level instead of individual tables.

Managing tables

In Amazon Redshift, you can create a collection of tables within a schema with related entities and attributes. Working backward from your business requirements, you can use different modeling techniques to create tables in Amazon Redshift. You can choose a **star** or **snowflake** schema by using **Normalized**, **Denormalized**, or **Data Vault** data modeling techniques.

In this recipe, we will create tables in the `finance` schema, insert data into those tables and cover the key concepts to leverage the **massively parallel processing** (**MPP**) and columnar architecture.

Getting ready

To complete this recipe you will need a SQL client, or you can use the Amazon Redshift query editor.

How to do it...

Let's explore how to create tables in Amazon Redshift.

1. Let's create a `customer` table in the `finance` schema with `customer_number`, `first_name`, `last_name`, and `date_of_birth` related attributes:

    ```
    CREATE TABLE finance.customer
    (
        customer_number    INTEGER,
        first_name         VARCHAR(50),
        last_name          VARCHAR(50),
        date_of_birth      DATE
    );
    ```

    > **Note**
    > The key ingredient when creating a customer table is to define columns and their corresponding data types. Amazon Redshift supports data types such as numeric, character, date, datetime with time zone, boolean, geometry, HyperLogLog, and super.

2. We will now insert 10 records into the customer table using a multi-value `insert` statement:

    ```
    insert into finance.customer values
    (1, 'foo', 'bar', '1980-01-01'),
    (2, 'john', 'smith', '1990-12-01'),
    (3, 'spock', 'spock', '1970-12-01'),
    (4, 'scotty', 'scotty', '1975-02-01'),
    (5, 'seven', 'of nine', '1990-04-01'),
    (6, 'kathryn', 'janeway', '1995-07-01'),
    (7, 'tuvok', 'tuvok', '1960-06-10'),
    (8, 'john', 'smith', '1965-12-01'),
    (9, 'The Doctor', 'The Doctor', '1979-12-01'),
    (10, 'B Elana', 'Torres', '2000-08-01');
    ```

3. You can now review the information on the customer table using the `svv_table_info` system view. Execute the following query:

```
select "schema", table_id, "table", encoded, diststyle,
sortkey1,  size, tbl_rows
from svv_Table_info
where "table" = 'customer'
and "schema" = 'finance';
```

This is the expected output:

```
schema table_id table encoded diststyle sortkey1 size
tbl_rows
finance 167482 customer Y AUTO(ALL) AUTO(SORTKEY) 14 10
```

Table_id is the object ID and the number of records in the table is 10 rows. The encoded column indicates the table is compressed. Amazon Redshift stores columns in 1 **megabyte (MB)** immutable blocks. The size of the table is 14 MB. Let's dive into the terminology and concept of `diststyle` and `sortkey`. The customer table is created with default sort key of AUTO, where Amazon Redshift handles the distribution style of the table on the computer nodes.

- `diststyle` is a table property that dictates how that table's data is distributed throughout the cluster.

- KEY: The value is hashed, and the same value goes to same location (slice) on the compute node.

- ALL: The full table data goes to the first slice of every compute node.

- EVEN: Round-robin across all the compute nodes.

- AUTO: When the table is small, it starts with an AUTO style, and when it becomes larger in size, Amazon Redshift converts it to an EVEN style.

Further information about distribution styles can be found at the following link:

https://docs.aws.amazon.com/redshift/latest/dg/c_choosing_
dist_sort.html

1. Let's run a query against the customer table to list customers who were born before 1980:

```
select *
from finance.customer
where extract(year from date_of_birth) < 1980;
```

2. You can also create a copy of the permanent table using **create table as** (**CTAS**). Let's execute the following query to create another table for a customer born in 1980:

```
create table finance.customer_dob_1980 as
select *
from finance.customer
where extract(year from date_of_birth) = 1980 ;
```

3. You can also create temporary tables—for example, to generate IDs in a data loading operation. The temporary tables can only be queried during the current session and are automatically dropped when the session ends. The temporary tables are created in the session-specific schema and are not visible to any other user. You can use a `create temporary table` command to do this. Execute the following three queries in single session:

```
create temporary table #customer(custid integer
IDENTITY(1,1), customer_number integer);
insert into #customer (customer_number) values(1);
select * from #customer;
```

This is the expected output:

```
custid   customer_number
1 1
```

4. Reconnect to the Amazon Redshift cluster using the SQL client. Reconnecting will create a new session. Now, try to execute the following query against the `#customer` temporary table. You will get an **ERROR: 42P01: relation "#customer" does not exist** error message as the temporary tables are only visible to the current session:

```
select * from #customer;
```

How it works...

When you create a table in Amazon Redshift, it stores the data on disk, column by column, on 1 MB blocks. Amazon Redshift by default compresses the columns, which reduces the storage footprint and the **input/output (I/O)** when you execute a query against the table. Amazon Redshift provides different distribution styles to spread the data across all the compute nodes, to leverage the MPP architecture for your workload. The metadata and the table summary information can be queried using the catalog table and summary view.

Amazon Redshift stores metadata about the customer table. You can query the pg_table_def catalog table to retrieve this information. You can execute the following query to view the table/column structure:

```
select * from pg_table_def where schemaname = 'finance';.
```

> **Important note**
>
> When data is inserted into a table, Amazon Redshift automatically builds, in memory, the metadata of the minimum and maximum values of each block. This metadata, known as a zone map, is accessed before a disk scan in order to identify which blocks are relevant to a query. Amazon Redshift does not have indexes; it does, however, have sort keys. Sort key columns govern how data is physically sorted for a table on disk and can be used as a lever to improve query performance. Sort keys will be covered in depth in the performance-tuning best practices chapter.

Managing views

View database objects allow the result of a query to be stored. In Amazon Redshift, views run each time a view is mentioned in a query. The advantage of using a view instead of a table is that it can allow access to only a subset of data on a table, join more than one table in a single virtual table, and act as an aggregated table, and it takes up no space on the database since only the definition is saved, hence making it convenient to abstract complicated queries. In this recipe, we will create views to store queries for the underlying tables.

Getting ready

To complete this recipe, you will need access to any SQL interface such as a SQL client or query editor.

How to do it...

Let's create a view using the CREATE VIEW command. We will use the following steps to create a view:

1. Create a finance.customer_vw view based on the results of the query on finance.customer:

```
CREATE VIEW finance.customer_vw
AS
SELECT customer_number,
       first_name,
       last_name,
       EXTRACT(year FROM date_of_birth) AS year_of_birth
FROM finance.customer;
```

2. To verify that a view has been created, you can use the following command:

```
SELECT table_schema as schema_name,
       table_name as view_name,
       view_definition
FROM information_schema.views
WHERE table_schema not in ('information_schema', 'pg_
catalog')
ORDER by schema_name,
         view_name;
```

> **Note**
>
> This script will provide an output of the views created under a particular schema and the SQL script for the view.

3. We can now select directly from the finance.customer_vw view, just like with any another database object, like so:

```
SELECT * from finance.customer_vw limit 5;
```

> **Note**
>
> Here, the `finance.customer_vw` view abstracts the `date_of_birth`
> **personally identifiable information** (**PII**) from the underlying table and
> provides the user an abstracted view of only the essential data for that year to
> determine the age group.

This is the expected output:

```
outputcustomer_number,first_name,last_name,year_of_birth
1 foo bar 1980
2 john smith 1990
3 spock spock 1970
4 scotty scotty 1975
5 seven of nine 1990
```

4. To delete the previously created view, you can use the following command:

```
DROP VIEW finance.customer_vw ;
```

Managing materialized views

A materialized view is a database object that persists the results of a query to disk. In
Amazon Redshift, materialized views allow frequently used complex queries to be stored
as separate database objects, allowing you to access these database objects directly, and
enabling faster query responses.

Employing materialized views is a common approach to powering repeatable queries in
a **business intelligence** (**BI**) dashboard, and avoids expensive computation each time.
Furthermore, materialized views allow an incremental refresh of the results, using the
underlying table data. In this recipe, we will create a materialized view to query the tables
and also to persist the results to fetch the data more quickly.

Getting ready

To complete this recipe, you will need access to any SQL interface such as a SQL client
or a query editor.

How to do it...

Let's create a materialized view using the CREATE MATERIALIZED VIEW command. We will use the following steps to create a materialized view, in order to store the precomputed results of an analytical query and also see how to refresh it:

1. Create a `finance.customer_agg_mv` materialized view using the results of the query based on `finance.customer`:

    ```
    CREATE MATERIALIZED VIEW finance.customer_agg_mv
    AS
    SELECT
            EXTRACT(year FROM date_of_birth) AS year_of_birth,
            count(1) customer_cnt
    FROM finance.customer
    group by EXTRACT(year FROM date_of_birth);
    ```

2. We can now select directly from `finance.customer`, just like with any another database object, like so:

    ```
    select * from finance.customer limit 5;
    ```

    This is the expected output:

    ```
    outputyear_of_birth,customer_cnt
    1975 1
    1979 1
    1995 1
    1970 1
    1965 1
    ```

3. You can verify the state of a materialized view by using a STV_MV_INFO system table (https://docs.aws.amazon.com/redshift/latest/dg/r_STV_MV_INFO.html):

    ```
    select * from STV_MV_INFO where name='customer_agg_mv';
    ```

    This is the expected output:

    ```
    outputdb_name,schema,name,updated_upto_xid,is_
    stale,owner_user_name,state,autorefresh, autorewrite
    vdwpoc   finance customer_agg_mv 24642401 f vdwadmin 1 f t
    ```

Here, `stale='f'` indicates the data is current, reflecting the `daily_product_reviews` underlying base table. This column can be used to refresh the materialized view when needed. Another key column in the `STV_MV_INFO` table is the `state` column, which indicates if an incremental refresh is possible (`state=1`) or not (`state=0`). In the materialized view we created a `state=1` state, which indicates a faster incremental refresh is possible.

4. Now, let's load more data into the underlying table `finance.customer`, using the following command, and check the `STV_MV_INFO` table:

```
insert into finance.customer values
(11, 'mark', 'bar', '1980-02-01'),
(12, 'pete', 'smith', '1990-2-01'),
 (13, 'woofy', 'spock', '1980-11-01'),
 (14, 'woofy jr', 'scotty', '1975-03-01'),
 (15, 'eleven', 'of nine', '1990-07-01');
```

5. Query the `STV_MV_INFO` table again to check the status of the materialized view:

```
select name,is_stale,state from STV_MV_INFO where
name='customer_agg_mv';
```

This is the expected output:

```
name,is_stale,state
customer_agg_mv
t 1
```

Note that `stale = 't'` indicates that the underlying data for the materialized view has changed, but it is possible to refresh it incrementally.

6. Refresh the materialized view using the `REFRESH MATERIALIZED VIEW` command and check the status again:

```
REFRESH MATERIALIZED VIEW finance.customer_agg_mv;
select name,is_stale, state from STV_MV_INFO where
name='customer_agg_mv';
```

This is the expected output:

```
name,is_stale,state
customer_agg_mv   f 1
```

As we can see from the preceding code snippet, `customer_agg_mv` is now updated to reflect the underlying table data.

How it works...

A materialized view can be updated with the latest data from the underlying tables by using the REFRESH MATERIALIZED VIEW command. When the materialized view is being refreshed, it executes a separate transaction to update the dataset. Amazon Redshift also supports an **autorefresh** option to keep the materialized view up to date as soon as possible after base tables change.

Managing stored procedures

Stored procedures in Amazon Redshift are user-created objects using a **Procedural Language/PostgreSQL (PL/pgSQL)** procedural programming language. Stored procedures support both **data definition language (DDL)** and **data manipulation language (DML)**. Stored procedures can take in input arguments but do not necessarily need to return results. **PL/pgSQL** also supports conditional logic, loops, and case statements. Stored procedures are commonly used to build reusable **extract, transform, load (ETL)** data pipelines and enable the **database administrator (DBA)** to automate routine administrative activities—for example, periodically dropping unused tables.

The **SECURITY** attribute controls who has privileges to access certain database objects.

Stored procedures can be created with security definer controls to allow execution of a procedure without giving access to underlying tables—for example, they can drop a table created by another user and enable the DBA to automate administrative activities.

Getting ready

To complete this recipe, you will need the following:

- Access to the **Amazon Web Services (AWS)** Management Console
- Access to any SQL interface such as a SQL client or query editor

How to do it...

In this recipe, we will start with creating a scalar Python-based UDF that will be used to parse an **Extensible Markup Language (XML)** input:

1. Connect to Amazon Redshift using the SQL client, and copy and paste the following code to create a sp_cookbook stored procedure:

```
Create schema cookbook;
create or replace procedure sp_cookbook(indate in date,
records_out INOUT refcursor) as
```

```
$$
declare
   integer_var int;
begin
   RAISE INFO 'running first cookbook storedprocedure on
date %',  indate;
   drop table if exists cookbook.cookbook_tbl;
   create table cookbook.cookbook_tbl
   (recipe_name varchar(50),
   recipe_date date
   );
   insert into cookbook.cookbook_tbl values('stored
procedure', indate);
   GET DIAGNOSTICS integer_var := ROW_COUNT;
   RAISE INFO 'rows inserted into cookbook_tbl = %',
integer_var;
     OPEN records_out FOR SELECT * FROM cookbook.cookbook_
tbl;
END;
$$ LANGUAGE plpgsql;
```

This stored procedure is taking two **parameters**: indate is the input, and records_out serves as both an input and output parameter. This stored procedure uses DDL and DML statements. The current user is the owner of the stored procedure and is also the owner of the cookbook.cookbook_tbl table.

> **Note**
>
> Some older versions of SQL client tools may produce an "unterminated dollar-quoted string at or near "$$" error. Ensure that you have the latest version of the SQL client—for example, ensure you are using version 124 or higher for the SQL Workbench/J client.

2. Now, let's execute the sp_cookbook stored procedure using the following statements:

```
call sp_cookbook(current_date, 'inputcursor');
fetch all from inputcursor;
```

This is the expected output:

```
Message
running first cookbook storedprocedure on date 2020-12-13
rows inserted into cookbook_tbl = 1
recipe_name recipe_date
stored procedure   2020-12-13 00:00:00
```

3. To view a definition of the previously created stored procedure, you can run the following statement:

```
SHOW PROCEDURE sp_cookbook(indate in date, records_out
INOUT refcursor);
```

4. We will now create another stored procedure with a security definer privilege:

```
create or replace procedure public.sp_self_
service(tblName in varchar(60)) as
            $$
begin
    RAISE INFO 'running sp_self_service to drop table %',
tblName;
      execute 'drop table if exists cookbook.' || tblName;
   RAISE INFO 'table dropped %',   tblName;
END;
$$ LANGUAGE plpgsql
SECURITY DEFINER;
```

5. Let's create a user and check whether they have a permission to drop the `cookbook.cookbook_tbl` table. The `user1` user does not have a permission to drop the table:

```
create user user1 with password 'Cookbook1';
grant execute on procedure public.sp_self_service(tblName
in varchar(60)) to user1;
```

```
set SESSION authorization  user1;
select current_user;
drop table cookbook.cookbook_tbl;
```

This is the expected output:

```
ERROR: 42501: permission denied for schema cookbook
```

6. When `user1` executes the `sp_self_service` stored procedure, the procedure runs with the security context of the owner of the procedure:

```
set SESSION authorization  user1;
select current_user;
call public.sp_self_service('cookbook_tbl');
```

This is the expected output:

```
running sp_self_service to drop table cookbook_tbl
table
```

This allows the user to drop the table without providing the full permissions for the tables in the cookbook schema.

How it works...

Amazon Redshift uses the PL/pgSQL procedural language for authoring the stored procedures. PL/pgSQL provides programmatic access that can be used to author control structures to the SQL language and allow complex computations. For example, you have a stored procedure that can create users and set up necessary access that meets your organizational needs—hence, rather than invoking several commands, this can now be done in a single step. You can find the complete reference to the PL/pgSQL procedural language at https://www.postgresql.org/docs/8.0/plpgsql.html and ready-to-use stored useful procedures at https://github.com/awslabs/amazon-redshift-utils/tree/master/src/StoredProcedures. The **SECURITY** access attribute of a stored procedure defines the privileges to access underlying database objects used. By default, an **INVOKER** is used to access the user privileges and the **SECURITY DEFINER** allows the procedure user to inherit the privileges of the owner.

Managing UDFs

Scalar UDF functions in Amazon Redshift are routines that are able to take parameters, perform calculations, and return the results. UDFs are handy when performing complex calculations that can be stored and reused in a SQL statement. Amazon Redshift supports UDFs that can be authored using either Python or SQL. In addition, Amazon Redshift also supports AWS Lambda UDFs that open up further possibilities to invoke other AWS services. For example, let's say the latest customer address information is stored in AWS DynamoDB—you can invoke an AWS Lambda UDF to retrieve this using a SQL statement in Amazon Redshift.

Getting ready

To complete this recipe, you will need the following:

- Access to the AWS console
- Access to any SQL interface such as a SQL client or query editor
- Access to create an AWS Lambda function
- Access to create an **Identity and Access Management** (**IAM**) role that can invoke AWS Lambda and attach it to Amazon Redshift

How to do it...

In this recipe, we will start with a scalar Python-based UDF that will be used to parse an XML input:

1. Connect to Amazon Redshift using the SQL client, and copy and paste the following code to create an f_parse_xml function:

```
CREATE OR REPLACE FUNCTION f_parse_xml
(xml VARCHAR(MAX), input_rank int)
RETURNS varchar(max)
STABLE
AS $$
    import xml.etree.ElementTree as ET
    root = ET.fromstring(xml)
    res = ''
    for country in root.findall('country'):
        rank = country.find('rank').text
        if rank == input_rank:
```

```
        res =   name = country.get('name') + ':' + rank
            break
    return res
$$ LANGUAGE plpythonu;
```

> **Important note**
>
> The preceding Python-based UDF takes in the XML data and uses the `xml.etree.ElementTree` library to parse it to locate an element, using the input rank. See `https://docs.python.org/3/library/xml.etree.elementtree.html` for more options that are available with this XML library.

2. Now, let's validate the `f_parse_xml` function using the following statement, by locating the country name that has the rank 2:

```
select
f_parse_xml('<data>         <country name="Liechtenstein">
<rank>2</rank>              <year>2008</year>
<gdppc>141100</gdppc>           <neighbor name="Austria"
direction="E"/>         <neighbor name="Switzerland"
direction="W"/> </country></data>', '2') as col1
```

This is the expected output:

```
col1
Liechtenstein:2
```

3. We will now create another AWS Lambda-based UDF. Navigate to the AWS Management Console and pick the AWS Lambda service and click on **Create function**, as shown in the following screenshot:

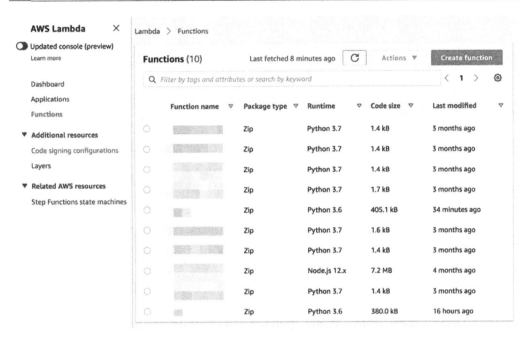

Figure 2.1 – Creating a Lambda function using the AWS Management Console

4. In the **Create function** screen, enter `rs_lambda` under **Function name**, choose a **Python 3.6** runtime, and click on **Create function**.

5. Under the **Function code textbox**, copy and paste the following code and press the **Deploy** button:

```
import json
def lambda_handler(event, context):
    ret = dict()
    ret['success'] = True
    ret['results'] = ["bar"]
    ret['error_msg'] = "none"
    ret['num_records'] = 1
    return json.dumps(ret)
```

In the preceding Python-based Lambda function, a sample result is returned. This function can further be integrated to call any other AWS service—for example, you can invoke AWS **Key Management Service** (**KMS**) to encrypt input data.

6. Navigate to AWS **IAM** in the AWS Management Console and create a new role, RSInvokeLambda, using the following policy statement by replacing [Your_AWS_Account_Number], [Your_AWS_Region] with your AWS account number/region and attaching the role to the Amazon Redshift cluster:

```
{
    "Version": "2012-10-17",
    "Statement": [
        {
            "Effect": "Allow",
            "Action": "lambda:InvokeFunction",
            "Resource": "arn:aws:lambda:[Your_AWS_
Region]:[Your_AWS_Account_Number]:function:rs_lambda"
        }
    ]
}
```

7. Connect to Amazon Redshift using the SQL client, and copy and paste the following code to create a f_redshift_lambda function that links the AWS Lambda rs_lambda function:

```
CREATE OR REPLACE EXTERNAL FUNCTION f_redshift_lambda
(bar varchar)
RETURNS varchar STABLE
LAMBDA 'rs_lambda'
IAM_ROLE 'arn:aws:iam::[Your_AWS_Account_Number]:role/
RSInvokeLambda';
```

8. You can validate the f_redshift_lambda function by using the following SQL statement:

```
select f_redshift_lambda ('input_str') as col1
--output
col1
bar
```

Amazon Redshift is now able to invoke the AWS Lambda function using a SQL statement.

How it works...

Amazon Redshift allows you to create a scalar UDF using either a SQL SELECT clause or a Python program in addition to the AWS Lambda UDF illustrated in this recipe. The scalar UDFs are stored with Amazon Redshift and are available to any user when granted the required access. You can find a collection of several ready-to-use UDFs that can be used to implement some of the complex reusable logic within a SQL statement at the following link: `https://github.com/aws-samples/amazon-redshift-udfs`.

3
Loading and Unloading Data

In this chapter, we will delve into the data loading process, which allows us to put transformed data from source systems into a target data warehouse table structure. While data can be loaded into Amazon Redshift using an `INSERT` statement (as in the case of other relational databases), it is more efficient to bulk load the data, given the volumes that a data warehouse handles. For example, in an ordering system-based data warehouse table, usually, the entire previous day's worth of data needs to be loaded rather than individual orders. Similarly, data from the data warehouse can be exported to other applications in bulk using the unload feature.

There are multiple ways of loading data into an Amazon Redshift cluster. The most common way is using the `COPY` command to load data from Amazon S3. This chapter will cover all the different ways you can load data into a Redshift cluster from different sources.

The following recipes will be covered in this chapter:

- Loading data from Amazon S3 using COPY
- Loading data from Amazon EMR
- Loading data from Amazon DynamoDB

- Loading data from remote hosts

- Updating and inserting data

- Unloading data to S3

Technical requirements

You will need the following technical requirements to complete the recipes in this chapter:

- Access to the AWS Console.

- An AWS administrator should create an IAM user by following *Recipe 1 – Creating an IAM user* in the *Appendix*. This IAM user will be used in some of the recipes in this chapter.

- An AWS administrator should create an IAM role by following *Recipe 3 – Creating an IAM role for an AWS service* in the *Appendix*. This IAM role will be used in some of the recipes in this chapter.

- An AWS administrator should deploy the AWS CloudFormation template (`https://github.com/PacktPublishing/Amazon-Redshift-Cookbook/blob/master/Chapter03/chapter_3_CFN.yaml`) and create two IAM policies:

   a. An IAM policy attached to the IAM user, which will give them access to Amazon Redshift, Amazon RDS, Amazon DynamoDB, Amazon S3, and Amazon EMR.

   b. An IAM policy attached to the IAM role, which will allow the Amazon Redshift cluster to access Amazon S3 and Amazon DynamoDB.

- Attach an IAM role to the Amazon Redshift cluster by following *Recipe 4 – Attaching an IAM role to the Amazon Redshift cluster* in the *Appendix*. Take note of the IAM role name as we will reference it in the recipes in this chapter as [Your-Redshift_Role].

- An Amazon Redshift cluster deployed in AWS region eu-west-1.

- Amazon Redshift cluster master user credentials.

- Access to any SQL interface, such as a SQL client or Amazon Redshift query editor.

- Create an Amazon S3 bucket for staging and unloading the data in specific recipes. We will reference it in the recipes in this chapter as [Your-Amazon_S3_Bucket].

- An AWS account number. We will reference it in the recipes in this chapter as [Your-AWS_Account_Id].

Loading data from Amazon S3 using COPY

Amazon Redshift is a **relational database management system** (**RDBMS**) that supports a number of data model structures, including **dimensional**, **denormalized**, and **aggregate** (rollup) structures. This makes it optimal for analytics.

In this recipe, we will set up two separate sample datasets in Amazon Redshift that are publicly available:

- A dimensional model by using a **Star Schema Benchmark** (**SSB**) (https://www.cs.umb.edu/~poneil/StarSchemaB.pdf), a retail system-based dataset.

- A denormalized model by using the Amazon.com customer product reviews dataset.

For loading the datasets, we will use the COPY command, which allows data to be copied from Amazon S3 to Amazon Redshift. This is the recommend approach for loading large amounts of data.

Getting ready

To complete this recipe, you will need to do the following:

- Deploy an Amazon Redshift cluster in AWS region eu-west-1.

- Create Amazon Redshift cluster master user credentials.

- Access any SQL interface, such as a SQL client or the Amazon Redshift Query Editor.

- Attach an IAM role to your Amazon Redshift cluster that can access Amazon S3.

How to do it...

We must create and load the following dimensional model, which is based on the SSB, to create an illustrative retail system:

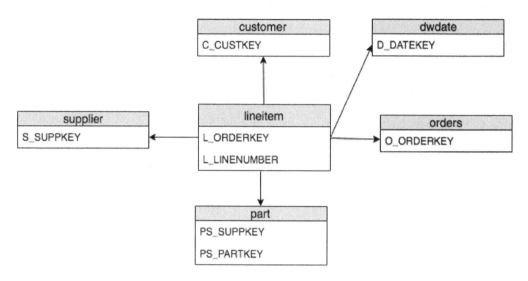

Figure 3.1 – SSB data model

Now, let's create some tables that mimic the preceding data model, as well as populate the data in the tables:

1. We will start by setting up the data in our Amazon S3 bucket. Download the Ssb_
    Table_Ddl.sql file from https://github.com/PacktPublishing/
    Amazon-Redshift-Cookbook/blob/master/Chapter03/Ssb_Table_
    Ddl.sql and copy and paste it into any SQL client tool. Then, execute it to create
    a dimensional model for the retail system dataset:

```
DROP TABLE IF EXISTS lineitem;
DROP TABLE IF EXISTS supplier;
DROP TABLE IF EXISTS part;
DROP TABLE IF EXISTS orders;
DROP TABLE IF EXISTS customer;
DROP TABLE IF EXISTS dwdate;
CREATE TABLE customer
(
   C_CUSTKEY        BIGINT NOT NULL,
   C_NAME           VARCHAR(25),
```

```
    C_ADDRESS          VARCHAR(40),

    C_NATIONKEY        BIGINT,

    C_PHONE            VARCHAR(15),

    C_ACCTBAL          DECIMAL(18,4),

    C_MKTSEGMENT       VARCHAR(10),

    C_COMMENT          VARCHAR(117)

...

CREATE TABLE dwdate

(

    d_datekey              INTEGER NOT NULL,

    d_date                 VARCHAR(19) NOT NULL,

    d_dayofweek            VARCHAR(10) NOT NULL,

    d_month                VARCHAR(10) NOT NULL,

    d_year                 INTEGER NOT NULL,

    d_lastdayinweekfl      VARCHAR(1) NOT NULL,

    d_lastdayinmonthfl     VARCHAR(1) NOT NULL,

    d_holidayfl            VARCHAR(1) NOT NULL,

    d_weekdayfl            VARCHAR(1) NOT NULL

);
```

2. Now, load the data from the public S3 bucket into the preceding tables. Use any SQL client tool and execute the following command by replacing the [Your-AWS_ Account_Id] and [Your-Redshift_Role] values shown in the *Technical requirements* section:

```
COPY customer from 's3://packt-redshift-cookbook/
customer/' iam_role 'arn:aws:iam::[Your-AWS_Account_
Id]:role/[Your-Redshift_Role]'  CSV gzip COMPUPDATE
PRESET;

COPY orders from 's3://packt-redshift-cookbook/orders/'
iam_role 'arn:aws:iam::[Your-AWS_Account_Id]:role/[Your-
Redshift_Role]'  CSV gzip COMPUPDATE PRESET;

COPY part from 's3://packt-redshift-cookbook/part/'
iam_role 'arn:aws:iam::[Your-AWS_Account_Id]:role/[Your-
Redshift_Role]'  CSV gzip COMPUPDATE PRESET;

COPY supplier from 's3://packt-redshift-cookbook/
supplier/' iam_role 'arn:aws:iam::[Your-AWS_Account_
Id]:role/[Your-Redshift_Role]'  CSV gzip COMPUPDATE
PRESET;
```

```
COPY lineitem from 's3://packt-redshift-cookbook/
lineitem/' iam_role 'arn:aws:iam::[Your-AWS_Account_
Id]:role/[Your-Redshift_Role]'  CSV gzip COMPUPDATE
PRESET;
```

```
COPY dwdate from 's3://packt-redshift-cookbook/dwdate/'
iam_role 'arn:aws:iam::[Your-AWS_Account_Id]:role/[Your-
Redshift_Role]'  CSV gzip COMPUPDATE PRESET dateformat
'auto';
```

> **Note**
>
> The script will take around 10 minutes to complete. Each table load will output `Load into table *** completed, *** record(s) loaded successfully` to acknowledge a successful execution.

3. Verify that all the tables have been loaded with the correct number of rows using the following command:

```
select count(1) from  lineitem; -- expected rows:
599037902
```

```
select count(1) from  supplier; -- expected rows: 1100000
```

```
select count(1) from  part; -- expected rows:20000000
```

```
select count(1) from  orders; -- expected rows: 76000000
```

```
select count(1) from  customer; -- expected rows:
15000000
```

```
select count(1) from  dwdate; -- expected rows: 2556
```

4. Now, the dimensional model is ready for querying. We can run an analytical query similar to the following to join the different tables of the dimensional model:

```
SELECT c_mktsegment,
       COUNT(o_orderkey) AS orders_count,
       SUM(l_quantity) AS quantity,
       SUM(l_extendedprice) AS extendedprice,
       COUNT(DISTINCT P_PARTKEY) AS parts_count,
       COUNT(DISTINCT L_SUPPKEY) AS supplier_count,
       COUNT(DISTINCT o_custkey) AS customer_count
FROM lineitem
   JOIN orders ON l_orderkey = o_orderkey
   JOIN customer c ON o_custkey = c_custkey
   JOIN dwdate
```

```
    ON d_date = l_commitdate
  AND d_year = 1992
   JOIN part ON P_PARTKEY = l_PARTKEY
   JOIN supplier ON L_SUPPKEY = S_SUPPKEY
GROUP BY c_mktsegment;
```

5. In addition to the dimensional model, let's also create a denormalized table using the Amazon product review data. Create the product review data table using the following code:

```
CREATE TABLE product_reviews(
  marketplace varchar(2),
  customer_id varchar(32),
  review_id varchar(24),
  product_id varchar(24),
  product_parent varchar(32),
  product_title varchar(512),
  star_rating int,
  helpful_votes int,
  total_votes int,
  vine char(1),
  verified_purchase char(1),
  review_headline varchar(256),
  review_body varchar(max),
  review_date date,
  year int,
  product_category varchar(32),
  insert_ts datetime default current_timestamp)
DISTSTYLE KEY
DISTKEY (customer_id)
SORTKEY (
  marketplace,
  product_category,
  review_date);
```

6. Now, let's load the review data into the `product_reviews` table by executing the following command in the SQL client:

```
COPY product_reviews
FROM 's3://packt-redshift-cookbook/reviews_parquet/'
iam_role 'arn:aws:iam::[Your-AWS_Account_Id]:role/[Your-
Redshift_Role]' PARQUET;
```

7. Now, the `product_reviews` table is ready for querying. Execute the following query to get the top 10 most voted products:

```
SELECT product_title,
       SUM(total_votes)
FROM product_reviews
WHERE product_category = 'Apparel'
GROUP BY product_title
ORDER BY SUM(total_votes) DESC LIMIT 10;
```

With that, we have used Amazon S3 to move the data into Amazon Redshift using the `COPY` command and set up a **dimensional** and **denormalized** dataset.

How it works...

The Amazon Redshift `COPY` command is used to load large datasets into Amazon Redshift from Amazon S3. This is the recommended approach as the `COPY` command takes advantage of the **massively parallel processing (MPP)** capabilities of the Amazon Redshift cluster to ingest the data into the Amazon Redshift table efficiently. The `COPY` command also provides several options for ingesting incoming files. This includes support for multiple files formats (CSV, Parquet, JSON, and so on) with error handling and the flexibility to ingest all kinds of structured data. Please see https://docs.aws.amazon.com/redshift/latest/dg/copy-parameters-data-source-s3.html for more details.

Please also see the best practices of the `COPY` command at https://docs.aws.amazon.com/redshift/latest/dg/c_loading-data-best-practices.html.

Loading data from Amazon EMR

Amazon **Elastic Map Reduce** (**EMR**) allows you to execute big data frameworks such as Apache Hadoop and Apache Spark on AWS managed infrastructure. Amazon EMR is used for both batch and near-real-time processing as part of an analytical data pipeline.

In this recipe, we will see how to leverage Amazon EMR to load data into the customer table on Amazon Redshift using the `COPY` command.

Getting ready

To complete this recipe, you will need to do the following:

- Ensure you have access to the AWS Console.

- Deploy an Amazon Redshift cluster in AWS region eu-west-1.

- Create Amazon Redshift cluster master user credentials.

- Gain access to any SQL interface, such as a SQL client or the Amazon Redshift Query Editor.

- Deploy an Amazon EMR cluster in AWS region eu-west-1. Refer to `https://docs.aws.amazon.com/emr/latest/ManagementGuide/emr-gs.html` to set up an EMR cluster.

- Ensure you have open connectivity between the Amazon EMR cluster and the Amazon Redshift cluster.

How to do it...

In this recipe, we will allow Amazon EMR to directly ingest data into Amazon Redshift. The following steps will guide you through the process of connecting to the Amazon EMR cluster to initiate data loading.

First, you must capture the Amazon Redshift public key and cluster IP addresses. To connect to the ingested data from the remote host (Amazon EMR), you will need to SSH information for the target Amazon Redshift cluster. You can obtain this by logging into the AWS Console, navigating to your Amazon Redshift cluster, selecting **Properties**, and clicking on **Connection Details**, as shown here:

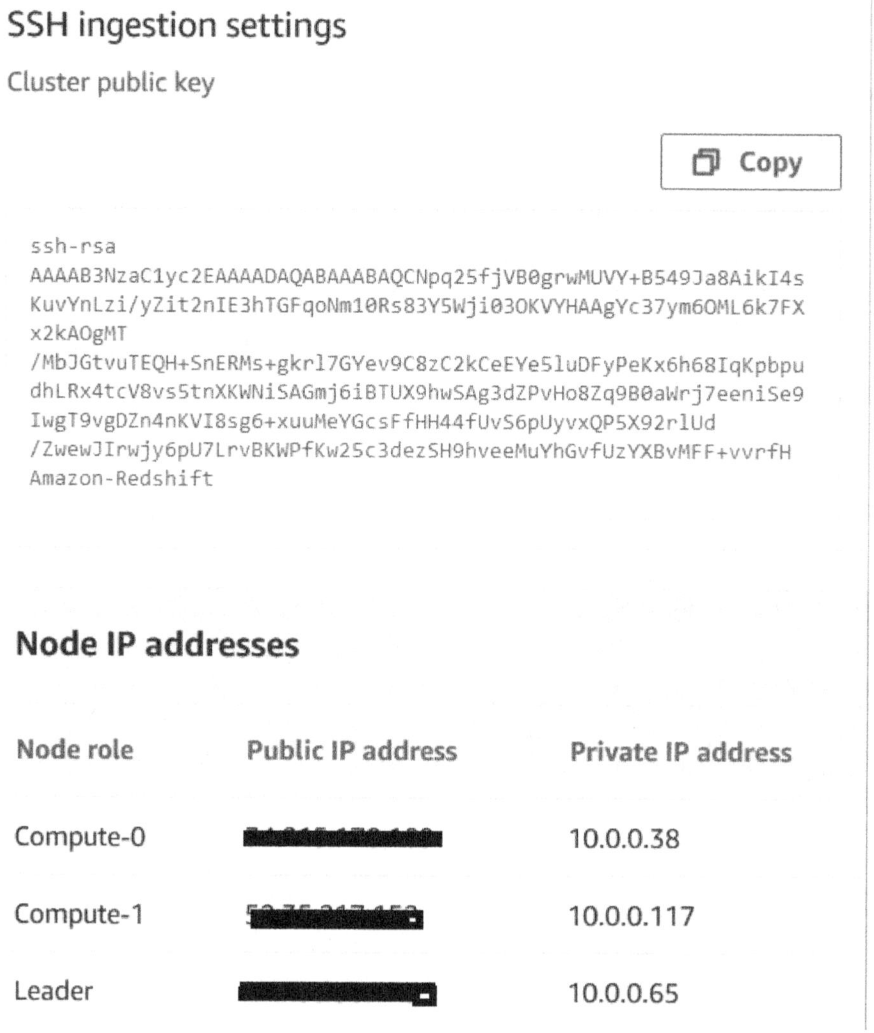

SSH ingestion settings

Cluster public key

🗐 Copy

```
ssh-rsa
AAAAB3NzaC1yc2EAAAADAQABAAABAQCNpq25fjVB0grwMUVY+B549Ja8AikI4s
KuvYnLzi/yZit2nIE3hTGFqoNm10Rs83Y5Wji03OKVYHAAgYc37ym6OML6k7FX
x2kAOgMT
/MbJGtvuTEQH+SnERMs+gkrl7GYev9C8zC2kCeEYe5luDFyPeKx6h68IqKpbpu
dhLRx4tcV8vs5tnXKWNiSAGmj6iBTUX9hwSAg3dZPvHo8Zq9B0aWrj7eeniSe9
IwgT9vgDZn4nKVI8sg6+xuuMeYGcsFfHH44fUvS6pUyvxQP5X92rlUd
/ZwewJIrwjy6pU7LrvBKWPfKw25c3dezSH9hveeMuYhGvfUzYXBvMFF+vvrfH
Amazon-Redshift
```

Node IP addresses

Node role	Public IP address	Private IP address
Compute-0	████████████████	10.0.0.38
Compute-1	████████████████	10.0.0.117
Leader	████████████████	10.0.0.65

Figure 3.2 – Capturing an Amazon Redshift cluster's public key and IP addresses

Now, follow these steps:

1. Add all the IP addresses for Amazon Redshift to the inbound rule in the security group of the Amazon EMR cluster for SSH with the TCP protocol on Port 22.

2. On each EMR node, add the Amazon Redshift public key to the following file while using SSH to connect to the host. You will need to use your key pair to connect:

```
/home/<ssh_username>/.ssh/authorized_keys
```

3. On the EMR cluster, download the data for the customer table from the S3 bucket. SSH into the EMR master node using the Hadoop user. Once you've logged in, run the following code to create hdfs and s3-dist-cp to copy the files from s3 to hdfs:

```
hadoop fs -mkdir /output/cust
s3-dist-cp --src s3://packt-redshift-cookbook/customer/
--dest hdfs:///output/customer/
```

4. Log into the Amazon Redshift cookbook cluster using the SQL client or Query Editor and create the customer table:

```
DROP TABLE IF EXISTS customer;
CREATE TABLE customer
(
C_CUSTKEYBIGINT NOT NULL,
C_NAMEVARCHAR(25),
C_ADDRESSVARCHAR(40),
C_NATIONKEYBIGINT,
C_PHONEVARCHAR(15),
C_ACCTBALDECIMAL(18,4),
C_MKTSEGMENT VARCHAR(10),
C_COMMENTVARCHAR(117)
)
diststyle ALL;
```

5. Frame the COPY command to load data into the Redshift customer table. In the COPY command, we are providing the Amazon EMR cluster ID and the HDFS path with *, which will load all the files on that path. The COPY command loads data in parallel into the Redshift table:

```
COPY customer from 'emr://[YOUR-EMR-CLUSTERID]/output/
cust/*'    '
iam_role 'arn:aws:iam::[Your-AWS_Account_Id]:role/[Your-
Redshift_Role]'
CSV
```

```
gzip
COMPUPDATE PRESET;
```

6. Execute the COPY command using the Redshift Query Editor.

7. Verify the record count of the data that was loaded into the part table:

```
Select count(*) from customer;
```

15000000 records have been loaded into the customer table.

Loading data from Amazon DynamoDB

Amazon DynamoDB is a NoSQL serverless, fully managed service. Amazon DynamoDB provides single-digit milliseconds performance at any scale. DynamoDB is designed to be used as an operational database in OLTP use cases where you know access patterns and can design your data model for them. When you want to perform analytics, you can complement Amazon DynamoDB using Amazon Redshift OLAP capabilities.

In this recipe, we will learn how data from the Amazon DynamoDB parts table can be copied to the Amazon Redshift table using the COPY command. We will use the full table copy approach in this recipe.

Amazon DynamoDB can also capture changes to the tables in DynamoDB streams. This can be leveraged to copy near-real-time data into Amazon Redshift tables via Amazon Lambda and the Amazon Kinesis Firehose service. This will be covered later in this book.

Getting ready

To complete this recipe, you will need to do the following:

- Ensure you have access to the AWS Console.

- Deploy an Amazon Redshift cluster in AWS region eu-west-1.

- Create Amazon Redshift cluster master user credentials.

- Access any SQL interface, such as a SQL client or the Amazon Redshift query editor.

- Deploy an Amazon DynamoDB table in AWS region eu-west-1. Please refer to https://docs.aws.amazon.com/amazondynamodb/latest/developerguide/GettingStarted.Python.html to set up the necessary AWS SDK for Python (Boto3). Then, use https://github.com/PacktPublishing/Amazon-Redshift-Cookbook/blob/master/Chapter03/CreateAndLoad_dynamodb.py to set up the sample part table.

- Attach an IAM role to an Amazon Redshift cluster that can access Amazon DynamoDB.
- Access the AWS CLI to get a record count from an Amazon DynamoDB table.

How to do it...

In this recipe, we will load data directly from Amazon DynamoDB into Amazon Redshift:

1. Let's start by making a CLI call to the DynamoDB table to verify the total number of items. Execute the following code on the command line. You will see a count of 20000 in the part table:

```
aws dynamodb scan --table-name part --select "COUNT"
        output:
            {
                "Count": 20000,
                "ScannedCount": 20000,
                "ConsumedCapacity": null }
```

2. Log into the Amazon Redshift cookbook cluster using a SQL client or the Query Editor and create the part table:

```
DROP TABLE IF EXISTS part;
CREATE TABLE part
(
    P_PARTKEY       BIGINT NOT NULL,
    P_NAME          VARCHAR(55),
    P_MFGR          VARCHAR(25),
    P_BRAND         VARCHAR(10),
    P_TYPE          VARCHAR(25),
    P_SIZE          INTEGER,
    P_CONTAINER     VARCHAR(10),
    P_RETAILPRICE   DECIMAL(18,4),
    P_COMMENT       VARCHAR(23)
)
diststyle ALL;
```

3. Frame the COPY command to load into the Amazon Redshift table part from the Amazon DynamoDB table part. In the COPY command, we are providing the name of the dynamodb table part:

```
COPY part from 'dynamodb://part'
iam_role 'arn:aws:iam::[Your-AWS_Account_Id]:role/[Your-Redshift_Role]'
readratio 50;
```

4. Execute the preceding COPY command using the Amazon Redshift Query Editor.

5. Verify the record count of the data that was loaded into the part table. 20000 records have been loaded into the part table:

```
Select count(*) from part;
--expected sample output
count(*)
20000
```

6. Let's review the columns values for the part table on Amazon Redshift:

```
Select p_partkey,p_name,p_mfgr from part limit 5;
--expected sample output
p_partkey p_name p_mfgr
800213 chartreuse steel indian burlywood
Manufacturer#2
1101041 red lemon khaki frosted blush Manufacturer#1
2500838 tan cream cyan lemon olive Manufacturer#2
12669574 bisque salmon honeydew violet steel
Manufacturer#2
12579584 pale linen thistle firebrick orange
Manufacturer#3
```

How it works...

In the COPY command, which is used to load data from Amazon DynamoDB, the column names in the Amazon Redshift table should match the attribute names in the DynamoDB part table. If the column name is not present in DynamoDB, then those columns are loaded as empty or NULL, based on the COPY command's emptyasnull option. If the attributes in DynamodDB are not present in the Amazon Redshift table, those attributes are discarded. Also, notice that you can specify the Amazon DynoamoDB readratio (in the preceding readratio of 50), which regulates the percentage of provisioned throughput that is consumed by the COPY command for the DynamoDB table part.

Loading data from remote hosts

The local datasets in a processing server can be loaded into an Amazon Redshift table using the COPY command and the ssh parameter. You can specify the command that Amazon Redshift can execute on the remote server, which will write to standard output. The COPY command will use this to load the data into the table in parallel.

In this recipe, we will learn how to connect to remote hosts to load the data present on the remote host in the part table.

Getting ready

To complete this recipe, you will need to do the following:

- Gain access to the AWS Console.
- Deploy an Amazon Redshift cluster in AWS region eu-west-1.
- Create Amazon Redshift cluster master user credentials.
- Gain access to any SQL interface, such as a SQL client or the Amazon Redshift Query Editor.
- Gain access to an Amazon EC2 Linux instance or any Unix or Linux server. You will need open connectivity between Amazon EC2 Linux or your local Linux/Unix server to Amazon Redshift cluster.
- Gain access to the AWS CLI to copy the data from S3 to a local server.
- Create an Amazon S3 bucket in eu-west-1. We will reference it as [Your-Amazon_S3_Bucket].
- Attach an IAM role to the Amazon Redshift cluster that can access Amazon S3.

How to do it...

In this recipe, we will let a remote host (such as Amazon EC2) directly ingest data into Amazon Redshift:

1. To connect to the ingest data from Amazon EMR, you will need SSH information for the target Amazon Redshift cluster. You can obtain this by logging into the AWS Console, navigating to your Amazon Redshift cluster, selecting **Properties**, and clicking on **Connection Details**, as shown here:

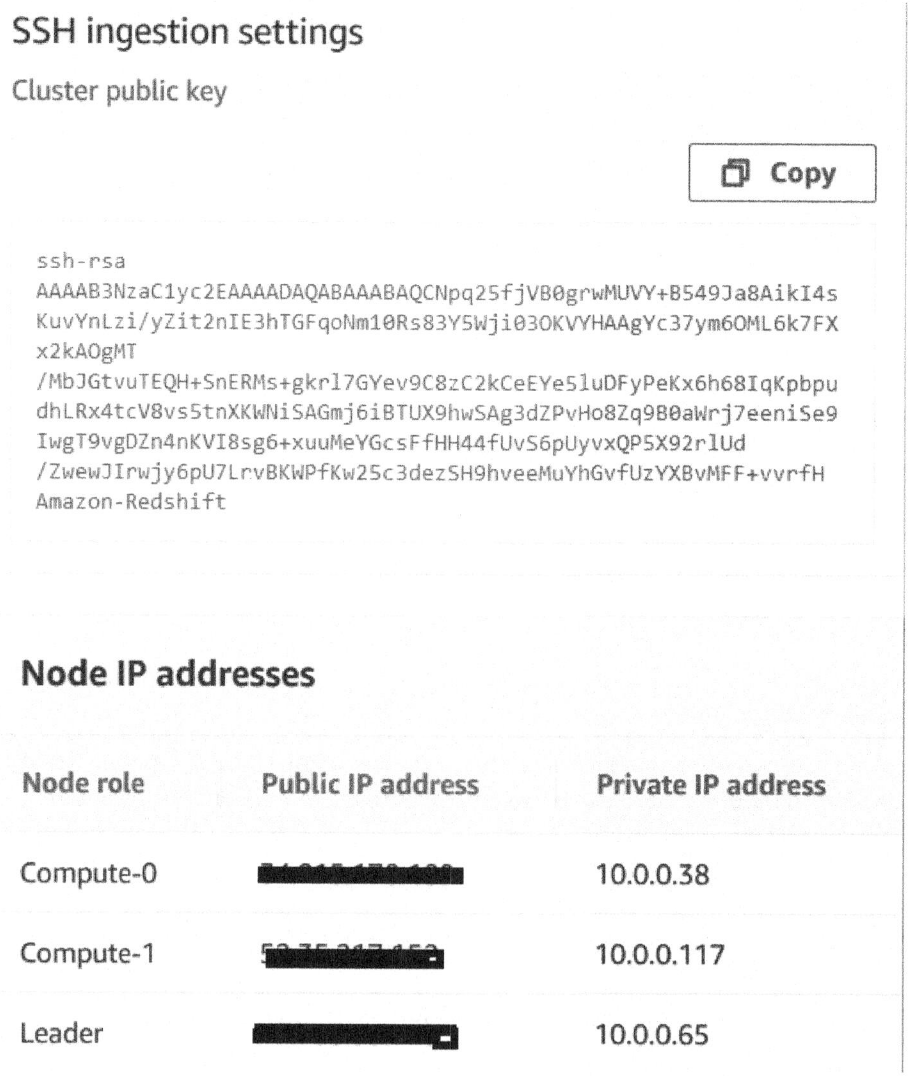

SSH ingestion settings

Cluster public key

Copy

```
ssh-rsa
AAAAB3NzaC1yc2EAAAADAQABAAABAQCNpq25fjVB0grwMUVY+B549Ja8AikI4s
KuvYnLzi/yZit2nIE3hTGFqoNm10Rs83Y5Wji03OKVYHAAgYc37ym6OML6k7FX
x2kAOgMT
/MbJGtvuTEQH+SnERMs+gkrl7GYev9C8zC2kCeEYe5luDFyPeKx6h68IqKpbpu
dhLRx4tcV8vs5tnXKWNiSAGmj6iBTUX9hwSAg3dZPvHo8Zq9B0aWrj7eeniSe9
IwgT9vgDZn4nKVI8sg6+xuuMeYGcsFfHH44fUvS6pUyvxQP5X92rlUd
/ZwewJIrwjy6pU7LrvBKWPfKw25c3dezSH9hveeMuYhGvfUzYXBvMFF+vvrfH
Amazon-Redshift
```

Node IP addresses

Node role	Public IP address	Private IP address
Compute-0	▉▉▉▉▉▉▉▉▉▉▉	10.0.0.38
Compute-1	▉▉▉▉▉▉▉▉▉	10.0.0.117
Leader	▉▉▉▉▉▉▉▉▉	10.0.0.65

Figure 3.3 – Capturing an Amazon Redshift cluster's public key and IP addresses

2. Add all the IP addresses for Amazon Redshift to the security group of Amazon EC2 Linux for port 22. If you are using local Unix or Linux, open the firewall for all the Redshift cluster IP addresses.

3. On the Linux host, add the Amazon Redshift public key:

```
/home/<ssh_username>/.ssh/authorized_keys
```

4. On the Linux host, create a directory to download the data for the part table from the S3 bucket:

```
mkdir /home/ec2-user/input/part
cd /home/ec2-user/input/part
aws s3 cp s3://packt-redshift-cookbook/part/ . --recursive
```

5. Capture the public key of your host from /etc/ssh/<ssh_host_rsa_key_ name>.pub. Amazon Redshift supports RSA keys.

6. Now, let's create the manifest file that will be referenced in the COPY command to load the value into Redshift. The manifest file is in JSON format; this file will be used by Amazon Redshift to connect to the ssh host:

```
{
    "entries": [
        {"endpoint":"<sh_endpoint_or_IP>",
        "command": "zcat /home/ec2-user/input/part/*.gz",
            "mandatory":true,
            "publickey": "<public_key> ",
            "username": "<host_user_name> "}
    ]
}
```

7. Save the manifest file as load_from_remote_host_manifest. Upload this file to your S3 bucket; that is, [Your-Amazon_S3_Bucket]. Use the same bucket where the sample data resides in the same region as your Redshift cluster.

8. Log into your Amazon Redshift cookbook cluster using a SQL client or the Query Editor and create the part table:

```
DROP TABLE IF EXISTS PART;
CREATE TABLE part
(
```

```
P_PARTKEY           BIGINT NOT NULL,
P_NAME              VARCHAR(55),
P_MFGR              VARCHAR(25),
P_BRAND             VARCHAR(10),
P_TYPE              VARCHAR(25),
P_SIZE              INTEGER,
P_CONTAINER         VARCHAR(10),
P_RETAILPRICE       DECIMAL(18,4),
P_COMMENT           VARCHAR(23)
)
diststyle ALL;
```

9. Frame the `copy` command to load into the Redshift `part` table. In the `copy` command, we are providing the manifest file on the S3 path. `COPY` will execute the `zcat` command through the host connection, and then load the output from the commands in parallel into the `part` table. The `COPY` command shown here is using the `SSH` option:

```
copy part
from 's3://[Your-Amazon_S3_Bucket]/load_from_remote_host_
manifest'
iam_role 'arn:aws:iam::[Your-AWS_Account_Id]:role/[Your-
Redshift_Role]'
CSV
ssh;
```

10. Execute the `copy` command.

11. Verify the record count of the data that's been loaded into the `part` table:

```
Select count(*) from part;
```

12. **20000000** records have been loaded into the `part` table.

Updating and inserting data

An **Extract Transform Load** (**ETL**) process is a common technique for refreshing the data warehouse of the source system. The ETL process can be executed as a batch/near-real-time process that allows us to stage the data from the source system and perform bulk refreshes of the Amazon Redshift data warehouse. Amazon Redshift, being an RDBMS-based system, allows data refreshes to occur in the form of UPDATE/INSERT/DELETE operations, broadly known as **Data Manipulation Language** (**DML**).

In this recipe, we will delve into some of the common ETL strategies for refreshing a dimensional model.

Getting ready

To complete this recipe, you will need to do the following:

- Gain access to the AWS Console.

- Deploy an Amazon Redshift cluster in AWS region eu-west-1.

- Create Amazon Redshift cluster master user credentials.

- Gain access to any SQL interface, such as a SQL client or the Amazon Redshift Query Editor.

- Set up a sample dimensional model.

How to do it...

This recipe will illustrate refreshing the part dimension, followed by the lineitem fact table. The dimensional tables will be refreshed first, followed by the fact table, to maintain the data's integrity. The complete script for this recipe is also available at https://github.com/PacktPublishing/Amazon-Redshift-Cookbook/blob/master/Chapter03/part.sql and https://github.com/PacktPublishing/Amazon-Redshift-Cookbook/blob/master/Chapter03/Insert_Update_Lineitem.sql. Let's start with the data refresh for the part dimension:

1. Open any SQL client tool and start the transaction for the part dimension table's refresh:

```
BEGIN TRANSACTION;
```

> **Tip**
> Using the transaction to update the data allows rollbacks if there is an error.
> End users do not see the intermediate state of the data change.

2. Create the staging table and load the incoming incremental data from the source:

```
/* Create a staging table to hold the input data. Staging
table is created with BACKUP NO option for faster inserts
and also since data is temporary */
DROP TABLE IF EXISTS stg_part;
CREATE TABLE stg_part
(
    NAME            VARCHAR(55),
    MFGR            VARCHAR(25),
    BRAND           VARCHAR(10),
    TYPE            VARCHAR(25),
    SIZE            INTEGER,
    CONTAINER       VARCHAR(10),
    RETAILPRICE     DECIMAL(18,4),
    COMMENT         VARCHAR(23)
)
BACKUP NO
;
COPY stg_part
FROM 's3://packt-redshift-cookbook/etl/part/dt=2020-08-
15/' iam_role 'arn:aws:iam::[Your-AWS_Account_Id]:role/
[Your-Redshift_Role]'csv gzip compupdate preset;
```

> **Tip**
> Notice that the incremental data for 2020-08-15 is loaded into the stg_
> part table.

3. Data can be merged into the part dimension table by performing an update
    (for existing matching records) and insert for the new records. An update can be
    performed using the natural key of the name attribute:

```
--Update all attributes for the existing parts
```

```
UPDATE part
SET p_mfgr = mfgr,
    p_brand = brand,
    p_type = TYPE,
    p_size = SIZE,
    p_container = container,
    p_retailprice = retailprice,
    p_comment = COMMENT
FROM stg_part
WHERE part.p_name = stg_part.name;
```

4. An insert will be performed for the new incoming records. When you're performing inserts, the referential key column is autogenerated:

```
-- Insert new parts, by auto-generating the p_partkey

INSERT INTO part (p_partkey, p_name, p_mfgr, p_brand, p_
type, p_size, p_container, p_retailprice, p_comment)
WITH max_partkey AS
   (SELECT max(p_partkey) max_partkey
    FROM part)
SELECT row_number() OVER (
       ORDER BY stg_part.name) + max_partkey AS p_partkey,
                         name,
                         mfgr,
                         brand,
                         TYPE,
                         SIZE,
                         container,
                         retailprice,
                         COMMENT
FROM stg_part
LEFT JOIN part ON (stg_part.name = part.p_name)
JOIN max_partkey ON (1=1)
WHERE part.p_name IS NULL ;
```

5.   The data refresh is now complete on the target `part` dimension, so we can commit the transaction using the following command:

```
--   commit and End transaction


END TRANSACTION;
```

> **Note**
>
> Similarly, you can repeat the preceding steps for other dimensional tables before starting the fact table.

6.   Now, let's refresh the `lineitem` fact table using the following script. Start the transaction for the `lineitem` fact table:

```
-- Start a new transaction
BEGIN TRANSACTION;
```

7.   Create the staging table so that it can hold the incoming incremental data, as shown in the following code:

```
-- Drop stg_lineitem if exists
DROP TABLE IF EXISTS stg_lineitem;
-- Create a stg_lineitem staging table and COPY data from
input S3 location with the refreshed incremental data
CREATE TABLE stg_lineitem
(
    orderkey          BIGINT,
    LINENUMBER        INTEGER NOT NULL,
    QUANTITY          DECIMAL(18,4),
    EXTENDEDPRICE     DECIMAL(18,4),
    DISCOUNT          DECIMAL(18,4),
    TAX               DECIMAL(18,4),
    RETURNFLAG        VARCHAR(1),
    LINESTATUS        VARCHAR(1),
    SHIPDATE          DATE,
    COMMITDATE        DATE,
    RECEIPTDATE       DATE,
    SHIPINSTRUCT      VARCHAR(25),
    SHIPMODE          VARCHAR(10),
```

```
   COMMENT VARCHAR(44),
    p_name            VARCHAR(55),
    s_name            VARCHAR(25)
)
BACKUP NO sortkey (RECEIPTDATE);
s_name varchar(25)) BACKUP NO sortkey (receiptdate);
COPY stg_lineitem FROM 's3://packt-redshift-cookbook/
etl/lineitem/shipdate_dt=2020-08-15/' iam_role
'arn:aws:iam::[Your-AWS_Account_Id]:role/[Your-Redshift_
Role]' csv gzip compupdate preset;
```

> **Tip**
> Notice that the incremental data for 2020-08-15 is loaded into the stg_
> lineitem table.

8. Now, let's delete any existing data (if any) for 2020-08-15 and refresh it with the current data for this date:

```
-- Delete any rows from target store_sales for the input
date for idempotency
DELETE FROM lineitem WHERE l_shipdate = '2020-10-15';
```

9. Insert the new incoming data for 2020-18-15 using the following --Insert statement:

```
--Insert data from staging table to the target TABLE
INSERT INTO lineitem (l_orderkey, l_partkey, l_suppkey,
l_linenumber, l_quantity, l_extendedprice, l_discount,
l_tax, l_returnflag, l_linestatus, l_shipdate, l_
commitdate, l_receiptdate, l_shipinstruct, l_shipmode,
l_comment)
WITH supplier_dim AS
   (SELECT DISTINCT s_name,s_suppkey FROM supplier),
part_dim AS
   (SELECT DISTINCT p_name, p_partkey FROM part)
SELECT orderkey AS l_orderkey,
       p_partkey AS l_partkey,
       s_suppkey AS l_suppkey,
```

```
        linenumber AS l_linenumber,
        quantity AS l_quantity,
        extendedprice AS l_extendedprice,
        discount AS l_discount,
        tax AS l_tax,
        returnflag AS l_returnflag,
        linestatus AS l_linestatus,
        shipdate AS l_shipdate,
        commitdate AS l_commitdate,
        receiptdate AS l_receiptdate,
        shipinstruct AS l_shipinstruct,
        shipmode AS l_shipmode,
        COMMENT AS l_comment
   FROM stg_lineitem stg
   LEFT OUTER JOIN part_dim prt ON prt.p_name = stg.p_name
   LEFT OUTER JOIN supplier_dim sup ON sup.s_name = stg.s_
   name;
```

> **Important note**
>
> Note that dimensional keys are derived from the dimensional table using the natural keys.

10. The data refresh is now complete on the target `lineitem` fact, so we can commit the transaction using the following code:

```
--   commit and End transaction
COMMIT;
```

> **Important note**
>
> Notice that all the data in both the dimension and fact tables is handled in bulk to update/insert all the incoming data in one go. This is a best practice since the effort to perform DML on a few rows versus several rows is almost the same.

11. At this point, you have a refreshed dimensional model that contains the latest data. This can be verified by executing the following `JOIN` query:

```
SELECT c_mktsegment,
       COUNT(o_orderkey) AS orders_count,
       SUM(l_quantity) AS quantity,
       SUM(l_extendedprice) AS extendedprice,
       COUNT(DISTINCT P_PARTKEY) AS parts_count,
       COUNT(DISTINCT L_SUPPKEY) AS supplier_count,
       COUNT(DISTINCT o_custkey) AS customer_count
FROM lineitem
  JOIN orders ON l_orderkey = o_orderkey
  JOIN customer c ON o_custkey = c_custkey
  JOIN part ON P_PARTKEY = l_PARTKEY
  JOIN supplier ON L_SUPPKEY = S_SUPPKEY
WHERE l_shipdate = '2020-10-15'
GROUP BY c_mktsegment;
```

The preceding ETL strategy can now be integrated with any workflow tool so that you can automatically refresh the data warehouse.

Unloading data to Amazon S3

Amazon Redshift can create a copy of the data on Amazon S3 using the UNLOAD command. The UNLOAD command splits the data across multiple files based on the node slices across the Redshift cluster.

This recipe will show you how to use UNLOAD data from an Amazon Redshift cluster in an Amazon S3 bucket.

Getting ready

To complete this recipe, you will need to do the following:

- Gain access to the AWS Console.

- Deploy an Amazon Redshift deployed in AWS region eu-west-1. Load the data, as referenced in the *Loading data from Amazon S3* recipe.

- Create Amazon Redshift cluster master user credentials.

- Gain access to any SQL interface, such as a SQL client or the Amazon Redshift Query Editor.

- Create an Amazon S3 bucket in eu-west-1. We will reference it as [Your-Amazon_S3_Bucket].

- Attach an IAM role to an Amazon Redshift cluster that can access Amazon S3.

How to do it...

To unload the data from Amazon Redshift into an Amazon S3 bucket, follow these steps:

1. Connect to the Redshift cluster using the SQL client of your choice.

2. Use the following command to unload the data from your Amazon Redshift cluster. Replace the values in [] with the corresponding values in your environment:

```
unload ('select * from orders')
to 's3://[Your-Amazon_S3_Bucket]/unload/orders_'
iam_role 'arn:aws:iam::[Your-AWS_Account_Id]:role/[Your-Redshift_Role]'
PARQUET;
```

Based on the number of slices in the cluster, the UNLOAD command will write data in Parquet format to multiple files in parallel. You can review the https://docs.aws.amazon.com/redshift/latest/dg/r_UNLOAD.html documentation for other parameters.

3. To validate the path for the unloaded data, you can use the following command, which looks at STL_UNLOAD_LOG:

```
select query, substring(path,0,100) as path
from stl_unload_log
where query=pg_last_query_id()
order by path limit 10;
```

```
--expected sample output
query   path
21585117 s3://[ Your-Amazon_S3_Bucket]/unload/
orders_000_part_000.parquet
21585117 s3://[ Your-Amazon_S3_Bucket]/unload/
orders_001_part_000.parquet
21585117 s3://[ Your-Amazon_S3_Bucket]/unload/
orders_002_part_000.parquet
..
```

4. To confirm that the data is available in Amazon S3, you can browse the Amazon S3 bucket and list the Parquet files that are provided in the output.

4
Data Pipelines

Companies build modern cloud-based data warehouses to either migrate from their on-premises data warehouses or to build new workloads. To hydrate data in these modern data warehouses, users can build data pipelines based on the source data. In this chapter, we will cover the different types of data pipelines that we can design on **Amazon Web Services** (**AWS**) with Amazon Redshift as a destination data warehouse.

The following recipes are discussed in this chapter:

- Ingesting data from transactional sources using **AWS Database Migration Service** (**AWS DMS**)
- Streaming data to Amazon Redshift via Amazon Kinesis Firehose
- Cataloging and ingesting data using AWS Glue

Technical requirements

Here are the technical requirements in order to complete the recipes in this chapter:

- Access to the AWS Management Console.
- AWS administrators should create an **Identity and Access Management** (**IAM**) user by following *Recipe 1 – Creating an IAM user* in the *Appendix* section. This IAM user will be deployed to perform some of the recipes in this chapter.

- AWS administrators should create an IAM role by following *Recipe 3 – Creating an IAM role for an AWS service* in the *Appendix*. This IAM role will be deployed to perform some of the recipes in this chapter.

- AWS administrators should deploy the AWS CloudFormation template (`https://github.com/PacktPublishing/Amazon-Redshift-Cookbook/blob/master/Chapter04/chapter_4_CFN.yaml`) to create two IAM policies:

  a. An IAM policy attached to the IAM user that will give the user access to Amazon Redshift, **Amazon Relational Database Service (Amazon RDS)**, Amazon Kinesis, Amazon Kinesis Data Firehose, Amazon CloudWatch Logs, AWS CloudFormation, AWS Secrets Manager, Amazon Cognito, **Amazon Simple Storage Service (Amazon S3)**, AWS DMS, and AWS Glue.

  b. An IAM policy attached to the IAM role that will allow an Amazon Redshift cluster to access Amazon S3.

- Attach the IAM role to an Amazon Redshift cluster by following *Recipe 4 – Attaching an IAM Role to the Amazon Redshift cluster* in the *Appendix* section. Take a note of the IAM role name, which we will refer to in the recipes as [`Your-Redshift_Role`].

- An Amazon Redshift cluster deployed in the `eu-west-1` AWS region.

- Amazon Redshift cluster master user credentials.

- Access to any **Structured Query Language** (**SQL**) interface such as a SQL client or the Amazon Redshift query editor.

- An Amazon RDS MySQL cluster deployed in the `eu-west-1` AWS region in the same **virtual private cloud** (**VPC**) as the Amazon Redshift cluster (refer to `https://aws.amazon.com/getting-started/hands-on/create-mysql-db/` for more information).

- An AWS DMS replication instance deployed in the `eu-west-1` AWS region in the same VPC as the Amazon Redshift cluster (refer to `https://docs.aws.amazon.com/dms/latest/sbs/CHAP_RDSOracle2Aurora.Steps.CreateReplicationInstance.html` for more information).

- A command line to connect to Amazon RDS MySQL (refer to `https://docs.aws.amazon.com/AmazonRDS/latest/UserGuide/USER_ConnectToInstance.html` for more information).

- Access to the **Kinesis Data Generator** (**KDG**), which is a **user interface** (**UI**) that helps to send test data to Amazon Kinesis. Use this blog post to configure the open source KDG: `https://aws.amazon.com/blogs/big-data/test-your-streaming-data-solution-with-the-new-amazon-kinesis-data-generator/`.

- An AWS account number, which we will refer to in the recipes as `[Your-AWS_Account_Id]`.

- An Amazon S3 bucket created in the `eu-west-1` region, which we will refer to in the recipes as `[Your-Amazon_S3_Bucket]`.

- The code files are referenced in the GitHub repository at `https://github.com/PacktPublishing/Amazon-Redshift-Cookbook/tree/master/Chapter04`.

Ingesting data from transactional sources using AWS DMS

When you have transactional data sources—either on-premises or on AWS RDS—and you want to replicate or migrate that data to your data warehouse in Amazon Redshift for consolidation or reporting, you can use AWS DMS. AWS DMS is a fully managed service that helps you to do full loading from your transactional source to the target data warehouse as well as near-real-time **change data capture** (**CDC**) from source to target.

In this recipe, we will do full replication of the `parts` table from Amazon RDS MySQL, serving as a transactional source to the Amazon Redshift database warehouse.

Getting ready

To complete this recipe, you will need the following:

- An Amazon Redshift cluster deployed in the `eu-west-1` AWS region.

- Amazon Redshift cluster master user credentials.

- An IAM user with access to Amazon Redshift, Amazon RDS, and AWS DMS.

- An Amazon RDS MySQL cluster deployed in the `eu-west-1` AWS region in the same VPC as the Amazon Redshift cluster (refer to `https://aws.amazon.com/getting-started/hands-on/create-mysql-db/` for more information).

- An AWS DMS replication instance deployed in the `eu-west-1` AWS region in the same VPC as the Amazon Redshift cluster (refer to `https://docs.aws.amazon.com/dms/latest/sbs/CHAP_RDSOracle2Aurora.Steps.CreateReplicationInstance.html` for more information).

- A command line to connect to Amazon RDS MySQL (refer to `https://docs.aws.amazon.com/AmazonRDS/latest/UserGuide/USER_ConnectToInstance.html` for more information). Open connectivity between your local client, such as **Amazon Elastic Compute Cloud (Amazon EC2)** Linux, to the Amazon RDS MySQL database.

- Open connectivity between Amazon RDS MySQL and AWS DMS instances.

- Note the VPC ID where Amazon Redshift and Amazon RDS are deployed.

How to do it...

This recipe will illustrate full replication of the `parts` table from Amazon RDS MySQL to the Amazon Redshift cluster using AWS DMS as the replication engine:

1. Let's connect to the Amazon RDS MySQL database using the command line installed on the AWS EC2 instance. Enter the password to connect to the database:

```
mysql -h [yourMySQLRDSEndPoint] -u admin -p;
```

2. We will create an `ods` database on MySQL and a `parts` table in the `ods` database:

```
create database ods;
CREATE TABLE ods.part
(
   P_PARTKEY        BIGINT NOT NULL,
   P_NAME           VARCHAR(55),
   P_MFGR           VARCHAR(25),
   P_BRAND          VARCHAR(10),
   P_TYPE           VARCHAR(25),
   P_SIZE           INTEGER,
   P_CONTAINER      VARCHAR(10),
   P_RETAILPRICE    DECIMAL(18,4),
   P_COMMENT        VARCHAR(23)
)
```

3. On your client server, download the part.tbl file from GitHub at https://github.com/PacktPublishing/Amazon-Redshift-Cookbook/blob/master/Chapter04/part.tbl.

4. We will now load this file into the ods.part table on the MySQL database. This will load 20000 records into the parts table:

```
LOAD DATA LOCAL INFILE 'part.tbl'
    INTO TABLE ods.part
    FIELDS TERMINATED BY '|'
    LINES TERMINATED BY '\n';
```

5. Let's verify the record count loaded into the ods.part table:

```
MySQL [(none)]> select count(*) from ods.part;
+----------+
| count(*) |
+----------+
|    20000 |
+----------+
1 row in set (0.00 sec)
```

6. Turn on binary logging on the RDS MySQL database by executing the following command:

```
call mysql.rds_set_configuration('binlog retention
hours', 24);
In your MySQL database instance in parameter group
Set the binlog_format parameter to ROW
```

Binary logging enables CDC for the AWS DMS service. You can get more details about turning on binary logging at this link: https://docs.aws.amazon.com/dms/latest/userguide/CHAP_Source.MySQL.html#CHAP_Source.MySQL.AmazonManag.

7. Now, we will go to the AWS DMS landing page to create a source and target for the replication instance. Refer to https://console.aws.amazon.com/dms/v2/home? for more information on this.

8. First, we will create a source endpoint for RDS MySQL. Navigate to **Endpoints** and click on **Create endpoint**. Select **Source endpoint** and check **Select RDS DB instance**. From the drop-down menu, select your RDS instance:

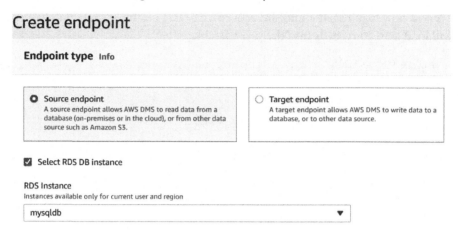

Figure 4.1 – Creating an AWS DMS source endpoint for MySQL database

9. Enter the password for your RDS MySQL database:

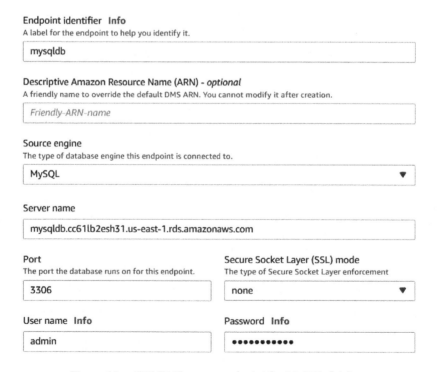

Figure 4.2 – AWS DMS source endpoint for MySQL database

10. Test your endpoint connection from the AWS DMS replication you created earlier on. Select a VPC and replication instance and click **Run test**. On completion, you will receive a **successful** connection message:

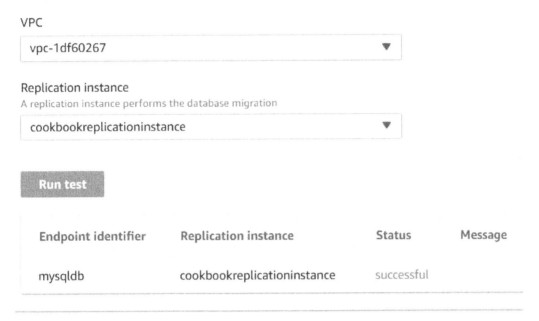

Figure 4.3 – AWS DMS source endpoint for MySQL database test connection

11. Secondly, we will create a target endpoint for the Amazon Redshift cluster. Click on **Create endpoint** and select **Target endpoint**. Populate the details of your Amazon Redshift cluster endpoint, including user ID, password, and database name. Test the connection using the pre-created database replication instance:

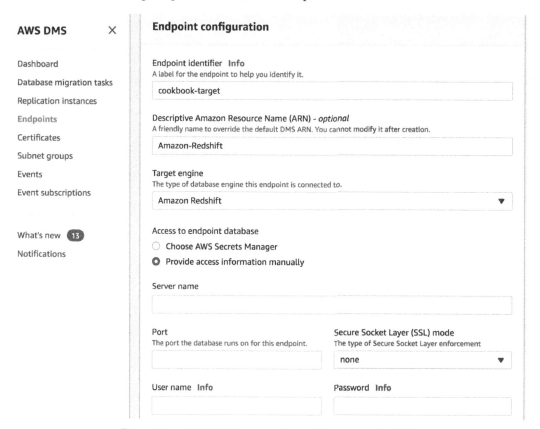

Figure 4.4 – AWS DMS target endpoint for Amazon Redshift

12. Now, we will create a database migration task. Navigate to **Database migration tasks** and click on **Create task**. Select a replication instance. For **Source database endpoint**, select **mysqldb**, and for **Target database endpoint**, select the **cookbooktarget** Amazon Redshift endpoint you created. For **Migration type**, select **Migrate existing data and replicate ongoing changes**. This will do a full load followed by ongoing CDC:

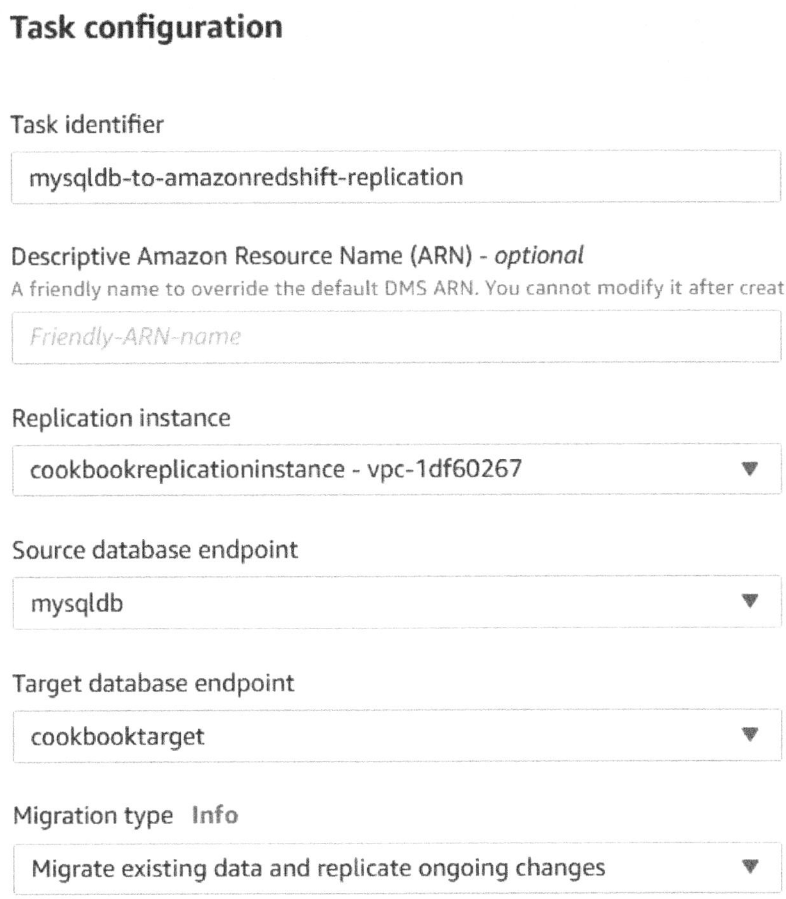

Task configuration

Task identifier

mysqldb-to-amazonredshift-replication

Descriptive Amazon Resource Name (ARN) - *optional*
A friendly name to override the default DMS ARN. You cannot modify it after creation.

Friendly-ARN-name

Replication instance

cookbookreplicationinstance - vpc-1df60267   ▼

Source database endpoint

mysqldb   ▼

Target database endpoint

cookbooktarget   ▼

Migration type   Info

Migrate existing data and replicate ongoing changes   ▼

Figure 4.5 – AWS DMS migration task

13. For **Target table preparation mode**, select **Do nothing**. AWS DMS assumes that the target tables have been pre-created by Amazon Redshift.

14. For **Table Mappings**, add the following rule. Enter `ods` as the schema name and a `%` character as a wildcard table name:

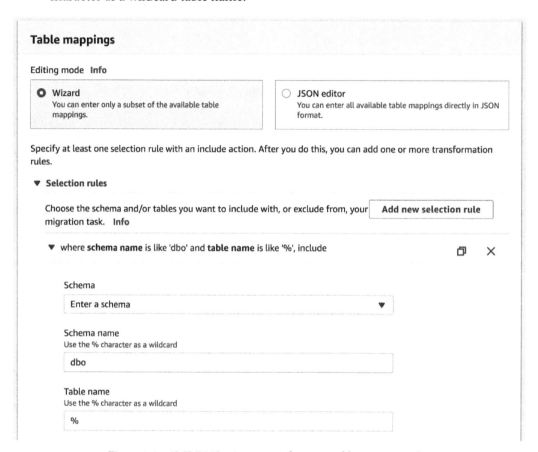

Figure 4.6 – AWS DMS migration task source table mapping rules

15. For transformation rules for the target, select the `ods` schema and table wildcard name and select an action to add a `stg_` prefix to the table name on Amazon Redshift. In the DMS task, you can apply some transformation rules (for example, convert to lowercase or remove columns):

▼ **Transformation rules**

	Add new transformation rule

You can use transformation rules to change or transform schema, table or column names of some or all of the selected objects.   **Info**

▼ where **schema name** is like 'ods' and **table name** is like '%', add-prefix   ☐   ✕

Target

Table	▼

Schema name

Enter a schema	▼

Schema name
Use the % character as a wildcard

ods

Table name
Use the % character as a wildcard

%

Action

Add prefix	▼	stg_

Figure 4.7 – AWS DMS migration task target transformation rule

16. In the **Migration task** startup configuration, select the **Manually later** option and click on **Create task**.

17. Once the task has a **Ready** status, click on the task. Then, under **Action**, select **Restart and resume**. With this, the replication instance has connected to the source and has replicated data to Amazon Redshift.

18. To view the status of the replication, click on **Table statistics**. The load state on completion will show **Table completed**. The total rows on the `ods.part` target Amazon Redshift table are **20,000**:

Table statistics (1)

Total rows include loaded source table rows from Inserts, Deletes, Updates, DDLs, and Full load rows.

Schema name	Table	Load state	Inserts	Deletes	Updates	DDLs	Full load rows	Total rows
ods	part	Table completed	0	0	0	0	20,000	20,000

Figure 4.8 – AWS DMS migration task status and full mode replicated record count

19. Let's insert the following records into the source MySQL database `part` table to see the CDC scenario:

```
insert into ods.part values
(20001,'royal red metallic
dim','Manufacturer#2','Brand#25','STANDARD BURNISHED
NICKEL',48,'SM JAR',920.00,'sts-1');
insert into ods.part values
(20002,'royal red metallic
dim','Manufacturer#2','Brand#26','STANDARD BURNISHED
NICKEL',48,'SM JAR',921.00,'sts-2');
insert into ods.part values
(20003,'royal red metallic
dim','Manufacturer#2','Brand#27','STANDARD BURNISHED
NICKEL',48,'SM JAR',922.00,'sts-3');
insert into ods.part values
(20004,'royal red metallic
dim','Manufacturer#2','Brand#28','STANDARD BURNISHED
NICKEL',48,'SM JAR',923.00,'sts-4');
insert into ods.part values
(20005,'royal red metallic
dim','Manufacturer#2','Brand#29','STANDARD BURNISHED
NICKEL',48,'SM JAR',924.00,'sts-5');
```

20. On the database migration task, let's check the CDC of the five newly inserted five records. The **Inserts** column shows **5**, and the **Total rows** column on the target now has **20,005** records:

Table statistics (1)

Total rows include loaded source table rows from Inserts, Deletes, Updates, DDLs, and Full load rows.

Schema name ▽	Table ▽	Load state ▽	Inserts ▽	Deletes ▽	Updates ▽	DDLs ▽	Full load rows ▽	Total rows ▽	Validation
ods	part	Table completed	5	0	0	0	20,000	20,005	Not enabled

Figure 4.9 – AWS DMS migration task status and CDC replicated record count

21. Let's confirm the record count on the `ods.stg_part` Amazon Redshift table. Execute the following query in the SQL client, and the output will be 20,005 records:

```
select count(*) from ods.stg_part;
```

22. You can choose to stop the database migration task by navigating to **Database migration tasks** > **Actions** > **Stop**.

How it works...

AWS DMS provides the capability to do homogenous (same database platform—for example, on-premises MySQL to Amazon RDS MySQL) and heterogeneous (different database platform) replication. In this recipe, we saw the scenario of heterogeneous replication, whereby the source is MySQL and the target is Amazon Redshift. Using an AWS DMS task, it first fully migrated the data to Amazon Redshift, and the task captured changes from the source transactional logs that got replicated to Amazon Redshift in near real time.

Streaming data to Amazon Redshift via Amazon Kinesis Firehose

Streaming datasets are continuous datasets that can originate from sources such as **internet of things** (**IoT**) devices, log files, gaming systems, and so on. Ingesting streamed data into Amazon Redshift allows the running of near-real-time analytics that can be combined with the historical/operational data to produce actionable reporting—for example, in a manufacturing shop, analyzing the data from several IoT sensors can help predict the failure of machinery and enable you to take preventive action.

In this recipe, we will simulate a streaming dataset using the www.amazon.com product review data to be ingested into Amazon Redshift using Amazon Kinesis Firehose. Amazon Kinesis Firehose provides out-of-the-box integration to capture the streaming dataset and land it into an Amazon Redshift table.

Getting ready

To complete this recipe, you will need the following:

- An Amazon Redshift cluster deployed in the eu-west-1 AWS region.

- Amazon Redshift cluster master user credentials.

- An IAM user with access to Amazon Redshift, Amazon Kinesis, Amazon Cognito, and Amazon S3.

- Access to any SQL interface such as a SQL client or the Amazon Redshift query editor.

- An Amazon S3 bucket created in the eu-west-1 region, which we will refer to as [Your-Amazon_S3_Bucket].

- An IAM role attached to an Amazon Redshift cluster that can access Amazon S3, which will refer to in the recipes as [Your-Redshift_Role].

- Access to the KDG, which is a UI that helps to send test data to Amazon Kinesis. Use this blog post to configure the open source KDG: https://aws.amazon.com/blogs/big-data/test-your-streaming-data-solution-with-the-new-amazon-kinesis-data-generator/.

- An AWS account number, which we will refer to in the recipes as [Your-AWS_Account_Id].

How to do it...

This recipe will stream the www.amazon.com customer product review dataset and ingest it into Amazon Redshift using Amazon Kinesis Firehose.

1. Navigate to the AWS Management Console and pick the **AWS Kinesis** service. In the left menu, choose **Data Firehose** and click on the **Create delivery stream** button, as shown in the following screenshot:

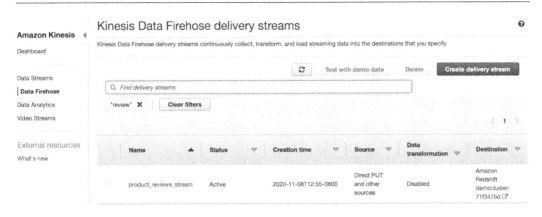

Figure 4.10 – Creating a Kinesis Data Firehose stream

2. Provide a delivery stream name (such as `product_reviews_stream`) and click **Next** until you get to the **Choose a destination** option.

3. Choose **Amazon Redshift** as the destination and configure the Amazon Redshift destination parameters, as shown in the following screenshot:

Cluster

redshift-cluster-1

Create new ⟋

View cluster **redshift-cluster-1** in Amazon Redshift ⟋

User name

awsuser

Password

•••••••••••

User must have INSERT permissions for the Amazon Redshift table

Database

dev

Table

product_reviews_stg

Columns - *optional*
Specify a comma-separated list of column names to load source data fields into specific target columns.
The order of the columns must match the order of the source data.

marketplace,customer_id,review_id,product_id,product_parent,product_title,star_rating,helpful_vo

Figure 4.11 – Configuring destination Amazon Redshift cluster

Here, provide the following respective parameters:

- **Cluster**—Choose an Amazon Redshift cluster to land the streaming dataset
- **User name**—Type the username that you chose when you set up the Amazon Redshift cluster
- **Password**—Type the password that you chose when you set up the Amazon Redshift cluster
- **Database**—Type the database name
- **Table**—Type `product_reviews_stg`
- **Columns - optional**—Leave this field empty
- **Intermediate S3 bucket**—Choose an existing S3 bucket or create a new one where data will be staged before being copied into Amazon Redshift (`[Your-Amazon_S3_Bucket]`)
- **Backup S3 bucket prefix - optional**—Type `/product_review_stg/`
- In the **COPY options – optional** section, type the following script:

```
COPY product_reviews_stg (marketplace,customer_id,review_
id,product_id,product_parent,product_title,star_rating,helpful_
votes,total_votes,vine,verified_purchase,review_
headline,review_body,review_date,year) FROM 's3://
[Your-Amazon_S3_Bucket/product_review_stg/manifest'
CREDENTIALS 'aws_iam_role=arn:aws:iam::[Your-AWS_Account_
Id]:role/[Your-Redshift_Role]' MANIFEST  JSON 'auto';
```

4. Navigate to the **Review** option and create an Amazon Kinesis Firehose stream.

5. Log in to the Amazon Redshift cluster using the SQL client tool and create a `product_reviews_stg` table that will hold the incoming streaming data:

```
CREATE TABLE product_reviews_stg
(
    marketplace          VARCHAR(2),
    customer_id          VARCHAR(32),
    review_id            VARCHAR(24),
    product_id           VARCHAR(24),
    product_parent       VARCHAR(32),
    product_title        VARCHAR(512),
    star_rating          INT,
```

```
helpful_votes          INT,
total_votes            INT,
vine                   CHAR(1),
verified_purchase      CHAR(1),
review_headline        VARCHAR(256),
review_body            VARCHAR(MAX),
review_date            DATE,
YEAR                   INT
)
DISTSTYLE KEY DISTKEY (customer_id) SORTKEY (review_date);
```

6. Now, let's use the Amazon KDG to produce streaming data and send it to the
    `product_reviews_stream` Kinesis Firehose stream, as follows:

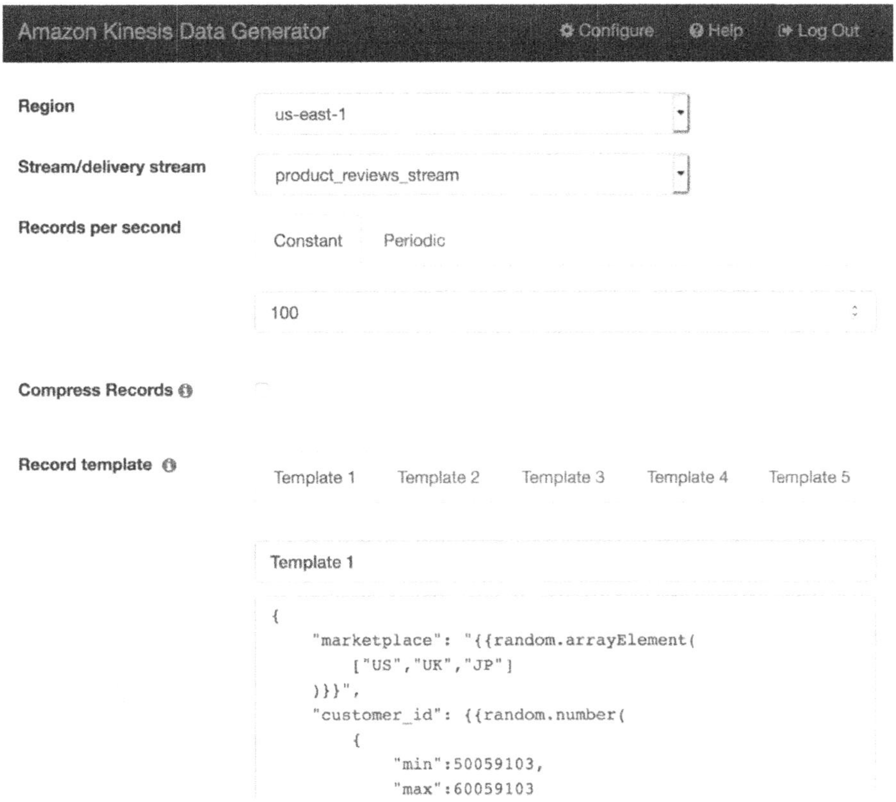

Figure 4.12 – Amazon KDG

Here, you will use the `product_review_stream` stream/delivery stream to send the streaming data and copy and paste the template from `https://github.com/PacktPublishing/Amazon-Redshift-Cookbook/blob/master/Chapter04/kinesis_data_generator_template.json` to generate the product review data:

```
{
    "marketplace": "{{random.arrayElement(
        ["US","UK","JP"]
    )}}",
    "review_headline": "{{commerce.productAdjective}}",
    "review_body": "{{commerce.productAdjective}}",
    "review_date": "{{date.now("YYYY-MM-DD")}}",
    "year":{{date.now("YYYY")}}
}
```

7. After a while, the streamed data should start landing into Amazon Redshift and can be verified by using the following code:

```
SELECT *
FROM product_reviews_stage;
```

How it works...

Amazon KDF allows data to be sourced and streamed into multiple destinations. It can capture, transform, and loadstreaming data into Amazon S3, Amazon Redshift, Amazon Elasticsearch Service, and Splunk destinations. KDF, being a fully managed service, can automatically scale to meet the growth of the data.

Cataloging and ingesting data using AWS Glue

Data that is staged in Amazon S3 can be cataloged using the AWS Glue service. Cataloging the data allows metadata to be attached and the AWS Glue Data Catalog to be populated. This process enriches the raw data, which can be queried as tables using many of the AWS analytical services—such as Amazon Redshift, **Amazon Elastic MapReduce** (**Amazon EMR**), and so on—for analytical processing. It is easy to perform this data discovery using the AWS Glue crawlers that can create and update the metadata automatically.

In this recipe, we will enrich the data to catalog and enable ingestion into Amazon Redshift.

Getting ready

To complete this recipe, you will need the following:

- An Amazon Redshift cluster deployed in the `eu-west-1` AWS region

- Amazon Redshift cluster master user credentials

- An IAM user with access to Amazon Redshift, Amazon S3, and AWS Glue

- An IAM role attached to an Amazon Redshift cluster that can access Amazon S3, which we will refer to in the recipes as `[Your-Redshift_Role]`

- Access to any SQL interface such as a SQL client or the Amazon Redshift query editor

- An Amazon S3 bucket for staging and unloading the data in specific recipes, which we will refer to in the recipes as `[Your-Amazon_S3_Bucket]`

- An AWS account number, which we will refer to in the recipes as `[Your-AWS_Account_Id]`

How to do it...

This recipe will use the Amazon.com customer product review dataset to be cataloged and ingested into Amazon Redshift:

1. Navigate to the AWS Management Console and pick the **AWS Glue** option, verifying you are in the same AWS region as the Amazon Redshift cluster. In the left menu on AWS Glue, choose **Add crawler** and type any crawler name, such as `product reviews dataset crawl`, and click **Next**.

2. In the data source, copy and paste the `s3://packt-redshift-cookbook/amazon-reviews-pds/parquet/` path into the **Include path** option, as shown in the following screenshot, and click **Next**:

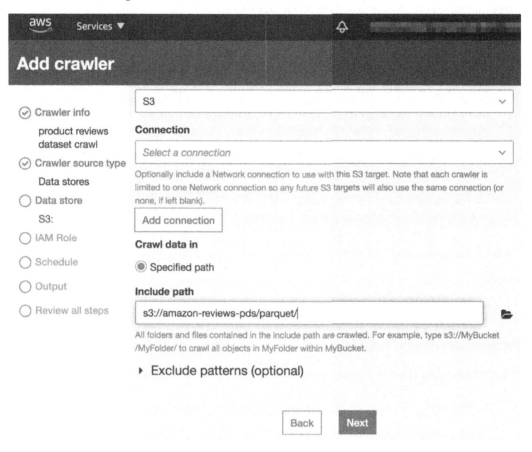

Figure 4.13 – Add crawler screen

3. Choose an IAM role to allow AWS Glue access to crawl and update the AWS Glue Data Catalog, and click on the **Next** button.

4. In the **Output** option, add a `reviews` database and a `product_reviews_src` prefix for the **Prefix added to tables** option, and then click **Next** and **Submit** to create a `product reviews dataset crawl` crawler:

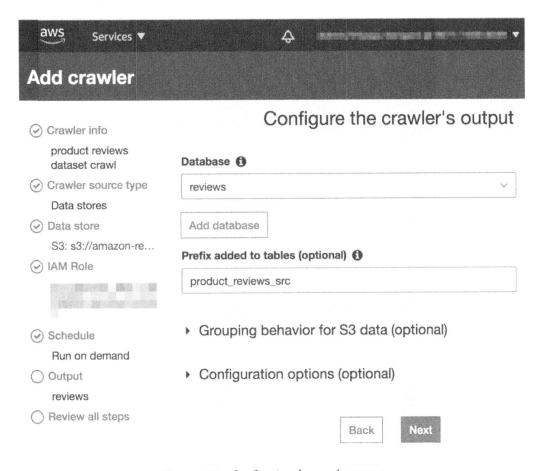

Figure 4.14 – Configuring the crawler output

5. Navigate to the **Crawlers** menu and pick the `product reviews dataset crawl` crawler and click **Run crawler**, as shown in the following screenshot, and wait until the status changes to **Success**:

Figure 4.15 – Monitoring the crawler status

6. Now, AWS Glue has crawled the product review dataset and discovered the table automatically. You can verify the table by navigating to the **Tables** option to view the `product_reviews_srcparquet` table in the list:

Figure 4.16 – Viewing the table created by crawler

7. Open any SQL client tool and connect to Amazon Redshift, and create a schema to point to the `reviews` AWS Glue catalog database using the following command, by replacing the `[Your-AWS_Account_Id]` and `[Your-Redshift_Role]` values:

```
CREATE external SCHEMA review_ext_sch FROM data catalog
DATABASE 'reviews' iam_role 'arn:aws:iam::[Your-AWS_
Account_Id]:role/[Your-Redshift-Role]' CREATE external
DATABASE if not exists;
```

8. Create a `product_reviews_stage` table that will hold the incoming crawled data:

```
CREATE TABLE product_reviews_stage
(
    marketplace       VARCHAR(2),
    customer_id       VARCHAR(32),
    review_id         VARCHAR(24),
    product_id        VARCHAR(24),
    product_parent    VARCHAR(32),
    product_title     VARCHAR(512),
```

```
    star_rating          INT,
    helpful_votes        INT,
    total_votes          INT,
    vine                 CHAR(1),
    verified_purchase    CHAR(1),
    review_headline      VARCHAR(256),
    review_body          VARCHAR(MAX),
    review_date          DATE,
    YEAR                 INT
)
DISTSTYLE KEY DISTKEY (customer_id) SORTKEY (review_
date);
```

9. Now, let's insert `Automotive` data from the crawled data into the `product_reviews_stage` table:

```
INSERT INTO product_reviews_stage
(
    marketplace,
    customer_id,
    review_id,
    product_id,
    product_parent,
    product_title,
    star_rating,
    helpful_votes,
    total_votes,
    vine,
    verified_purchase,
    review_headline,
    review_body,
    review_date,
    year
)
SELECT marketplace,
       customer_id,
```

```
        review_id,
        product_id,
        product_parent,
        product_title,
        star_rating,
        helpful_votes,
        total_votes,
        vine,
        verified_purchase,
        review_headline,
        review_body,
        review_date,
        year
FROM review_ext_sch.reviewparquet
WHERE product_category = 'Automotive';
```

10. The `public.product_reviews_stage` table is now ready to hold the incoming `Automotive` dataset, which can be verified by using the following command:

```
SELECT *
FROM product_reviews_stage;
```

How it works...

AWS Glue provides a crawler that can automatically figure out the structure of data in Amazon S3. AWS Glue maintains the metadata catalog that can be accessed across other AWS analytical services, such as Amazon Redshift. Amazon Redshift can query the data in Amazon S3 directly using the Amazon Redshift **Spectrum** feature, which allows data to be ingested into local Redshift tables.

5
Scalable Data Orchestration for Automation

Amazon Web Services (**AWS**) provides a rich set of native services to integrate a workflow. These workflows may involve multiple tasks that can be managed independently, thereby taking advantage of purpose-built services and decoupling them.

In this chapter, we will primarily focus on workflows such as **extract, transform, load** (**ETL**) processes that are used to refresh a data warehouse. We will illustrate different options that are available using the individual recipes, but these are interchangeable depending on your use case. For example, in your workflow, you can call an AWS Python shell (`https://docs.aws.amazon.com/glue/latest/dg/add-job-python. html`) instead of the Amazon Redshift Data **application programming interface** (**API**) in cases where you might want to reuse your existing Python code base.

The following recipes are discussed in this chapter:

- Scheduling queries using the Amazon Redshift query editor
- Event-driven applications using EventBridge and the Amazon Redshift Data API
- Event-driven applications using AWS Lambda

- Orchestrating using AWS Step Functions

- Orchestrating using **Amazon Managed Workflows for Apache Airflow (Amazon MWAA)**

Technical requirements

Here are the technical requirements to complete the recipes in this chapter:

- Access to the AWS Management Console.

- AWS administrators should create an **Identity and Access Management (IAM)** user by following *Recipe 1– Creating an IAM User,* in the *Appendix.* This IAM user will be deployed to perform some of the recipes in this chapter.

- AWS administrators should create an IAM role by following *Recipe 3 – Creating an IAM Role for an AWS service* in the *Appendix.* This IAM role will be deployed to perform some of the recipes in this chapter.

- AWS administrators should deploy the AWS CloudFormation template (`https://github.com/PacktPublishing/Amazon-Redshift-Cookbook/blob/master/Chapter05/chapter_5_CFN.yaml`) to create two IAM policies:

  a. An IAM policy attached to the IAM user that will give the user access to Amazon Redshift, **Amazon Elastic Compute Cloud (Amazon EC2)**, AWS CloudFormation, **Amazon Simple Storage Service (Amazon S3)**, **Amazon Simple Notification Service (Amazon SNS)**, Amazon MWAA, Amazon EventBridge, AWS CloudWatch, AWS CloudWatch Logs, AWS Glue, AWS Lambda, and AWS State Functions.

  b. An IAM policy attached to the IAM role that will allow an Amazon Redshift cluster to access Amazon S3, AWS Lambda, and Amazon EventBridge.

- Attach an IAM role to an Amazon Redshift cluster by following *Recipe 4 – Attaching an IAM Role to the Amazon Redshift cluster* in the *Appendix.* Make a note of the IAM role name, as we will refer to this in the recipes as `[Your-Redshift_Role]`.

- An Amazon Redshift cluster deployed in the `eu-west-1` AWS region.

- Amazon Redshift cluster master user credentials.

- Access to any **Structured Query Language (SQL)** interface such as a SQL client or the Amazon Redshift query editor.

- An AWS account number, which we will refer to in the recipes as `[Your-AWS_Account_Id]`.

- An Amazon S3 bucket created in the `eu-west-1` region, which we will refer to as `[Your-Amazon_S3_Bucket]`.

- The code files are referenced in the GitHub repository at `https://github.com/PacktPublishing/Amazon-Redshift-Cookbook/tree/master/Chapter05`.

Scheduling queries using the Amazon Redshift query editor

The Amazon Redshift console allows users to schedule queries on a Redshift cluster. Users can schedule long-running or time-sensitive queries, refresh materialized views at regular intervals, and load or unload data.

In this recipe, we will look at the steps required to schedule a query using the query editor.

Getting ready

To complete this recipe, you will need the following:

- An Amazon Redshift cluster deployed in the `eu-west-1` AWS region.

- An IAM user with access to Amazon Redshift, the Amazon Redshift query editor, and Amazon EventBridge.

- An IAM role attached to the Amazon Redshift cluster that can access Amazon EventBridge, which we will refer to in the recipes as `[Your-Redshift_Role]`.

- We will reuse the `product_review_mv` materialized view that was set up using the *Managing materialized views* recipe in *Chapter 2, Data Management*.

How to do it...

In this recipe, we will automate a refresh of the `product_review_mv` materialized view so that the data is up to date when the base tables change:

1. Connect to the Amazon Redshift cluster using the query editor on the AWS Management Console. You will notice that the **Schedule** button is not clickable in this instance:

Figure 5.1 – Connecting to Amazon Redshift cluster using the query editor

2. In Command Prompt under **Query 1**, type the name of the query that you want to schedule:

```
REFRESH MATERIALIZED VIEW product_review_mv;
```

3. After entering the query, click on the **Schedule** button, as follows:

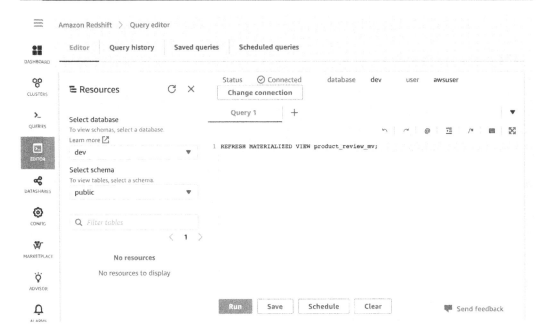

Figure 5.2 – Scheduling materialized view refresh using the query editor

4. Click on the **Schedule** button to open the **Schedule query** window. In the **Schedule query** window, there are four sections: **Scheduler permissions**, **Query information**, **Scheduling options**, and **Monitoring**.

5. In the **Scheduler permissions** section, enter the following details:

- **IAM role**—Select the role created that has access to the scheduled query [Your-Redshift_Role].

- **Authentication**—There are two modes of authentication: **Temporary credentials** and **AWS Secrets Manager**. By default, **Temporary credentials** is selected; this uses the GetClusterCredentials IAM permission and the db user to generate the temporary credentials. You can also select **AWS Secrets Manager**, where you can use secrets stored in AWS Secrets Manager.

- **Cluster**—Select the Amazon Redshift cluster.

- **Database name**—Enter the database name.

- **Database user**—Enter the database user if you're selecting **Temporary credentials**:

Scheduler permissions

IAM role

This IAM role allows the scheduled query to assume permissions on your behalf. It must trust principals for CloudWatch events (events.amazonaws.com). **Learn more** ⬀

| RedshiftQueryScheduler | ▼ | View ⬀ |

Authentication Learn more ⬀

🔘 **Temporary credentials**
Use the GetClusterCredentials IAM permission and your database user to generate temporary access credentials.

⭕ **AWS Secrets Manager**
Use a stored secret to authenticate access.

Cluster

| redshift-cluster-1 (Available) | ▼ |

Database name

| dev |

Database user
Enter a user name authorized to access your database.

| awsuser |

Figure 5.3 – Setting up the schedule options for refresh

6. In the **Query information** section, enter the following details:

- **Scheduled query name**—Enter a recognizable name for the query.

- **SQL query**—You can type the query in Command Prompt or use the **Upload query** button to ingest a SQL statement from the local client:

Query information

Scheduled query name

datalake-schedule-query-1

The name must have 1-64 characters. Valid characters: A-Z, a-z, 0-9, .(dot), -(hypen), and _(underscore).

SQL query
If the query doesn't explicitly reference a schema, then the default schema is used.

REFRESH MATERIALIZED VIEW product_review_mv;

🔼 **Upload query**

Choose a file to upload an SQL statement.

Figure 5.4 – Setting up the schedule name and query

7. In the **Scheduling options** section, you can schedule a query by selecting **Run frequency** or **Cron format**:

Scheduling options

Schedule query by:

⦿ Run frequency
○ Cron format

Repeat by:

Day ▼

Repeat every:

1   day or days

Value must be an integer from 1-999.

Repeat at time (UTC):

05:00

The schedule repeats every 1 day at 05:00 (UTC).

Figure 5.5 – Setting up the schedule interval

8. In the **Monitoring** section, you can optionally configure SNS notifications.

9. Click on **Save changes** to save the schedule.

How it works...

The **Schedule** option in the Amazon Redshift query editor is a convenient way to run a SQL statement using the Amazon Redshift console. You can create a schedule to run your SQL statement at time intervals that match your business needs. When it's time for a scheduled query to run, Amazon EventBridge (`https://aws.amazon.com/eventbridge/`) invokes the query.

Event-driven applications using Amazon EventBridge and the Amazon Redshift Data API

Event-driven data pipelines are increasingly used by organizations, whereby applications run in response to events. Event-driven architectures are loosely coupled and distributed. This provides the benefit of decoupling producer and consumer processes, allowing greater flexibility in application design.

An example of an event-driven application is an automated workflow being triggered on delivery of the data from the source system, which creates a completion event that is captured by the event bus and triggers the processing of data in downstream applications. At the end of this workflow, another event gets initiated to notify end users about the completion of those transformations and that they can start analyzing the transformed dataset.

In this recipe, you will see the use of Amazon EventBridge serving as an event bus. Amazon EventBridge is a fully managed serverless event bus service that simplifies connecting with a variety of your sources. EventBridge delivers a stream of real-time data from your own applications, **Software-as-a-Service (SaaS)** applications, and AWS services, and routes that data to targets such as AWS Lambda. You can set up routing rules to determine where to send your data to build application architectures that react in real time to all of your data sources.

Getting ready

To complete this recipe, you will need the following:

- An Amazon Redshift cluster deployed in the eu-west-1 AWS region. Note the cluster ID—we will refer to this as [Your-Redshift_Cluster].

- Amazon Redshift cluster master user credentials. Note the username—we will refer to this as [Your-Redshift_User].

- Access to any SQL interface such as a SQL client or the Amazon Redshift query editor.

- An IAM user with access to Amazon SNS, Amazon EventBridge, and AWS Lambda.

- An IAM role with access to AWS Lambda—we will refer to this in the recipes as [Your-Redshift_Role].

- An AWS account number—we will refer to this in the recipes as [Your-AWS_Account_Id].

How to do it...

This recipe will use EventBridge to schedule the running of a Redshift data pipeline for the parts table. Lambda functions will use the Amazon Redshift Data API to make an asynchronous call. On completion of the code execution, the pipeline will send an Amazon SNS notification.

1. Create a product review table in the Amazon Redshift database using the SQL client:

```
CREATE TABLE daily_product_reviews
(
    marketplace          VARCHAR(2),
    customer_id          VARCHAR(32),
    review_id            VARCHAR(24),
    product_id           VARCHAR(24),
    product_parent       VARCHAR(32),
    product_title        VARCHAR(512),
    star_rating          INT,
    helpful_votes        INT,
    total_votes          INT,
    vine                 CHAR(1),
```

```
verified_purchase    CHAR(1),
review_headline      VARCHAR(256),
review_body          VARCHAR(MAX),
review_date          DATE,
YEAR                 INT
)
DISTSTYLE KEY DISTKEY (customer_id) SORTKEY (review_date);
```

2. Create a `daily_product_review_fact_mv` materialized view using the results of the query based on `daily_product_reviews`:

```
CREATE MATERIALIZED VIEW public.daily_product_review_fact_mv
AS
SELECT marketplace,
       product_id,
       COUNT(1) as count_rating,
       SUM(star_rating) as sum_rating,
       SUM(helpful_votes) AS total_helpful_votes,
       SUM(total_votes) AS total_votes,
       review_date
FROM public.daily_product_reviews
GROUP BY marketplace,
         product_id,
         review_date;
```

3. Let's create a stored procedure that will enable us to build the ETL pipeline:

```
CREATE OR REPLACE PROCEDURE products_review_etl()
        AS $$
          BEGIN
 truncate public.product_reviews_daily;
        COPY public.product_reviews_daily FROM 's3://
packt-redshift-cookbook/amazon-reviews-pds/parquet/product_
category=Home/'
 iam_role 'arn:aws:iam::055122512284:role/redshift-spectrum'
              PARQUET ;
```

```
        REFRESH MATERIALIZED VIEW public.daily_product_
review_fact_mv;
        END;
        $$ LANGUAGE plpgsql;
```

4. Navigate to the AWS Management Console and pick **Amazon SNS**. From the menu on the left-hand side, click on **Topics** and choose **Standard**. Name the topic `products-review-communication`. This SNS topic will be used for communication on the status of the data pipeline. Also, note down the **Amazon Resource Name (ARN)** value—let's call this `[Your-SNS_ARN]`, as follows:

Amazon SNS 〉 Topics 〉 products-review-communication

products-review-communication   Edit   Delete   Publish message

Details

Name
products-review-communication

Display name
-

ARN
arn:aws:sns:▒▒▒▒▒▒▒▒▒▒▒▒▒▒▒▒products-review-communication

Topic owner
▒▒▒▒▒▒▒▒▒

Type
Standard

Figure 5.6 – Creating an Amazon SNS subscription

5. To subscribe to the `products-review-communication` topic, create a subscription. Select the ARN for the `products-review-confirmation` topic. Use the protocol email and give it your email ID. Select **Create subscription**:

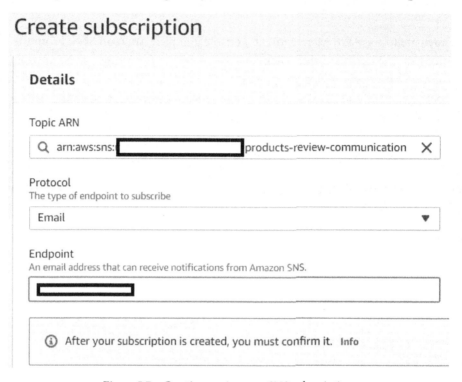

Figure 5.7 – Creating an Amazon SNS subscription

6. You will receive an email to confirm the subscription for the `product-review-communication` topic. Select **Subscription confirmed**.

7. Next, in the pipeline, we will create a lambda function that will execute the stored procedure using the Redshift Data API. This function also checks the status of the query execution and sends a notification on the status of the execution.

8. Navigate to the AWS Management Console, pick **AWS Lambda**, choose **Functions** from the left-hand menu, and create a function, as follows:

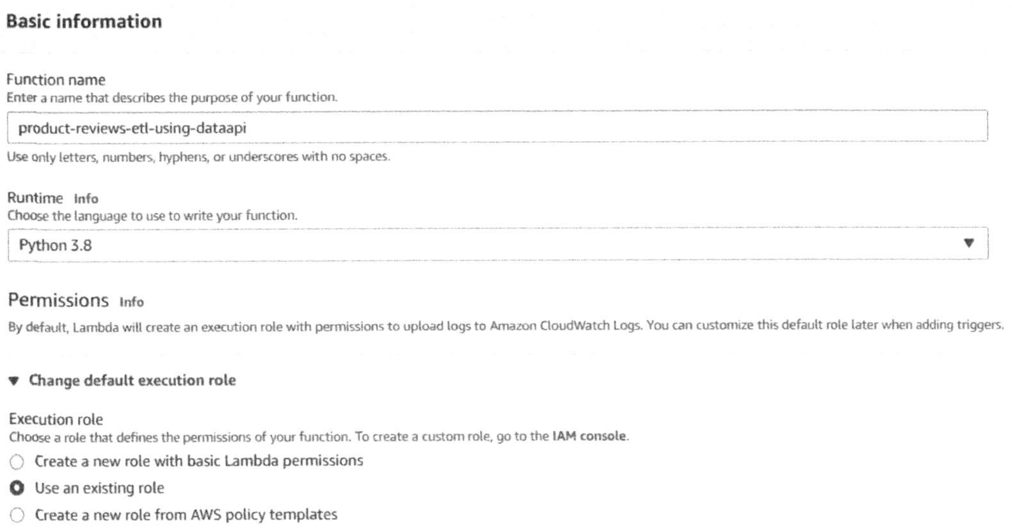

Basic information

Function name
Enter a name that describes the purpose of your function.

```
product-reviews-etl-using-dataapi
```

Use only letters, numbers, hyphens, or underscores with no spaces.

Runtime Info
Choose the language to use to write your function.

```
Python 3.8                                                                              ▼
```

Permissions Info

By default, Lambda will create an execution role with permissions to upload logs to Amazon CloudWatch Logs. You can customize this default role later when adding triggers.

▼ **Change default execution role**

Execution role
Choose a role that defines the permissions of your function. To create a custom role, go to the **IAM console**.

○ Create a new role with basic Lambda permissions

● Use an existing role

○ Create a new role from AWS policy templates

Figure 5.8 – Creating an AWS Lambda function

Here is some basic information as shown in the preceding screenshot:

- **Function name**: `product-reviews-etl-using-dataapi`.

- **Runtime**: `Python 3.8`.

- **Change default execution role**: Choose the lambda role you created in the *Getting ready* section of the recipe .

  Function code: Copy the code for the function from `https://github.com/PacktPublishing/Amazon-Redshift-Cookbook/blob/master/Chapter05/src/event-bridge-lambda-function.py`.

- Choose **Deploy.**

- **Change basic settings**: Set the lambda timeout to `30 seconds`.

Let's now create a scheduler event rule to trigger the `product-reviews-etl-using-dataapi` lambda function. Navigate to AWS Management Console, pick **Amazon EventBridge**, and choose **Rules** from the left-hand menu, then select **Default** from the **Event bus** dropdown and click on **Create rule**. Then, select the following options in the **Rules** section:

- **Name**: `schedule-productsreview-etl-execution`

- **Define pattern**: `Schedule`

- **Cron expression**: `0 20 ? * MON-FRI *`

> **Note**
>
> This rule will trigger at 3 A.M. **Coordinated Universal Time (UTC)** from Monday to Friday.

9. For **Select targets**, choose **Lambda function** and pick `product-reviews-executesql` from the drop-down menu, as follows:

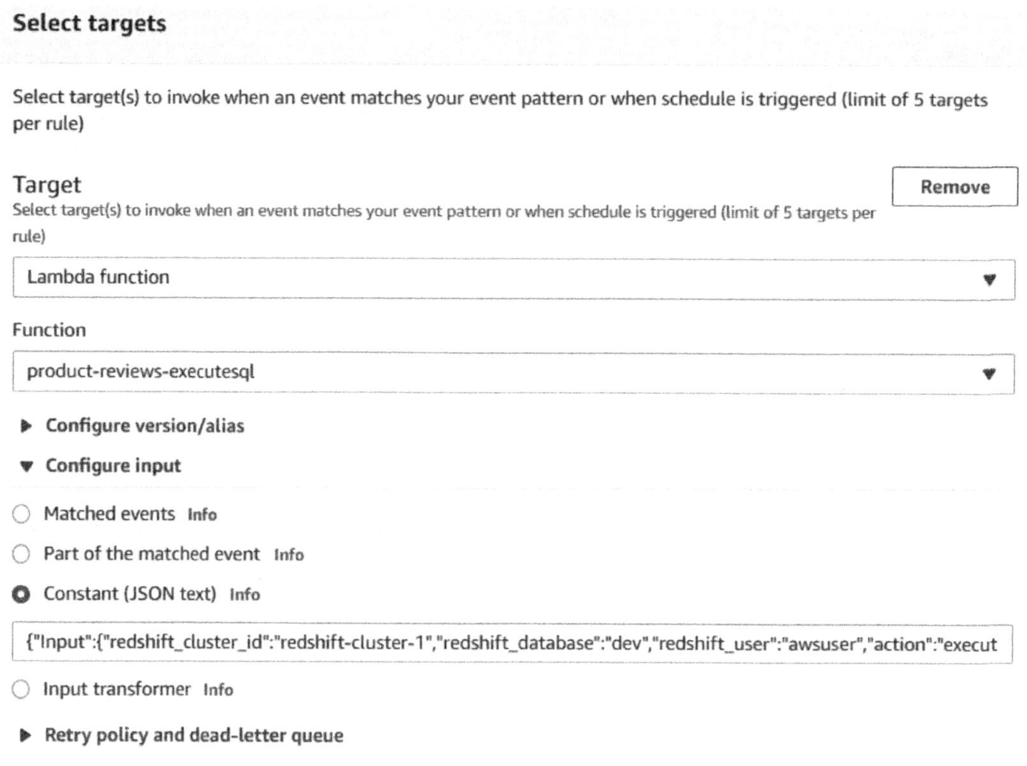

Select targets

Select target(s) to invoke when an event matches your event pattern or when schedule is triggered (limit of 5 targets per rule)

Target	Remove

Select target(s) to invoke when an event matches your event pattern or when schedule is triggered (limit of 5 targets per rule)

Lambda function	▼

Function

product-reviews-executesql	▼

▶ **Configure version/alias**

▼ **Configure input**

○ Matched events Info

○ Part of the matched event Info

● Constant (JSON text) Info

{"Input":{"redshift_cluster_id":"redshift-cluster-1","redshift_database":"dev","redshift_user":"awsuser","action":"execut

○ Input transformer Info

▶ **Retry policy and dead-letter queue**

Figure 5.9 – Selecting targets for the Amazon EventBridge rules

- Under **Configure input**, select **Constant (JSON text)** and provide the following, replacing [Your-Redshift_Cluster], [Your-Redshift_User], and [Your-SNS_ARN] with the respective values, and then click **Create**:

```
{"Input":{"redshift_cluster_id":"[Your-Redshift_
Cluster]","redshift_database":"dev","redshift_user":"[Your-
Redshift_User]","action":"execute_sql","sql_text":"call
products_review_etl();","sns_topic_arn":"[Your-SNS_ARN]"}}
```

10. Let's create another rule to check the status of the stored procedure execution completion. Click on **Rules** from the left-hand menu and select the following options:

Name

notify-productreview-execution-status

Maximum of 64 characters consisting of lower/upper case letters, ., -, _.

Description - *optional*

Enter description

Define pattern

Build or customize an Event Pattern or set a Schedule to invoke Targets.

○ Event pattern Info
   Build a pattern to match events

○ Schedule Info
   Invoke your targets on a schedule

Event matching pattern
You can use pre-defined pattern provided by a service or create a custom pattern

○ Pre-defined pattern by service

● Custom pattern

Event pattern   [Save]   [Cancel]

```
{
  "source": [
   "aws.redshift-data"
  ],
  "detail": {
   "principal": [
    "arn:aws:sts:          ssumed-
role/schedule-productsreview-etl-execution/product-
reviews-etl-using-dataapi"
   ]
```

Figure 5.10 – Creating a notify-productreview-execution-status rule

- **Name**: `notify-productreview-execution-status`

- **Define Pattern**: **Event pattern**

- **Event matching pattern**: **Custom pattern**

- **Event Pattern**: Provide the following, replacing `[Your-AWS_Account_Id]` and `[Your-Redshift_Role]` with the respective value, and choose **Save**:

```
{
  "source": [
    "aws.redshift-data"
```

```
    ],
    "detail": {
        "principal": [
            "arn:aws:sts::[Your-AWS_Account_Id]:assumed-role/[Your-
Redshift_Role]/product-reviews-executesql"
        ]
    }
}
```

11. Set the target as the `product-reviews-executesql` lambda function,
    as follows:

Target   [**Remove**]
Select target(s) to invoke when an event matches your event pattern or when schedule is triggered (limit of 5 targets per
rule)

```
Lambda function                                                          ▼
```

Function

```
product-reviews-executesql                                              ▼
```

▶ **Configure version/alias**

▼ **Configure input**

○ Matched events Info

○ Part of the matched event Info

○ Constant (JSON text) Info

● Input transformer Info

```
{"body":"$.detail"}
```

```
1","redshift_database":"dev","redshift_user":"awsuser","action":"notify","subject":"Extract Load Transform process
completed in Amazon Redshift","body":<body>,"sns_topic_arn":"arn:aws:sns:us-west-
                                                               "}}
```

Figure 5.11 – Configuring targets for the notify-productreview-execution-status rule

- Choose **Input transformer** and enter `{"body":"$.detail"}` in the **Input
  path** field.

- In the **Input template** field, provide the following value. In the next textbox, enter the following by replacing [Your-Redshift_Cluster], [Your-Redshift_User], and [Your-SNS_ARN] with the respective values, and then click on **Create**:

```
{"Input":{"redshift_cluster_id":"[Your-Redshift_
Cluster]","redshift_database":"dev","redshift_user":"[Your-
Redshift_User]","action":"notify","subject":"Extract
Load Transform process completed in Amazon
Redshift","body":[body],"sns_topic_arn":"[Your-SNS_ARN]"}}
```

12. When the set schedule is met, the Lambda function will trigger. To validate that the event pipeline is working correctly, navigate to the AWS Management Console and select **CloudWatch**. From the left-hand menu, choose **Log Groups** and filter for the `product-reviews-executesql` lambda function:

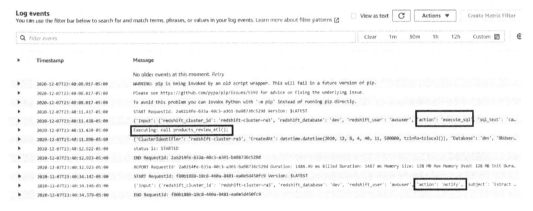

Figure 5.12 – Verifying the Lambda function trigger using Cloudwatch

13. On completion of the query, you will receive an email notification on the completion status:

Figure 5.13 – Email notification on completion of the event

14. Let's also validate the query execution on Amazon Redshift. In the AWS Management Console, navigate to **Amazon Redshift** and click on **Query monitoring**—notice the `product_review_etl` call in the list to confirm successful execution:

Figure 5.14 – Verifying query execution using the Amazon Redshift console

How it works...

Amazon EventBridge is used to orchestrate the product review data pipeline. Here is the architecture of this setup:

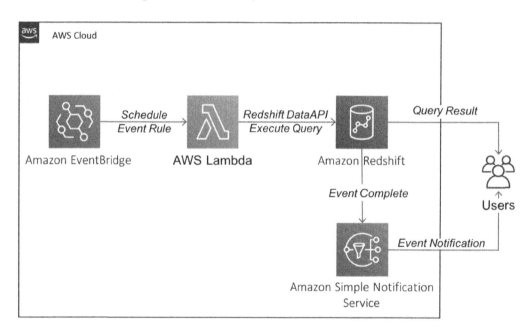

Figure 5.15 – Architecture of Amazon EventBridge setup

This workflow uses **Amazon EventBridge** to invoke the AWS Lambda function based on a schedule. AWS Lambda executes the data pipeline queries through the Amazon Redshift Data API. Amazon Redshift publishes custom notifications through Amazon SNS for their completion, and notifies the users. You are able to integrate a serverless decoupled pipeline that is scalable.

EventBridge allows you to connect applications using events. An event is a trigger when the system state changes that can be used to drive a workflow such as an ETL process. This also allows you to integrate your own AWS applications with microservices, SaaS applications, and custom applications as event sources that publish events to an event bus.

Event-driven applications using AWS Lambda

AWS Lambda helps you to build event-driven microservices. This serverless process can be invoked using a variety of events such as when a file arrives, when a notification is received, and so on. This helps build a decoupled data workflow that can be invoked as soon as the upstream dependencies are met, instead of a schedule-based workflow.

For example, let's say we have a website that is continuously sending the clickstream logs every 15 minutes into Amazon S3. Instead of accumulating all the log files and processing them at midnight in a typical ETL process, Amazon S3 can send an event to a Lambda function when an object is created and processed immediately. This provides several advantages, such as processing in smaller batch sizes to meet a **service-level agreement** (**SLA**) and also to have the data current within the data warehouse.

There are several ways to invoke an AWS Lambda function using an event—you can find more information about this at `https://docs.aws.amazon.com/lambda/latest/dg/lambda-invocation.html`.

Getting ready

To complete this recipe, you will need the following:

- An Amazon Redshift cluster deployed in the `eu-west-1` AWS region—note that we will refer to the cluster ID as `[Your-Redshift_Cluster]`

- Amazon Redshift cluster master user credentials—note that we will refer to the username as `[Your-Redshift_User]`

- Access to any SQL interface such as a SQL client or the Amazon Redshift query editor

- An IAM user with access to Amazon Redshift, Amazon S3, and AWS Lambda

- An Amazon S3 bucket created in the `eu-west-1` region—we will refer to this as `[Your-Amazon_S3_Bucket]`

- An AWS account number—we will refer to this in the recipes as `[Your-AWS_Account_Id]`

How to do it...

In this recipe, we will use Python-based AWS Lambda to `COPY` data into Amazon Redshift as soon as the file arrives at the Amazon S3 location.

1. The AWS Lambda package is already available at `https://github.com/PacktPublishing/Amazon-Redshift-Cookbook/blob/master/Chapter05/src/my-lambda-deployment-package.zip`. Download this deployment package to your local folder.

2. Navigate to the AWS Management Console and pick the **AWS Lambda** service, and click on **Create function**, as follows:

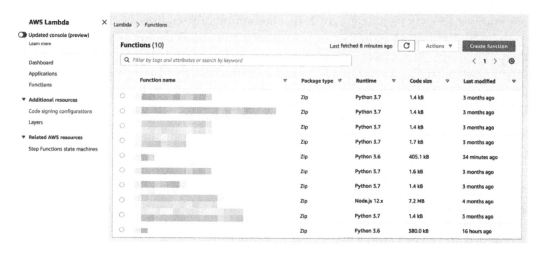

Figure 5.16 – Creating an AWS Lambda function using the AWS Management Console

3. In the **Create function** screen, enter `lambda_function` under **Function name** and set the **Runtime** option to **Python 3.6**, and then click on **Create function**:

Figure 5.17 – Creating an AWS Lambda lambda_function function

4. Click on the **Actions** button and choose the **Upload a .zip file** option. Select the `my-lambda-deployment-package.zip` file from your local folder and click on **Save**. Now, the lambda code and the Python package will be successfully imported.

5. Click on the `lambda_function.py` file and edit the values for the following parameters to point to your Amazon Redshift cluster:

```
db_database = "[database]"
db_user = "[user]"
db_password = "[password]"
db_port = "[port]"
db_host = "[host]"
iam_role = "'arn:aws:iam::[Your-AWS_Account_Id]:role/[Your-Redshift-Role]"
```

Click on **Deploy** to save the changes.

6. You can now test the `lambda_function` function by clicking on the **Test** option. In the **Test** option, choose **Create new test event**, and in the **Event** template, choose `hello-world` and provide an event name of `myevent`, and then copy and paste the following test stub event value:

```
{
    "Records": [
        {
            "eventVersion": "2.1",
            "eventTime": "2030-12-06T18:43:42.795Z",
```

```
    "s3": {
      "s3SchemaVersion": "1.0",
      "configurationId": "test",
      "bucket": {
        "name": "packt-redshift-cookbook"
      },
      "object": {
        "key": "part/000.gz",
        "size": 540
      }
    }
  }
]
}
```

> **Note**
> This test event will output the bucket name and key and will also perform
> a COPY operation into Amazon Redshift to create a `stg_part` table and
> ingest data from `s3://packt-redshift-cookbook/part/000.gz`

7. Now, let's create an Amazon S3 triggered event so that files can be automatically
   copied into Amazon Redshift as they get put into your S3 location. Navigate to
   the **Amazon S3** service in the AWS Management Console, click on the `[Your-Amazon_S3_Bucket]` bucket, select **Properties**, and then click on **Event
   notifications**, as follows:

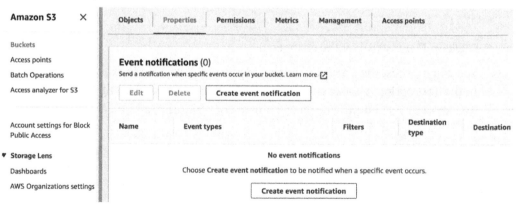

Figure 5.18 – Creating event notifications from Amazon S3

8. On the **Create event notification** screen, set up the event details as follows:

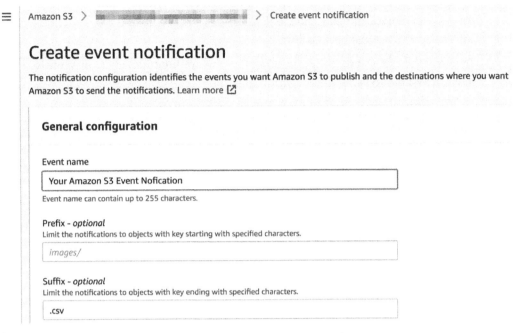

Figure 5.19 – Configuring the event notification

Here are the event details as shown in the preceding screenshot;

- **Event name**: Any event name of your choice
- **Prefix**: Your S3 folder location where you plan to put the files to be copied—for example, `events/`
- **Suffix**: `.csv`
- **Event types**: Check `Put`
- **Destination**: `Lambda Function`
- **Specify Lambda function**: Choose the `lambda_function` function from the list

    Now, click on **Save changes**.

9. Download the `s3://packt-redshift-cookbook/part/000.gz` and `s3://packt-redshift-cookbook/part/001.gz` public S3 files to your location folder.

10. Navigate to your `[Your-Amazon_S3_Bucket]` Amazon S3 bucket and upload `000.gz` from your local folder, followed by `001.gz`.

11. From the AWS Management Console, navigate to AWS **Lambda** and select the `lambda_function` function. Click on **Monitoring**, and you will notice that there are two invocations of the Lambda function that copied the uploaded files automatically to Amazon Redshift.

12. To verify the execution of the `lambda_function` function, click on **View logs in CloudWatch** to show the execution logs.

How it works...

The AWS Lambda deployment package bundles the Python function code and the dependent `psycopg2` library (`https://www.psycopg.org/`) that is used to connect to Amazon Redshift. You can build this deployment package from scratch using the instructions in `https://docs.aws.amazon.com/lambda/latest/dg/python-package.html` and `https://pypi.org/project/aws-psycopg2/`. You can include any other dependent packages that you may need to meet your organizational requirements when creating this deployment package.

Also, as a best practice, you can enhance the `lambda_function` code to retrieve the Amazon Redshift credentials using AWS Secrets Manager, as illustrated at `https://docs.aws.amazon.com/code-samples/latest/catalog/python-secretsmanager-secrets_manager.py.html`.

Orchestrating using AWS Step Functions

AWS Step Functions allows you to author a workflow where each step is decoupled but the application state can be maintained. AWS Step Functions is integrated with multiple AWS services to allow flexibility to call the specific service in each of the tasks.

You can see a list of natively supported integrations here: `https://docs.aws.amazon.com/step-functions/latest/dg/concepts-service-integrations.html`. AWS Step Functions supports the Amazon States Language, which allows a workflow to be authored and maintained like a **JavaScript Object Notation** (**JSON**) file. You can harness AWS Step Functions to execute any complex ETL workflow in Amazon Redshift.

Getting ready

To complete this recipe, you will need the following:

- An Amazon Redshift cluster deployed in the eu-west-1 AWS region—note that we will refer to the cluster ID as [Your-Redshift_Cluster]

- Amazon Redshift cluster master user credentials—note that we will refer to the username as [Your-Redshift_User]

- Access to any SQL interface such as a SQL client or the Amazon Redshift query editor

- An IAM user with access to Amazon Redshift and AWS Lambda

How to do it...

In this recipe, we will use AWS Step Functions to orchestrate a simple ETL workflow that will submit queries to Amazon Redshift asynchronously using the Amazon Redshift Data API. We will start by creating an AWS Lambda function that will be used to submit a status poll for the queries.

1. Navigate to the AWS Management Console and pick the **AWS Lambda** service, and then click on **Create function**, as follows:

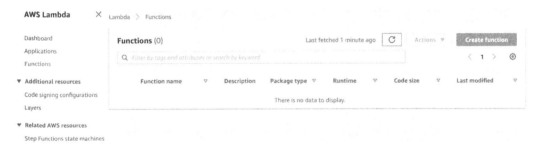

Figure 5.20 – Creating an AWS Lambda function using the AWS Management Console

2. In the **Create function** screen, enter submit_redshift_query under **Function name** and choose Python 3.6 as the **Runtime** option, and then click on **Create function**.

3. In the function code for lambda_function.py, copy and paste the code from https://github.com/PacktPublishing/Amazon-Redshift-Cookbook/blob/master/Chapter05/src/stepfunction/lambda_submit_redshift_query.py, and click on **Deploy** to save the function.

4. In the **Permissions** tab of the AWS Lambda function, click on the auto- created `submit_redshift_query-role-***` role name, as follows:

Figure 5.21 – Configuring the permissions for the AWS Lambda function

5. In **IAM**, which opens in a different tab, copy and paste the policy available at `https://github.com/PacktPublishing/Amazon-Redshift-Cookbook/blob/master/Chapter05/src/stepfunction/lambda_execute_policy.json` by clicking on **Add inline policy**.

6. Click on **Test** and press **Configure events**, choose **Create new test event**, and pick the `hello-world` event template:

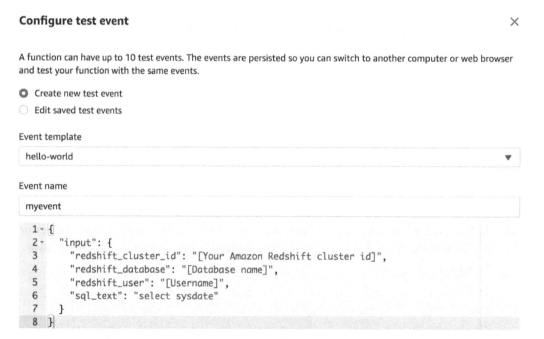

Figure 5.22 – Setting up a test event for the AWS Lambda function

7. In the **Event name** field, copy the following sample input, replacing the `[Your-Redshift_Cluster]`, `[Your-Redshift_DB]`, and `[Your-Redshift_User]` parameter values with your Amazon Redshift cluster, and then press the **Create** button:

```
{
  "input": {
    "redshift_cluster_id": "[Your-Redshift_Cluster]",
    "redshift_database": "[Your-Redshift_DB]",
    "redshift_user": "[Your-Redshift_User]",
    "sql_text": "select sysdate"
  }
}
```

8. Press the **Test** button, and you should be able to see the sample query was submitted in the execution results, as per the following code snippet shown for a successful submission:

```
START RequestId: 43df694d-3716-474f-b279-cd7b976ef05c Version:
$LATEST
{'input': {'redshift_cluster_id': 'democluster-71f3476d',
'redshift_database': 'dev', 'redshift_user': 'demo', 'sql_
text': 'select sysdate'}}
{'ClusterIdentifier': 'democluster-71f3476d', 'CreatedAt':
datetime.datetime(2020, 12, 9, 0, 47, 2, 353000,
tzinfo=tzlocal()), 'Database': 'dev', 'DbUser': 'demo', 'Id':
'0ce38431-be55-4c4b-97c8-230624a01c76', 'ResponseMetadata':
{'RequestId': 'dbabb5dc-8de8-4f59-80f9-367319eeaecb',
'HTTPStatusCode': 200, 'HTTPHeaders': {'x-amzn-requestid':
'dbabb5dc-8de8-4f59-80f9-367319eeaecb', 'content-type':
'application/x-amz-json-1.1', 'content-length': '150', 'date':
'Wed, 09 Dec 2020 00:47:02 GMT'}, 'RetryAttempts': 0}}
END RequestId: 43df694d-3716-474f-b279-cd7b976ef05c
```

9. Repeat *Steps 1-8* to create another AWS Lambda function named `poll_redshift_query` using the following code:

    AWS Lambda code—`https://github.com/PacktPublishing/Amazon-Redshift-Cookbook/blob/master/Chapter05/src/stepfunction/lambda_poll_redshift_query.py`

    AWS Lambda test event—`https://github.com/PacktPublishing/Amazon-Redshift-Cookbook/blob/master/Chapter05/src/stepfunction/lambda_poll_redshift_query_test.json`

10. Let's now start creating an AWS step function to orchestrate a simple workflow to submit and monitor the job using the AWS Lambda functions we have created. Navigate to the AWS Management Console and pick the **Step Functions** service. Click on **Create state machine**, as follows:

Figure 5.23 – Creating a Step Functions state machine

11. Pick **Author code snippet** and **Standard** to copy and paste the following code in the **Definition** field available at `https://github.com/PacktPublishing/Amazon-Redshift-Cookbook/blob/master/Chapter05/src/stepfunction/stepfunction_job_redshift.json` and then click **Next**:

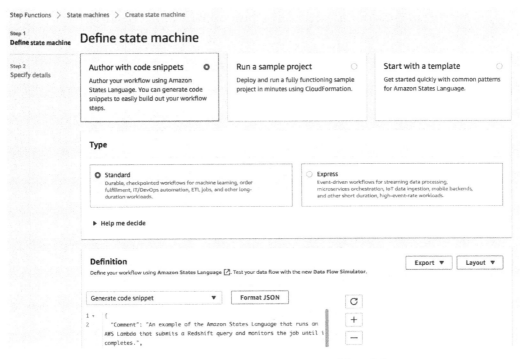

Figure 5.24 – Setting up the step function workflow definition

12. Under the **Permissions** tab, click on **Create new role** and click **Next** to create an AWS Step Functions state machine.

13. Click on **Start execution**, and under the input provide the following details, which are also available at `https://github.com/PacktPublishing/Amazon-Redshift-Cookbook/blob/master/Chapter05/src/stepfunction/stepfunction_job_redshift_test.json`:

```
{
  "input": {
    "redshift_cluster_id": "[Your-Redshift_Cluster]",
    "redshift_database": "[Your-Redshift_DB]",
    "redshift_user": "[Your-Redshift_User]",
    "sql_text": "select sysdate"
  },
  "wait_time": "3"
}
```

14. Now, you can monitor the execution of this workflow on the **Details** tab, as follows:

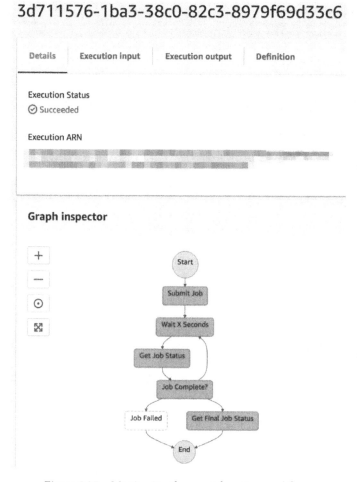

Figure 5.25 – Monitoring the event function workflow

How it works...

AWS Step Functions uses the Amazon States Language, which is JSON-based. You can author most kinds of ETL process and drive a workflow that can wait for dependency between each task and also allow for parallelism when needed. An AWS state machine can either be triggered through an event or be scheduled for automation.

For more information, see the Amazon States Language specification at https://docs.aws.amazon.com/step-functions/latest/dg/concepts-amazon-states-language.html.

Orchestrating using Amazon MWAA

Amazon MWAA is a managed service that allows you to build an end-to-end automated data pipeline using Apache Airflow. Apache Airflow is used to programmatically create workflows, to schedule, and to monitor. An entire data pipeline can be decomposed into a series of smaller tasks with the required dependencies to coordinate the execution of the tasks as part of a workflow. Workflows in Airflow are authored as **directed acyclic graphs** (**DAGs**) using the Python programming language. The workflow's functionality can be extended through a set of powerful plugins. The monitoring of the workflow is done through the **user interface** (**UI**), and the workflow's functionality is extended through a set of powerful plugins.

In this recipe, we will build the underlying infrastructure used for Apache Airflow, using Amazon MWAA. After the infrastructure is built, we will build a data pipeline for the parts table.

Getting ready

To complete this recipe, you will need the following:

- An Amazon Redshift cluster deployed in the eu-west-1 AWS region—note that we will refer to the cluster ID as [Your-Redshift_Cluster]

- Amazon Redshift cluster master user credentials—note that we will refer to the username as [Your-Redshift_User]

- Access to any SQL interface such as a SQL client or the Amazon Redshift query editor

- An IAM user with access to Amazon Redshift and MWAA

- An Amazon S3 bucket created in the eu-west-1 region—we will refer to this as [Your-Amazon_S3_Bucket]

How to do it...

In this recipe, we will set up a data pipeline using Apache Airflow that will connect to Amazon Redshift to orchestrate a workflow.

1. Browse to the Amazon S3 console and select [Your-Amazon_S3_Bucket]. Create a folder called airflow within the bucket. We will use this folder to store the Airflow DAGs and requirements file providing a list of dependencies needed to run the Python DAG.

2. You can use the **command-line interface (CLI)** or the S3 console to upload the files. Upload the `https://github.com/PacktPublishing/Amazon-Redshift-Cookbook/blob/master/Chapter05/src/requirements.txt` requirements file to the `s3:// [Your-Amazon_S3_Bucket]/airflow` bucket location.

3. Download the DAG script from `https://github.com/PacktPublishing/Amazon-Redshift-Cookbook/blob/master/Chapter05/src/redshift_parts_airflow_dag.py`. For `load_sql`, replace the name of the S3 bucket and the IAM role in the script. Save it and upload the workflow Python script (DAG) to the newly created `dags` folder in your airflow bucket:

Figure 5.26 – Setting up Apache Airflow DAG

4. We are now ready to build the infrastructure and setup needed for Apache Airflow. Navigate to the AWS Management Console in the `eu-west-1` AWS region and pick **MWAA**. Choose **Create environment**.

    Name the environment `MyAirflowEnvironment`.

    Choose the latest version of MWAA.

5. For the S3 bucket, specify the `s3:// [Your-Amazon_S3_Bucket` bucket. The bucket would need to be in the same region in which you are creating the MWAA.

    DAGs folder: `s3:// [Your-Amazon_S3_Bucket]/airflow/dags`

    Requirements file: `s3:// [Your-Amazon_S3_Bucket]/airflow/requirements.txt`

You can see these settings in the following screenshot:

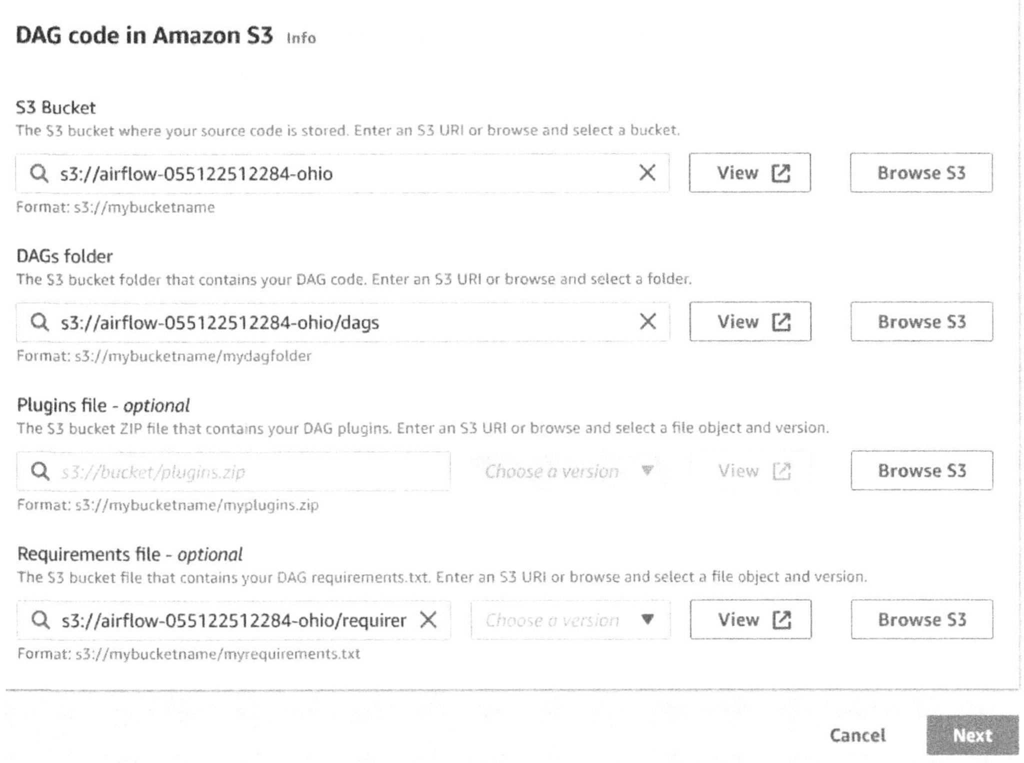

DAG code in Amazon S3 Info

S3 Bucket
The S3 bucket where your source code is stored. Enter an S3 URI or browse and select a bucket.

| Q s3://airflow-055122512284-ohio   ✕ | View ☑ | Browse S3 |

Format: s3://mybucketname

DAGs folder
The S3 bucket folder that contains your DAG code. Enter an S3 URI or browse and select a folder.

| Q s3://airflow-055122512284-ohio/dags   ✕ | View ☑ | Browse S3 |

Format: s3://mybucketname/mydagfolder

Plugins file - *optional*
The S3 bucket ZIP file that contains your DAG plugins. Enter an S3 URI or browse and select a file object and version.

| Q s3://bucket/plugins.zip | Choose a version ▼ | View ☑ | Browse S3 |

Format: s3://mybucketname/myplugins.zip

Requirements file - *optional*
The S3 bucket file that contains your DAG requirements.txt. Enter an S3 URI or browse and select a file object and version.

| Q s3://airflow-055122512284-ohio/requirer ✕ | Choose a version ▼ | View ☑ | Browse S3 |

Format: s3://mybucketname/myrequirements.txt

Cancel   Next

Figure 5.27 – Configuring the source Amazon S3 bucket

6. Choose **Next**. If you have an existing VPC, choose from the drop-down menu.
    If you do not have an existing VPC, choose **Create MWAA VPC**. This will launch
    a CloudFormation template, create a stack, and on completion, navigate back to the
    MWAA setup step.

From the drop-down menu, select the VPC and the subnets. Make the web server have **Public network** access:

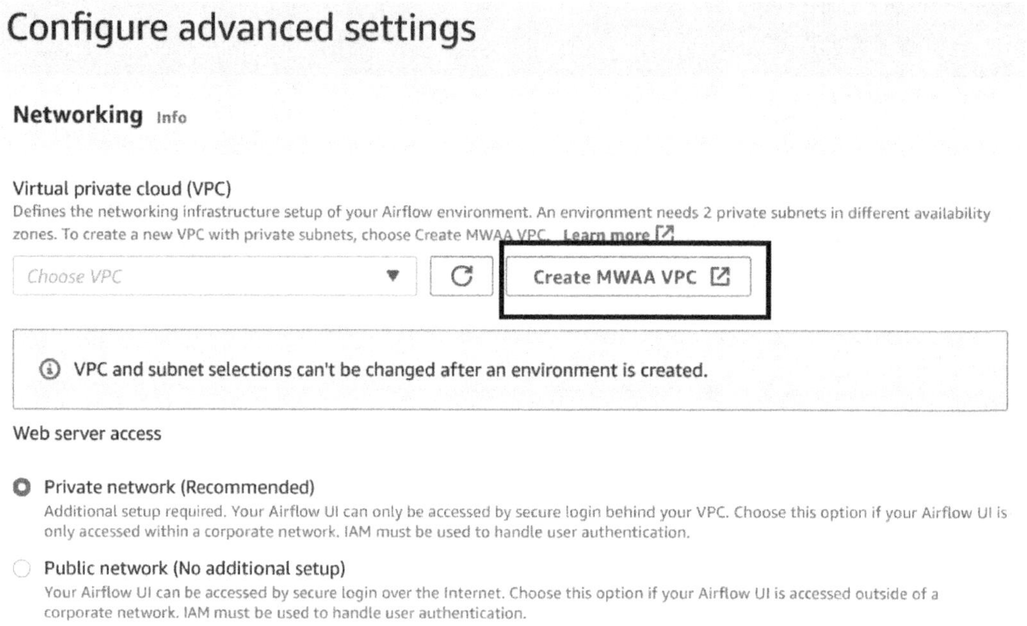

Configure advanced settings

Networking Info

Virtual private cloud (VPC)
Defines the networking infrastructure setup of your Airflow environment. An environment needs 2 private subnets in different availability zones. To create a new VPC with private subnets, choose Create MWAA VPC. **Learn more** [↗]

| Choose VPC ▾ | C | **Create MWAA VPC** [↗] |

ⓘ VPC and subnet selections can't be changed after an environment is created.

Web server access

◉ Private network (Recommended)
  Additional setup required. Your Airflow UI can only be accessed by secure login behind your VPC. Choose this option if your Airflow UI is only accessed within a corporate network. IAM must be used to handle user authentication.

○ Public network (No additional setup)
  Your Airflow UI can be accessed by secure login over the Internet. Choose this option if your Airflow UI is accessed outside of a corporate network. IAM must be used to handle user authentication.

Figure 5.28 – Setting up the network access to connect to Amazon Redshift

7. Select the mw1.small instance type. Keep the rest at their default settings for the IAM role:

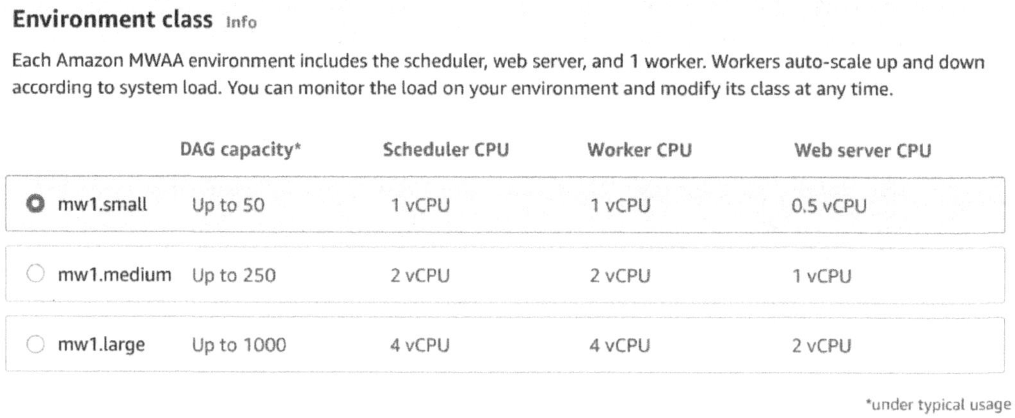

Environment class Info

Each Amazon MWAA environment includes the scheduler, web server, and 1 worker. Workers auto-scale up and down according to system load. You can monitor the load on your environment and modify its class at any time.

	DAG capacity*	Scheduler CPU	Worker CPU	Web server CPU
◉ mw1.small	Up to 50	1 vCPU	1 vCPU	0.5 vCPU
○ mw1.medium	Up to 250	2 vCPU	2 vCPU	1 vCPU
○ mw1.large	Up to 1000	4 vCPU	4 vCPU	2 vCPU

*under typical usage

Figure 5.29 – Configuring the Amazon EC2 instance for the Airflow environment

8. Choose **Create environment**. On completion of the setup, it will make the environment available with Apache Airflow. We are now ready to execute the workflow.

9. Select **Open Airflow UI** from the environment:

Figure 5.30 – Setting up the Airflow environment

10. From the UI, click on **Admin** and choose **Connections**. We will configure the connection for the Amazon Redshift cluster that will be used in the workflow tasks:

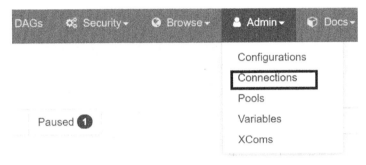

Figure 5.31 – Setting up the Amazon Redshift connection

11. Navigate to the `conn_id` Postgres and click **Edit**.

12. Specify your Redshift cluster endpoint, username, password, and port number. Click **Save**:

Figure 5.32 – Configuring the Amazon Redshift connection properties

13. Now that the setup is complete, from the UI click on **DAGs**—this will list the `parts-redshift-datapipeline-dag` DAG that you had uploaded to the S3 bucket:

Figure 5.33 – Configuring the Airflow DAG

14. Let's check the DAG. Firstly, click on the DAG name. This workflow has three tasks—the first will create a `parts_stg` table using `PostgresOperator`, the second will use the `COPY` command to load the `parts` sample data from S3, and in the final step, it will check the record count in the `parts_stg` table using `PythonOperator`:

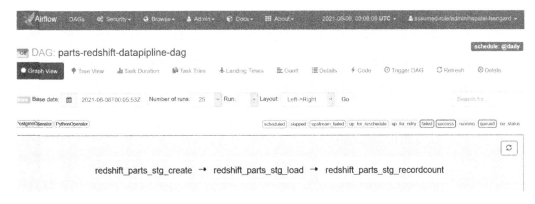

Figure 5.34 – Verifying the DAG setup on Airflow

15. Click on **DAGs** in the UI and toggle the DAG to an **On** state—this will put the DAG in schedule:

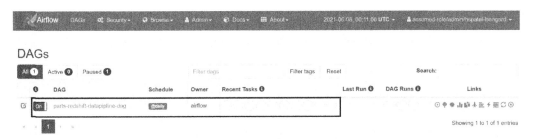

Figure 5.35 – Scheduling the workflow execution

16. This will start the execution. Click on the green number under **DAG runs**.

17. The workflow will execute as per the set dependency. It will run redshift_ parts_stg_create first and when that's finished, it will run the second task. When redshift_parts_stg_load has completed successfully, it will execute redshift_parts_stg_recordcount. This is the monitoring step:

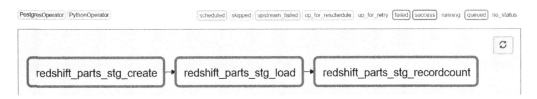

Figure 5.36 – Verifying the execution of the workflow

18. Let's validate the logs for the copy and record count step. Click on `redshift_parts_stg_load`. Then, select **Task Instance Details**:

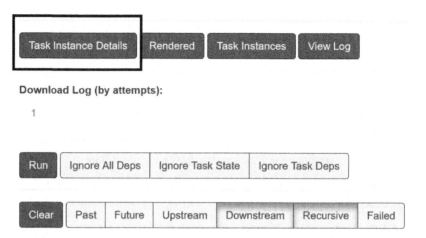

Figure 5.37 – Viewing the task execution details

19. Capture the `log_url`, open a new browser window, and paste the **Uniform Resource Locator (URL)**. The copy task completed successfully—this is logged in the logs and you can verify how many records got loaded:

```
[2021-06-08 01:45:40,789] {{taskinstance.py:880}} INFO -
------------------------------------------------------------------------
[2021-06-08 01:45:40,815] {{taskinstance.py:881}} INFO - Starting attempt 1 of 1
[2021-06-08 01:45:40,838] {{taskinstance.py:882}} INFO -
------------------------------------------------------------------------
[2021-06-08 01:45:40,885] {{taskinstance.py:901}} INFO - Executing <Task(PostgresOperator): redshift_parts_stg_load> on 2021-06-06T00:00:00+00:00
[2021-06-08 01:45:40,915] {{standard_task_runner.py:54}} INFO - Started process 2049 to run task
[2021-06-08 01:45:40,915] {{standard_task_runner.py:54}} INFO - Started process 2049 to run task
[2021-06-08 01:45:40,947] {{logging_mixin.py:112}} INFO - Failed to emit log record
[2021-06-08 01:45:41,035] {{logging_mixin.py:112}} WARNING - Traceback (most recent call last):
[2021-06-08 01:45:41,062] {{logging_mixin.py:112}} WARNING -   File "/usr/local/airflow/config/cloudwatch_logging.py", line 91, in emit
  self.handler.emit(record)
[2021-06-08 01:45:41,091] {{logging_mixin.py:112}} WARNING -   File "/usr/local/lib/python3.7/site-packages/watchtower/__init__.py", line 205, in emit
  self._submit_batch([cwl_message], stream_name)
[2021-06-08 01:45:41,121] {{logging_mixin.py:112}} WARNING -   File "/usr/local/lib/python3.7/site-packages/watchtower/__init__.py", line 173, in _submit_batch
  self.sequence_tokens[stream_name] = response["nextSequenceToken"]
[2021-06-08 01:45:41,151] {{logging_mixin.py:112}} WARNING - KeyError: 'nextSequenceToken'
[2021-06-08 01:45:41,179] {{standard_task_runner.py:78}} INFO - Job 72: Subtask redshift_parts_stg_load
[2021-06-08 01:45:41,377] {{logging_mixin.py:112}} INFO - Running %s on host %s <TaskInstance: parts-redshift-datapipline-dag.redshift_parts_stg_load 2021-06-06T00:00:00+00
[2021-06-08 01:45:41,684] {{postgres_operator.py:62}} INFO - Executing: copy public.part_stg from 's3://packtcookbook-hsp/ssb/part/' iam_role 'arn:aws:iam::          :ro]
[2021-06-08 01:47:19,410] {{postgres_operator.py:67}} INFO - INFO:  Load into table 'part_stg' completed, 20000000 record(s) loaded successfully.

[2021-06-08 01:47:19,504] {{taskinstance.py:1070}} INFO - Marking task as SUCCESS.dag_id=parts-redshift-datapipline-dag, task_id=redshift_parts_stg_load, execution_date=20
```

Figure 5.38 – Verifying the task execution detailed logs

20. Similarly, capture the log for the final task and verify the log as a data quality check. This record count of the `parts_stg` table is 20000000 records:

```
[2021-06-08 01:47:22,807] {{taskinstance.py:670}} INFO - Dependencies all met for <TaskInstance: parts-redshift-datapipline-dag.redshift_parts_stg_recordcount 2021-06-06T0
[2021-06-08 01:47:22,836] {{taskinstance.py:880}} INFO -
-----------------------------------------------------------------------------
[2021-06-08 01:47:22,865] {{taskinstance.py:881}} INFO - Starting attempt 1 of 1
[2021-06-08 01:47:22,893] {{taskinstance.py:882}} INFO -
-----------------------------------------------------------------------------
[2021-06-08 01:47:22,942] {{taskinstance.py:901}} INFO - Executing <Task(PythonOperator): redshift_parts_stg_recordcount> on 2021-06-06T00:00:00+00:00
[2021-06-08 01:47:22,976] {{standard_task_runner.py:54}} INFO - Started process 2055 to run task
[2021-06-08 01:47:22,976] {{standard_task_runner.py:54}} INFO - Started process 2055 to run task
[2021-06-08 01:47:23,008] {{logging_mixin.py:112}} INFO - Failed to emit log record
[2021-06-08 01:47:23,101] {{logging_mixin.py:112}} WARNING - Traceback (most recent call last):
[2021-06-08 01:47:23,132] {{logging_mixin.py:112}} WARNING -   File "/usr/local/airflow/config/cloudwatch_logging.py", line 91, in emit
    self.handler.emit(record)
[2021-06-08 01:47:23,159] {{logging_mixin.py:112}} WARNING -   File "/usr/local/lib/python3.7/site-packages/watchtower/__init__.py", line 205, in emit
    self._submit_batch([cwl_message], stream_name)
[2021-06-08 01:47:23,186] {{logging_mixin.py:112}} WARNING -   File "/usr/local/lib/python3.7/site-packages/watchtower/__init__.py", line 173, in _submit_batch
    self.sequence_tokens[stream_name] = response["nextSequenceToken"]
[2021-06-08 01:47:23,211] {{logging_mixin.py:112}} WARNING - KeyError: 'nextSequenceToken'
[2021-06-08 01:47:23,244] {{standard_task_runner.py:78}} INFO - Job 73: Subtask redshift_parts_stg_recordcount
[2021-06-08 01:47:23,389] {{logging_mixin.py:112}} INFO - Running %s on host %s <TaskInstance: parts-redshift-datapipline-dag.redshift_parts_stg_recordcount 2021-06-06T00:
[2021-06-08 01:47:23,875] {{redshift_parts_airflow_dag.py:39}} INFO - Data quality on table public.part_stg check passed with 20000000 records
[2021-06-08 01:47:23,903] {{python_operator.py:114}} INFO - Done. Returned value was: None
[2021-06-08 01:47:23,952] {{taskinstance.py:1070}} INFO - Marking task as SUCCESS.dag_id=parts-redshift-datapipline-dag, task_id=redshift_parts_stg_recordcount, execution_
```

Figure 5.39 – Verifying the task execution for the parts_stg table

How it works...

Amazon MWAA simplifies the setup needed to build and orchestrate a data pipeline using Apache Airflow. Apache Airflow provides the means to build a reusable data pipeline programmatically.

6
Data Authorization and Security

Amazon Redshift provides out-of-the-box features that enable you to build data warehouses to meet the requirements of the most security-sensitive organizations. In AWS, security is the highest priority and is a shared responsibility (`https://aws.amazon.com/compliance/shared-responsibility-model/`) between AWS and you. Using an Amazon Redshift managed service, the data center and network architecture come out of the box to meet the requirements of security-sensitive organizations. You can now configure the data and cluster management controls to meet your organization's requirements. Data can be encrypted to keep your data secure in transit and at rest using industry-standard encryption techniques. Amazon Redshift resources are controlled in the four different levels of cluster management (creating and configuring the cluster), cluster connectivity, database access to objects, and temporary/single sign-on.

Specifically, the following topics are covered in this chapter:

- Managing infrastructure security
- Data encryption at rest
- Data encryption in transit
- Column-level security
- Loading and unloading encrypted data

- Managing superusers
- Managing users and groups
- Managing federated authentication
- Using IAM authentication to generate database user credentials
- Managing audit logs
- Monitoring Amazon Redshift

Technical requirements

Here are the technical requirements in order to complete the recipes in this chapter:

- Access to the AWS Console.
- The AWS Administrator should create an IAM user by following *Recipe 1 – Creating an IAM user* in the *Appendix*. This IAM user will be used for some of the recipes in this chapter.
- The AWS administrator should create an IAM role by following *Recipe 3 – Creating an IAM role for an AWS service* in the *Appendix*. This IAM role will be used for some of the recipes in this chapter.
- The AWS administrator should deploy the AWS CloudFormation template (`https://github.com/PacktPublishing/Amazon-Redshift-Cookbook/blob/master/Chapter06/chapter_6_CFN.yaml`) to create two IAM policies:

  a. An IAM policy attached to the IAM user that will give them access to Amazon Redshift, Amazon S3, AWS Secrets Manager, Amazon CloudWatch, Amazon CloudWatch Logs, Amazon EC2, Amazon Simple Notification Service (SNS) AWS Identity and Access Management (IAM), AWS Key Management Service (KMS), AWS Glue, and **Amazon Virtual Private Cloud (Amazon VPC)**

  b. An IAM policy attached to the IAM role that will allow the Amazon Redshift cluster to access Amazon S3.

- Attach the IAM role to the Amazon Redshift cluster by following *Recipe 4 – Attaching an IAM role to the Amazon Redshift cluster* in the *Appendix*. Take note of the IAM role name; we will reference it in the recipes as [`Your-Redshift_Role`].
- An Amazon Redshift cluster deployed in AWS Region `eu-west-1`.
- Amazon Redshift cluster masteruser credentials.
- Access to any SQL interface such as a SQL client or the Amazon Redshift Query Editor.

- Your AWS account number; we will reference it in recipes as [Your-AWS_Account_Id].

- An Amazon S3 bucket created in eu-west-1; we will reference it as [Your-Amazon_S3_Bucket].

- The code files referenced in the GitHub repository at https://github.com/PacktPublishing/Amazon-Redshift-Cookbook/tree/master/Chapter06.

Managing infrastructure security

Amazon VPC allows you to launch Amazon Redshift clusters in a logically isolated virtual network in which you define the IP address range and subnets and configure the infrastructure security. When you provision an Amazon Redshift cluster, it is locked down by default, so nobody has access to it. To grant inbound access to an Amazon Redshift cluster, you associate the cluster using the security group. Having your Amazon Redshift cluster by following the least access security principle is
a best practice.

Getting ready

To complete this recipe, you will need the following setup:

- An IAM user with access to Amazon VPC, Amazon EC2, and Amazon Redshift
- Access to any SQL interface such as a SQL client or the Amazon Redshift Query Editor

How to do it

In this recipe, you will launch an Amazon Redshift cluster inside a custom VPC and subnet using the following steps:

1. Navigate to the AWS Console and select the **VPC** service. Click on **Launch VPC Wizard** and choose the default **VPC with a Single Public Subnet** option. Enter the following values and click on the **Create VPC** button:

- **IPv6 CIDR block – Amazon provided IPv6 CIDR block**
- **VPC name** – vpc-redshift
- **Subnet name** – subnet-redshift
- **Service endpoints – com.amazonaws.eu-west-1.s3**

Choosing the service endpoints from Amazon S3 allows the traffic to and from Amazon Redshift to be within the VPC, rather than the default of transcending the internet:

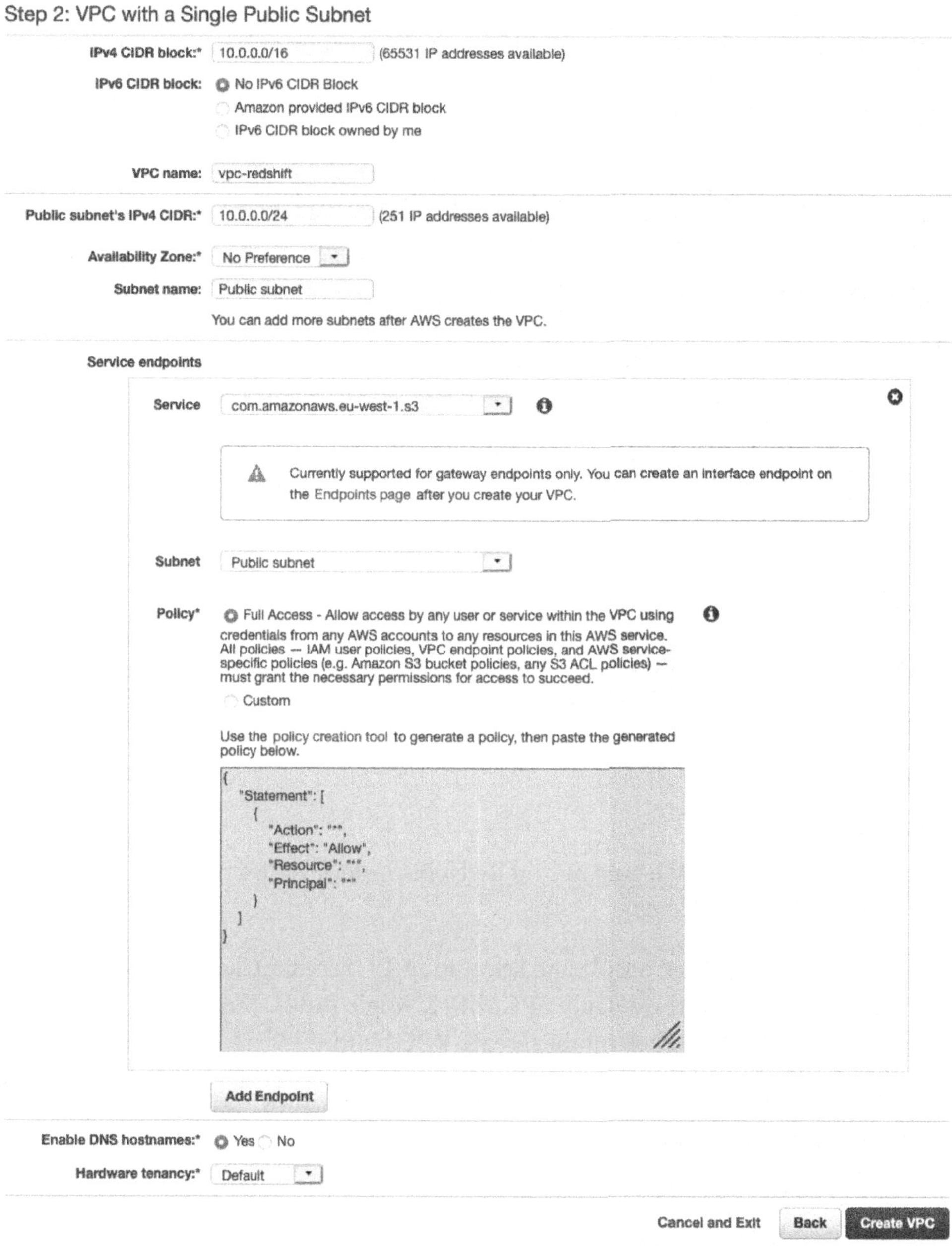

Step 2: VPC with a Single Public Subnet

IPv4 CIDR block:*	10.0.0.0/16	(65531 IP addresses available)
IPv6 CIDR block:	⦿ No IPv6 CIDR Block	
	○ Amazon provided IPv6 CIDR block	
	○ IPv6 CIDR block owned by me	
VPC name:	vpc-redshift	
Public subnet's IPv4 CIDR:*	10.0.0.0/24	(251 IP addresses available)
Availability Zone:*	No Preference ▼	
Subnet name:	Public subnet	

You can add more subnets after AWS creates the VPC.

Service endpoints

Service   com.amazonaws.eu-west-1.s3 ▼   ❶   ⊗

⚠ Currently supported for gateway endpoints only. You can create an interface endpoint on the Endpoints page after you create your VPC.

Subnet   Public subnet ▼

Policy*   ⦿ Full Access - Allow access by any user or service within the VPC using   ❶
credentials from any AWS accounts to any resources in this AWS service. All policies — IAM user policies, VPC endpoint policies, and AWS service-specific policies (e.g. Amazon S3 bucket policies, any S3 ACL policies) — must grant the necessary permissions for access to succeed.

○ Custom

Use the policy creation tool to generate a policy, then paste the generated policy below.

```
{
    "Statement": [
        {
            "Action": "*",
            "Effect": "Allow",
            "Resource": "*",
            "Principal": "*"
        }
    ]
}
```

Add Endpoint

Enable DNS hostnames:*	⦿ Yes ○ No
Hardware tenancy:*	Default ▼

Cancel and Exit   Back   Create VPC

Figure 6.1 – Creating a VPC and subnet for Amazon Redshift

2. Navigate to **Your VPCs** on the left-hand menu and note the **VPC ID** associated with `vpc-redshift`. Click on the **Security Group** in the left-hand menu and click on the security group associated with the VPC ID. Click on the **Edit inbound Rules**, remove the default rules selection, and choose **My IP** as shown in the following screenshot:

VPC > Security Groups > sg-0dee93e3cba936411 - default > Edit inbound rules

Edit inbound rules Info

Inbound rules control the incoming traffic that's allowed to reach the instance.

Inbound rules Info					
Type Info	**Protocol** Info	**Port range** Info	**Source** Info	**Description - optional** Info	
All traffic ▼	All	All	My IP ▼ 🔍		Delete
			54.240.197.226/32 ✕		

Add rule

⚠ NOTE: Any edits made on existing rules will result in the edited rule being deleted and a new rule created with the new details. This will cause traffic that depends on that rule to be dropped for a very brief period of time until the new rule can be created.

Cancel   Preview changes   **Save rules**

Figure 6.2 – Editing the inbound rules for the security group

In the list of **inbound Rules**, instead of an individual IP's address, configuring the CIDR IP's ranges provides flexibility for allowing connections within your organization.

> **Note**
>
> You can learn more about setting up a VPC by using this working with VPC guide: `https://docs.aws.amazon.com/vpc/latest/userguide/working-with-vpcs.html#add-ipv4-cidr`.

3.   Navigate to the Amazon redshift console, click on the **CONFIG** menu and choose **Subnet groups**. Click on **Create subnet group**, choose `vpc-redshift` and **Add all the subnets for this VPC**, provide any friendly description, and click on **Create cluster subnet group** as shown in the following screenshot:

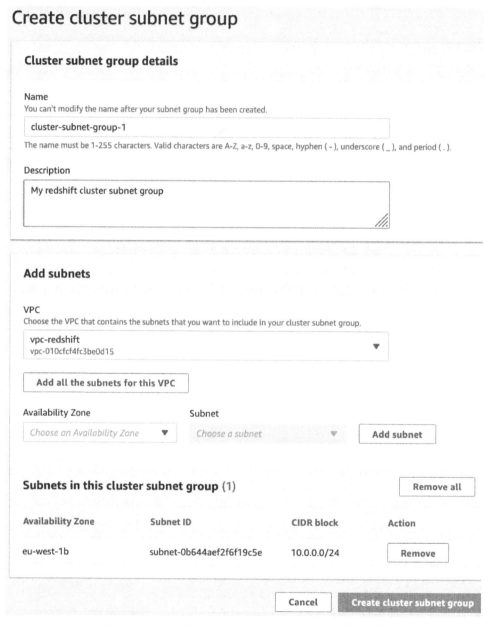

Figure 6.3 – Creating a subnet group for Amazon Redshift

4. Click on the **CLUSTERS** menu and navigate to **Amazon Redshift** > **Clusters** > **Create cluster**. Navigate to the **Additional configurations** section and toggle off the **Use default** option. Choose **vpc-redshift** in the **Virtual private cloud** (**VPC**) dropdown as shown in the following screenshot and click on **Create cluster**:

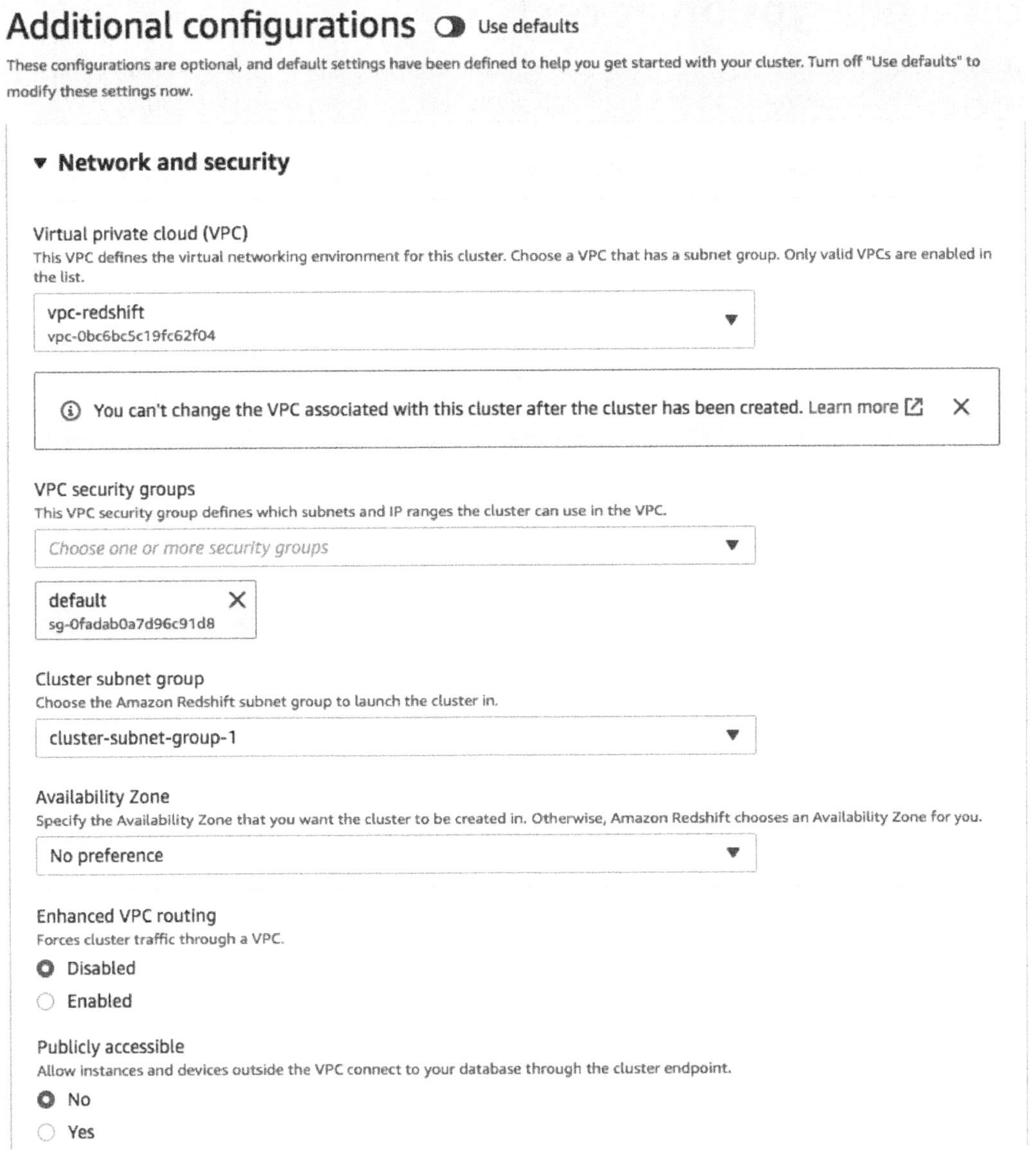

Additional configurations ⬤ Use defaults

These configurations are optional, and default settings have been defined to help you get started with your cluster. Turn off "Use defaults" to modify these settings now.

▼ Network and security

Virtual private cloud (VPC)

This VPC defines the virtual networking environment for this cluster. Choose a VPC that has a subnet group. Only valid VPCs are enabled in the list.

```
vpc-redshift
vpc-0bc6bc5c19fc62f04                                          ▼
```

ⓘ You can't change the VPC associated with this cluster after the cluster has been created. Learn more ⌐↗   ✕

VPC security groups

This VPC security group defines which subnets and IP ranges the cluster can use in the VPC.

```
Choose one or more security groups                             ▼
```

```
default                    ✕
sg-0fadab0a7d96c91d8
```

Cluster subnet group

Choose the Amazon Redshift subnet group to launch the cluster in.

```
cluster-subnet-group-1                                         ▼
```

Availability Zone

Specify the Availability Zone that you want the cluster to be created in. Otherwise, Amazon Redshift chooses an Availability Zone for you.

```
No preference                                                  ▼
```

Enhanced VPC routing

Forces cluster traffic through a VPC.

◉ Disabled
○ Enabled

Publicly accessible

Allow instances and devices outside the VPC connect to your database through the cluster endpoint.

◉ No
○ Yes

Figure 6.4 – Configuring the network and security when creating the Amazon Redshift cluster

5. Connect to the SQL client using the `masteruser` credentials to verify the connection. You can refer to the *Connecting using SQL client* section in *Chapter 1, Getting Started with Amazon Redshift*, for step-by-step instructions.

Data encryption at rest

Amazon Redshift by default provides you with the option to encrypt the cluster at rest, using an AES algorithm with 256-bit key. Key management can be performed by AWS KMS or your hardware security module. When an Amazon Redshift cluster is encrypted at rest, it provides block-level encryption. When the cluster is encrypted, the metadata and snapshots are also encrypted. This enables you to meet your security requirements to comply with PCI, SOX, HIPAA, and GDPR, depending on your needs.

Amazon Redshift uses envelope encryption using a robust four-tier hierarchy of encryption keys: the master key, **cluster encryption key (CEK)**, **database encryption key (DEK)**, and data encryption keys:

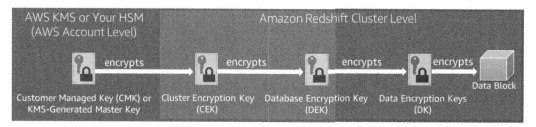

Figure 6.5 – Amazon Redshift envelope encryption

Getting ready

To complete this recipe, you will need the following setup:

- An IAM user with access to Amazon KMS and Amazon Redshift

- Reference to encryption at rest in AWS documentation: `https://docs.aws.amazon.com/redshift/latest/mgmt/working-with-db-encryption.html`

- Reference to AWS CLI for Redshift: `https://docs.aws.amazon.com/cli/latest/reference/redshift/index.html`

- Reference to Amazon Redshift API: `https://docs.aws.amazon.com/redshift/latest/APIReference/Welcome.html`

How to do it

In this recipe, we will see options to encrypt a new and an existing Amazon Redshift cluster.

Let's see the option to turn on encryption while creating an Amazon Redshift cluster:

1. Navigate to the Amazon redshift console and choose **Create cluster**. Scroll to **Additional configurations** and toggle the defaults. This will allow you to expand **Database configurations**. You have two options to choose from: AWS KMS or HSM. When you choose AWS KMS, you have the option to use the default Redshift key or use the key from an existing AWS account or a different AWS account:

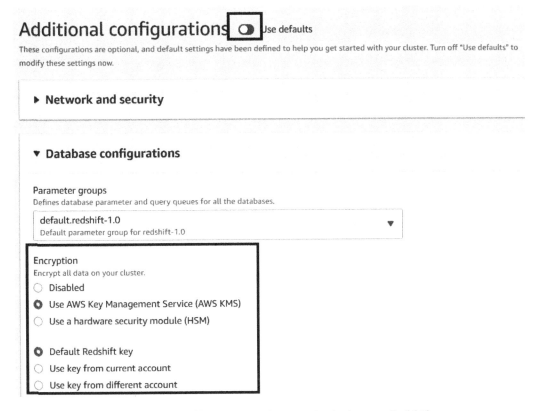

Figure 6.6 – Enabling AWS KMS encryption in Amazon Redshift

2. You can also create a cluster with encryption using the AWS CLI or Amazon Redshift API call.

   Let's see the option to turn on encryption for an existing Amazon Redshift cluster.

3.   Navigate to the Amazon redshift console. Click on the existing cluster. Choose the **Modify** action:

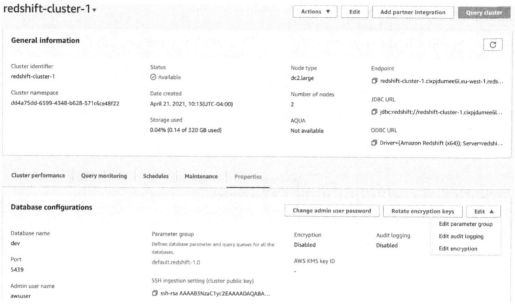

Figure 6.7 – Modifying encryption for an existing Amazon Redshift cluster

4.   Expand **Data configurations**. You can enable encryption using KMS with this one-click option. One-click conversion to HSM is not supported. To convert to HSM, you will need to create a new Amazon Redshift cluster with HSM encryption and unload and load data from the old to the new cluster:

▼ **Database configurations**

Parameter groups
Defines database parameter and query queues for all the databases.

default.redshift-1.0
Default parameter group for redshift-1.0

Encryption
Encrypt all data on your cluster.
○ Disabled
◉ Use AWS Key Management Service (AWS KMS)
○ Use a hardware security module (HSM)

◉ Default Redshift key
○ Use key from current account
○ Use key from different account

Figure 6.8 – Enabling AWS KMS encryption in Amazon Redshift

5.   When you modify a cluster, Amazon Redshift will provision a new cluster in the background and change the main cluster to read-only mode. Amazon Redshift will then do a binary transfer of the data from the main cluster to the newly provisioned cluster. When the transfer of the data is completed, Amazon Redshift will change the existing **Domain Name Service (DNS)** to point to the endpoint of the new cluster. The old cluster is then deleted. The duration of this process is dependent on the amount of data in the main cluster.

6.   The AWS CLI and Amazon Redshift API support conversion to a KMS-encrypted cluster.

Using the Amazon redshift console, navigate to the existing Amazon Redshift cluster. Choose **Actions** and select **Rotate encryption**:

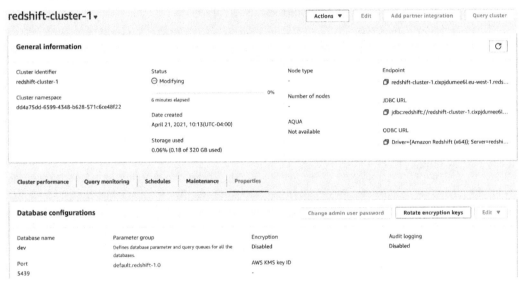

Figure 6.9 – Clusters

7. You will see the following dialog box. Amazon Redshift will rotate the Cluster Encryption Key for the cluster and the snapshot. The **data encryption key (DEK)** for the cluster is changed, but the DEK cannot be changed for the snapshots that are on S3. During key rotation, the cluster is put in ROTATING_KEY state until Amazon Redshift decrypts and re-encrypts the data. You can set the frequency of rotation to meet your organizational needs. You can balance the plan of rotating the keys along with availability considerations for your cluster:

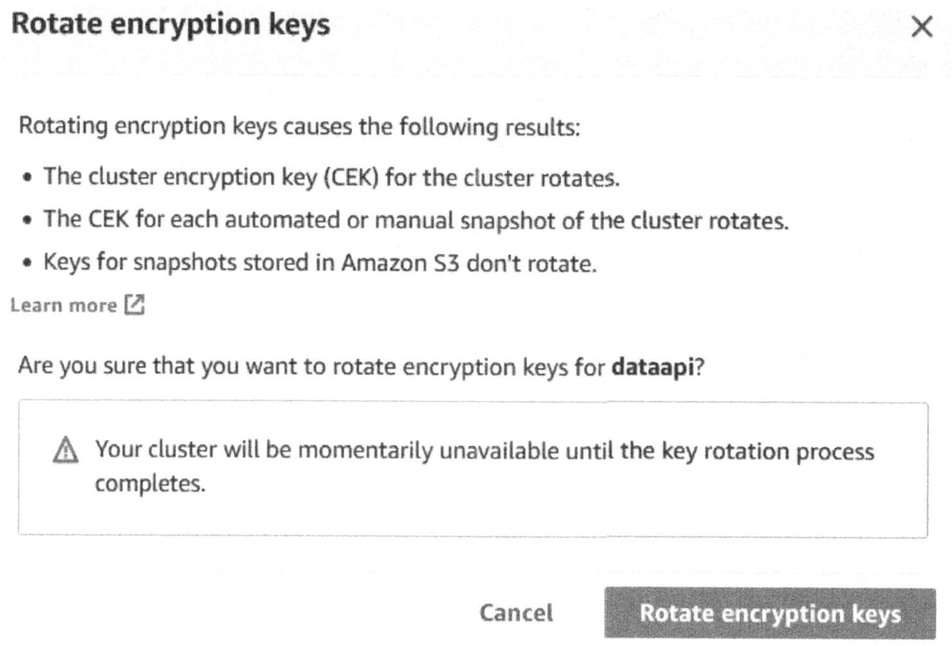

Rotate encryption keys   X

Rotating encryption keys causes the following results:

- The cluster encryption key (CEK) for the cluster rotates.
- The CEK for each automated or manual snapshot of the cluster rotates.
- Keys for snapshots stored in Amazon S3 don't rotate.

Learn more ⎘

Are you sure that you want to rotate encryption keys for **dataapi**?

⚠ Your cluster will be momentarily unavailable until the key rotation process completes.

Cancel   **Rotate encryption keys**

Figure 6.10 – Amazon Redshift rotating the AWS KMS keys

8. You can rotate the encryption keys using the AWS CLI and Amazon Redshift API.

Data encryption in transit

With Amazon Redshift, you can encrypt your data in transit. Enabling the SSL allows SQL clients to encrypt the data in transit using the certificates. In addition, the AWS CLI, SDK, and the API client can communicate using the HTTS endpoints. For communication between AWS services such as Amazon S3, DynamoDB, and so on, Amazon Redshift uses hardware-accelerated SSL.

Getting ready

To complete this recipe, you will need the following:

- An IAM user with access to Amazon Redshift.

- Download the JDBC driver from `https://docs.aws.amazon.com/redshift/latest/mgmt/configure-jdbc-connection.html`.

- SQL client using JDBC or ODBC connection; this recipe uses SQL Workbench/J: `http://www.sql-workbench.net/`.

- Create a new parameter group for your Amazon Redshift cluster: `https://docs.aws.amazon.com/redshift/latest/mgmt/managing-parameter-groups-console.html`.

How to do it

In this recipe, we will enable the SSL connection in Amazon Redshift and the SQL Workbench client to establish an SSL connection:

1. To configure the Amazon Redshift cluster to require an SSL connection, navigate to the Amazon redshift console. Choose your Amazon Redshift cluster and select the **Properties** tab. Scroll to the database configuration and select the parameter group:

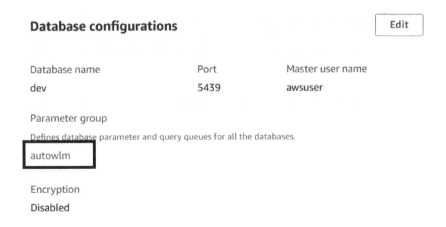

Figure 6.11 – Picking the parameter group associated with your Amazon Redshift cluster

2. Clicking on the parameter group will bring you to the workload management configuration page. Set **require_ssl** to **true**. Choose **Save**. Navigate to the Redshift cluster, when the cluster is in the pending-reboot state, and reboot the cluster by selecting **Reboot under action**:

Figure 6.12 – Enabling the require_sql parameter in the parameter group

3. When **require_ssl** is set to **true**, Amazon Redshift accepts connections that are TLS encrypted. When **sslMode** is set to **verify-ca**, then the server is verified by checking the certificate chain up to the root certificate bundled with the Amazon Redshift JDBC/ODBC driver. When **sslMode** is set to **verify-full**, the server hostname provided in the connection will be compared to the name stored in the server certificate. If the hostname matches, the connection is successful, else it will be rejected.

4. Connect to the Amazon Redshift cluster using your SQL client; this recipe is using SQLWorkbench/J. Get the cluster connection jdbc URL from the cluster's properties tab, connection details. We are using `sslMode=verify-full`:

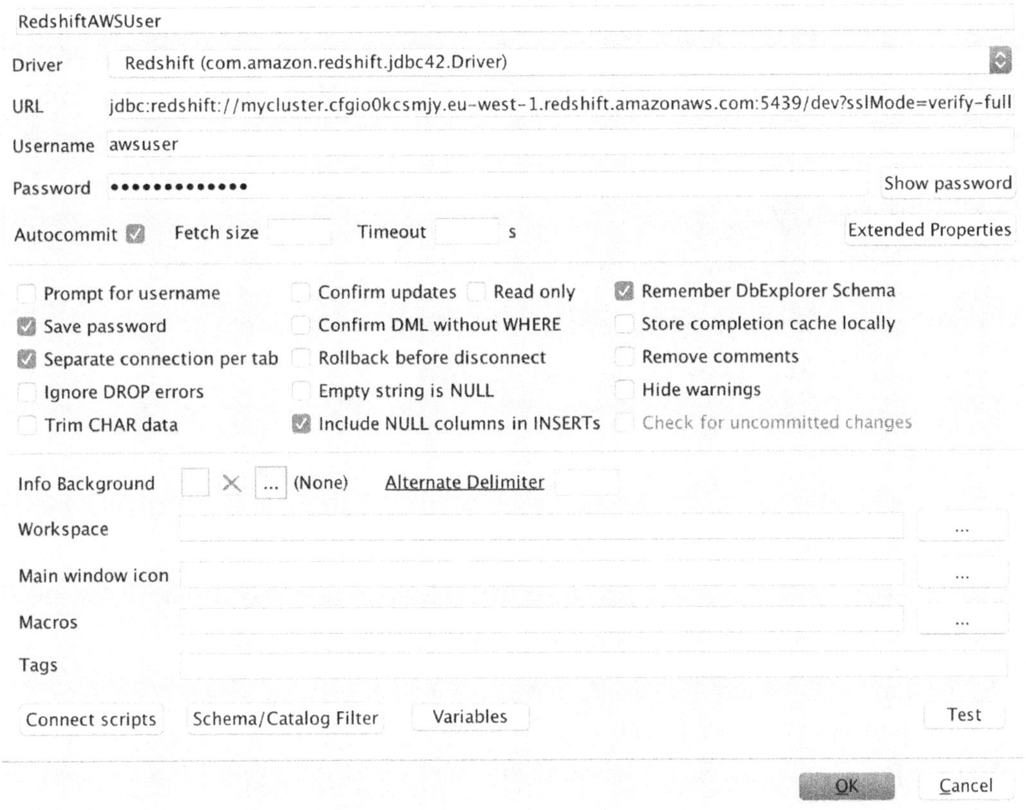

Figure 6.13 – Connecting to Amazon Redshift with SQL Workbench using SSL

5. Let's validate whether the connection is using **sslMode**. Run the following code:

```
select * from stl_connection_log
order by recordtime desc
limit 2;
```

Here is the output of the preceding code:

event	recordtime	remotehost	remoteport	pid	dbname	username	authmethod	duration	sslversion	sslcipher
set application_name ...	2021-06-07 16:06:24.62	::ffff:205.251.233.182 ...	9387 ...	40025	datalake ...	datalake ...	password ...	900836	TLSv1.2 ...	ECDHE-RSA-AES256-GCM-SHA384
initiating session ...	2021-06-07 16:06:00.60	::ffff:205.251.233.182 ...	9387 ...	40025	datalake ...	datalake ...	password ...	0	TLSv1.2 ...	ECDHE-RSA-AES256-GCM-SHA384

Figure 6.14 – Verifying the SSL connection using the STL_CONNECTION_LOG

We have now successfully connected to Amazon Redshift using a TLS-encrypted connection.

Column-level security

Amazon Redshift supports fine-grained data security with column-level controls. Column-level security can be applied to local tables, views, and materialized views. Applying column-level security allows you to restrict access to **personally identifiable information (PII)** or **payment card information (PCI)** to selected people. For instance, you can grant the finance or human resources team access to sensitive information but restrict access to the sales and marketing team.

Getting ready

To complete this recipe, you will need the following:

- An Amazon Redshift cluster deployed in AWS Region eu-west-1
- Amazon Redshift cluster masteruser credentials
- Access to any SQL interface such as a SQL client or the Amazon Redshift Query Editor

How to do it

In this recipe, we will use a customer table. Using column-level access control, a sales user will be restricted from accessing the phone number column:

1. Connect to the Amazon Redshift cluster using the SQL client or Query Editor. Create a customer table using the following code:

```
CREATE TABLE public.customer
(
    C_CUSTKEY       BIGINT NOT NULL,
    C_NAME          VARCHAR(25),
    C_NATIONKEY     BIGINT,
    C_PHONE         VARCHAR(15),
    C_ACCTBAL       DECIMAL(18,4),
    C_MKTSEGMENT    VARCHAR(10),
    C_COMMENT       VARCHAR(117)
);
```

2. Insert the following records into the customer table:

```
Insert into public.customer values
(1, 'customer-0001', 1, '123-123-1234', 111.11,
```

```
'MACHINERY', 'FIRST ORDER'),
(2, 'customer-0002', 2, '122-122-1234', 222.11,
'HOUSEHOLD', 'SECOND ORDER');
```

3. Let's create the sales user:

```
CREATE user sales with password 'Sales1234';
```

4. Grant access to the `sales` users on all the columns in the `customer` table except the C_PHONE column:

```
GRANT SELECT (C_CUSTKEY, C_NAME, C_NATIONKEY, C_ACCTBAL,
C_MKTSEGMENT, C_COMMENT) ON public.customer TO sales;
```

5. Let's verify the column-level access for sales users. Run the following code. You will receive the error message permission denied, as sales users do not have access to the C_PHONE column:

```
SET SESSION AUTHORIZATION 'sales';
SELECT CURRENT_USER;
SELECT * FROM public.customer;
--output
ERROR: 42501: permission denied for relation customer
```

6. Let's select the columns in the `SELECT` statement the `sales` users have access to:

```
SET SESSION AUTHORIZATION 'sales';
SELECT CURRENT_USER;
SELECT C_CUSTKEY, C_NAME, C_NATIONKEY, C_ACCTBAL, C_
MKTSEGMENT, C_COMMENT FROM public.customer;
```

Here is the output of the preceding code:

c_custkey	c_name	c_nationkey	c_acctbal	c_mktsegment	c_comment
1	customer-0001	1	111.11	MACHINERY	FIRST ORDER
2	customer-0002	2	222.11	HOUSEHOLD	SECOND ORDER

Figure 6.15 – Verifying the successful selection of the PII columns

How it works

Using the GRANT and REVOKE statements, you can enable or disable column-level access control to Amazon Redshift users or groups on tables, views, or materialized views. You can learn about the GRANT and REVOKE syntax for fine-grained access control at https://docs.aws.amazon.com/redshift/latest/dg/r_GRANT.html and https://docs.aws.amazon.com/redshift/latest/dg/r_REVOKE.html.

Loading and unloading encrypted data

Amazon S3 allows to have your data (for example, your source data files) to be encrypted using **server-side encryption with Amazon S3-managed keys (SSE-S3)** or **AWS KMS-managed keys (SSE-KMS)**. In addition, you can perform client-side encryption using a client-side symmetric master key. Amazon Redshift supports loading the encrypted data into the local table. Similarly, you can unload Amazon Redshift data to Amazon S3 as encrypted files using a customer-managed symmetric master key.

Getting ready

To complete this recipe, you will need the following setup:

- An IAM user with access to Amazon Redshift and AWS KMS.

- An Amazon Redshift cluster deployed in AWS Region eu-west-1.

- Amazon Redshift cluster masteruser credentials.

- Access to any SQL interface such as a SQL client or the Amazon Redshift Query Editor.

- An IAM role attached to the Amazon Redshift cluster that can access Amazon S3; we will reference it in the recipes as [Your-Redshift_Role].

- The AWS CLI configured on local client.

- An AWS account number; we will reference it in recipes as [Your-AWS_Account_Id].

- An Amazon S3 bucket created in eu-west-1; we will reference it as [Your-Amazon_S3_Bucket].

- Copy the customer table data to your Amazon S3 bucket using the following command, replacing [Your-Amazon_S3_Bucket] with your bucket name:

```
aws s3 cp s3://packt-redshift-cookbook/customer/ s3://
[Your-Amazon_S3_Bucket]/Chapter6/customer/
```

How to do it

In this recipe, we will COPY encrypted data from Amazon S3 and also load as encrypted files:

1. Let's start by creating a master encryption key using AWS KMS that will be used to encrypt and decrypt the data by Amazon S3. Navigate to AWS KMS from the AWS Console and select **Configure key** as shown:

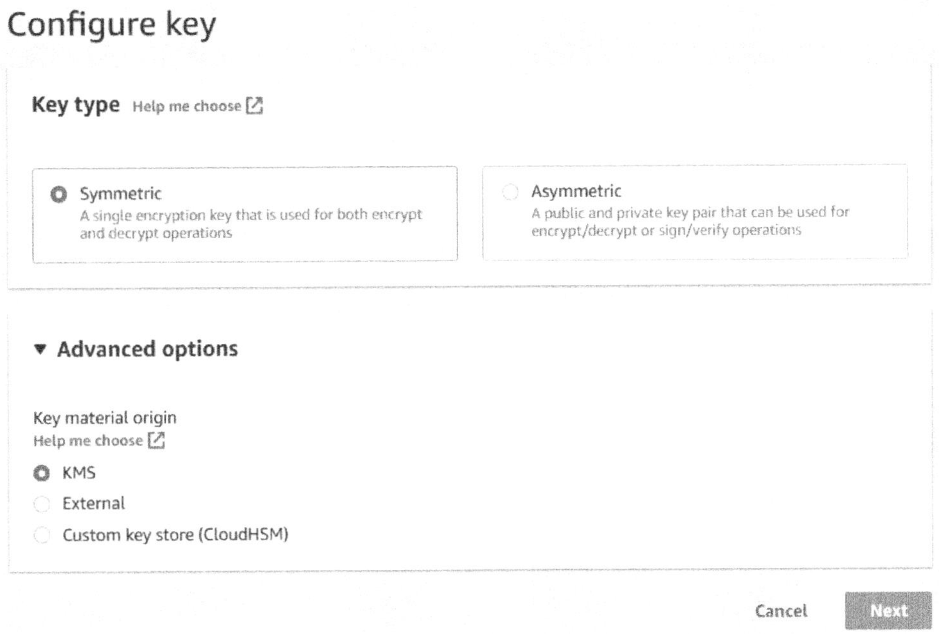

Configure key

Key type Help me choose ☐

○ **Symmetric**
A single encryption key that is used for both encrypt and decrypt operations

○ **Asymmetric**
A public and private key pair that can be used for encrypt/decrypt or sign/verify operations

▼ **Advanced options**

Key material origin
Help me choose ☐

● KMS
○ External
○ Custom key store (CloudHSM)

Cancel   Next

Figure 6.16 – Creating an AWS KMS symmetric key

> **Note**
> AWS KMS allows you to manage the encryption key. You can create, store, rotate, and control access to them.

2. Enter the name of the alias as `cookbook-kms`:

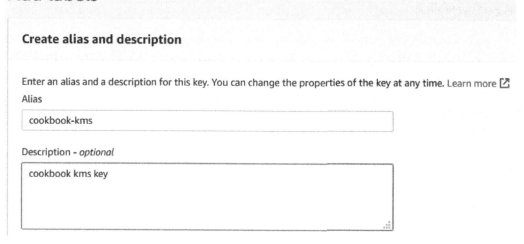

Figure 6.17 – Creating an alias for the AWS KMS encryption key

3. Select the user and the Redshift customizable role that will have access to the key. Review the policy and click **Finish**.

4. Make a note of the **ARN** of the KMS key and **Key ID**:

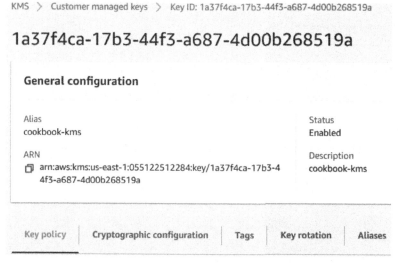

Figure 6.18 – Capturing the ARN for the AWS KMS key

5. Navigate to Amazon S3 path `s3://[Your_AmazonS3_Bucket]/Chapter6/customer/` and click on the **Edit server-side encryption** action:

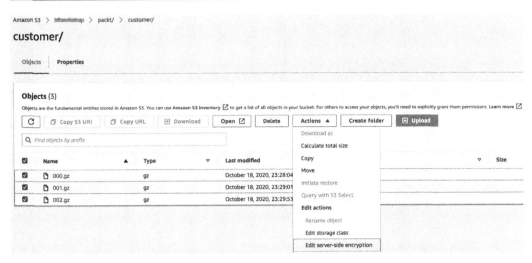

Figure 6.19 – Verifying the server-side encryption

6. Click **Enable** server-side encryption. For **Encryption key type**, select **SSE-KMS**. Select the ARN of the cookbook-kms key. Choose **Save changes**. This will encrypt the customer files on S3:

Server-side encryption settings

Server-side encryption protects data at rest. **Learn more** ☑

Server-side encryption

○ Disable

◉ Enable

Encryption key type
To upload an object with a customer-provided encryption key (SSE-C), use the AWS CLI, AWS SDK, or Amazon S3 REST API.

○ Amazon S3 key (SSE-S3)
An encryption key that Amazon S3 creates, manages, and uses for you. Learn more ☑

◉ AWS Key Management Service key (SSE-KMS)
An encryption key protected by AWS Key Management Service (AWS KMS). Learn more ☑

AWS KMS key

○ AWS managed key (aws/s3)
arn:aws:kms:us-east-1:055122512284:alias/aws/s3

◉ Choose from your KMS master keys

○ Enter KMS master key ARN

KMS master key

arn:aws:kms▮▮▮▮▮▮▮▮▮▮▮▮▮▮key/1a37f... ▼   C   Create key ☑

Figrue 6.20 – Encrypting the customer data using a KMS key

7. Now let's connect to the Amazon Redshift cluster using a SQL client or the Query Editor and create the `customer` table:

```
CREATE TABLE public.customer
(
    C_CUSTKEY        BIGINT NOT NULL,
    C_NAME           VARCHAR(25),
    C_ADDRESS        VARCHAR(40),
    C_NATIONKEY      BIGINT,
    C_PHONE          VARCHAR(15),
    C_ACCTBAL        DECIMAL(18,4),
    C_MKTSEGMENT     VARCHAR(10),
    C_COMMENT        VARCHAR(117)
)
diststyle ALL;
```

8. Let's now load the encrypted customer data using the COPY command using the following command:

```
COPY customer from 's3:// s3://[Your-Amazon_S3_Bucket]/
Chapter6/customer/' iam_role 'arn:aws:iam::[Your-
AWS_Account_Id]:role/[Your-Redshift_Role]'  CSV gzip
COMPUPDATE PRESET;
```

> **Note**
>
> Observe in the COPY command that Amazon Redshift is automatically able to identify that the file is encrypted and communicates with KMS automatically to retrieve the correct master key. This KMS key is used to decrypt the data key and is used by the COPY command for loading.

9. Now let's unload the encrypted data to Amazon S3 using a user-provided master key. Execute the following command to unload the data:

```
unload ('select * from customer') TO 's3:// [Your-
Amazon_S3_Bucket]/Chapter6/customer_encrypted/' iam_role
'arn:aws:iam::[Your-AWS_Account_Id]:role/[Your-Redshift_Role]'
master_symmetric_key 'EXAMPLEMASTERKEYtkbjk/OpCwtYSx/M4/
t7DMCDIK722' encrypted;
```

> **Note**
> Similar to the UNLOAD command, you can also copy the data that was encrypted using a master key. Please see `https://docs.aws.amazon.com/redshift/latest/dg/c_loading-encrypted-files.html`.

The preceding command unloads the `customer` table to a set of encrypted files using the specified master symmetric key.

Managing superusers

A superuser allows you to get all the access on Amazon Redshift, independent of all permission checks, and is used for administrative tasks. For example, you can create other users, execute diagnostic queries on system tables, and take action as needed. Superuser access has to be granted sparingly; do not use this for day-to-day work.

The `masteruser` is a special type of superuser that you set up when launching the cluster.

Getting ready

To complete this recipe, you will need the following setup:

- An IAM user with access to Amazon Redshift
- An Amazon Redshift cluster deployed in AWS Region `eu-west-1`
- Amazon Redshift cluster masteruser credentials
- Access to any SQL interface such as a SQL client or the Amazon Redshift Query Editor

How to do it

In this recipe, we will illustrate how to create a superuser and use it to list all the active SQL statements, and demonstrate how to terminate a particular statement:

1. Connect to Amazon Redshift using the SQL client using the masteruser credentials and execute the following statement to create another superuser, replacing `[masteruser_password]` with the password of your choice:

```
create user myadmin createuser password '[masteruser_
password]';
```

If you have forgotten the `masteruser` credentials, you can navigate to the Amazon Redshift AWS Console and click on your `cluster-id` (**Amazon Redshift** → **Clusters** → **YOUR_CLUSTER**) and click on the **Actions** dropdown and click on **Change masteruser password** to reset it to a new value.

2. Now, use the preceding superuser `myadmin` to reconnect to Amazon Redshift using the SQL Workbench/J client. Execute the following statement to see the list of all the `Running` SQL statements:

```
SELECT pid,
       TRIM(user_name),
       starttime,
       duration,
       SUBSTRING(query,1,50) AS stmt
FROM stv_recents
WHERE status = 'Running';
```

Here is the expected sample output:

```
Pid     btrim      starttime    duration       stmt
18764   user_a     2021-03-28 18:39:49.355918   3000 select
part_id, seller_id
18790    user_b    2021-03-28 18:39:49.355918   60      Insert
into parts(
```

The query from `user_a` is taking up over 3,000 seconds to execute and is likely to consume resources (that can be confirmed using the AWS Console), so we assume you would like to terminate this query.

3. Execute the following statement to terminate the query with `pid = 18764`:

```
set query_group to 'superuser';
cancel 18764;
```

Using the optional `query_group` to `'superuser'` allows access to the special superuser queue and has the query execute immediately. Please also refer to `https://docs.aws.amazon.com/redshift/latest/dg/cm-c-wlm-queue-assignment-rules.html`.

Managing users and groups

Users and groups are the building blocks for access management of the objects in the Amazon Redshift cluster. Users get authenticated into the Amazon Redshift cluster and privileges for objects can be managed at the group level for managing access in a scalable manner. Users can be members of one of multiple groups and inherit the access privileges granted to the groups. Users can also be individually granted privileges.

Getting ready

To complete this recipe, you will need the following setup:

- An IAM user with access to Amazon Redshift
- An Amazon Redshift cluster deployed in AWS Region eu-west-1
- Amazon Redshift cluster masteruser credentials
- Access to any SQL interface such as a SQL client or the Amazon Redshift Query Editor

How to do it

In this recipe, we will illustrate how to create users and groups for the schema set up in *Chapter 2, Data Management*. There are two groups – finance_grp and audit_grp – that will be created and users will be added to those groups:

1. Connect to Amazon Redshift using the SQL client using the masteruser or the superuser credentials and execute the following statement to create the following users, replacing [financeuser_password] and [audituser_password] with the passwords of your choice:

    ```
    create user financeuser1 with password '[financeuser_
    password]' createdb connection limit 30;
    create user audituser1 with password '[audituser_
    password]'syslog unrestricted;
    ```

    The audituser1 user is provided syslog unrestricted access that allows visibility to system tables to list queries and transactions performed by other users, which is restricted by default.

2. Create the finance schema and finance and audit groups so that object privileges can be managed separately:

```
create schema if not exists finance;
create group finance_grp with user financeuser1;
create group audit_grp with user audituser1;
```

3. Grant access to objects in the finance schema to the preceding groups:

```
GRANT USAGE on SCHEMA finance TO GROUP finance_grp, GROUP
audit_grp;
GRANT ALL ON schema finance to GROUP finance_grp;
ALTER DEFAULT PRIVILEGES IN SCHEMA finance GRANT ALL
   ON tables
   TO group finance_grp;
GRANT SELECT ON ALL TABLES IN SCHEMA finance TO GROUP
audit_grp;
ALTER DEFAULT PRIVILEGES IN SCHEMA finance GRANT SELECT
   ON tables
   TO group audit_grp;
```

4. Execute the following statement to verify the user membership to the groups:

```
SELECT
pg_group.groname
g,pg_group.grosysid
,pg_user.*
FROM pg_group, pg_user
WHERE pg_user.usesysid = ANY(pg_group.grolist)
ORDER BY 1,2
;
```

Here is the expected sample output:

```
groname,grosysid,usename,usesysid,usecreatedb,
usesuper,usecatupd,passwd,valuntil,useconfig
finance_grp  106    financeuser1   127   false   *******
audit_grp    107
audituser1127   false    ********
```

Hence, in the preceding setup, the users in `finance_grp` are able to perform all the DDL/DML (`SELECT`/`INSERT`/`UPDATE`/`DELETE`) operations, the `audit_grp` users are able to perform only the `SELECT` operations to isolate the access control managed through the individual groups. You can learn more about the `GRANT` access options at `https://docs.aws.amazon.com/redshift/latest/dg/r_GRANT.html`.

Managing federated authentication

Amazon Redshift allows easy integration of multiple **Identity Providers (IdPs)** such as Microsoft Azure Active Directory, **Active Directory Federation Services (ADFS)**, Okta, Ping Identity, AWS SSO, and any SAML v2. You can manage the authentication and authorization of the users and objects using the IdPs without the need to maintain local database users. This provides seamless extension of your corporate policies to Amazon Redshift and a convenient way to govern them centrally. For example, users just use their corporate credentials to get into Amazon Redshift. In addition, Amazon Redshift also supports multi-factor authentication using the federation to provide additional security when authenticating.

Getting ready

To complete this recipe, you will need the following setup:

- An IAM user with access to Amazon Redshift and AWS IAM
- An Amazon Redshift cluster deployed in AWS Region `eu-west-1`
- Amazon Redshift cluster masteruser credentials
- Access to any SQL interface such as a SQL client or the Amazon Redshift Query Editor
- The latest JDBC driver AWS SDK that can be downloaded from `https://docs.aws.amazon.com/redshift/latest/mgmt/configure-jdbc-connection.html#jdbc-previous-versions-with-sdk`
- Your AWS account number; we will reference it in recipes as [Your-AWS_Account_Id]

How to do it

In this recipe, we will integrate the Okta idP with Amazon Redshift:

1. Navigate to the Okta portal at `https://www.okta.com/free-trial/` and create a 30-day free trial, by specifying a domain name of your choice. Let's call this [your-okta-domain].

2. Create the following sample user and group by navigating to the **Directory** tab at `https://mailpackt-cookbook-admin.okta.com/admin/users` as follows:

- **User**: `bob west` (bob@mail.com)

- **Group**: `dwgroup`

    Add user `bob west` to the group `dwgroup`:

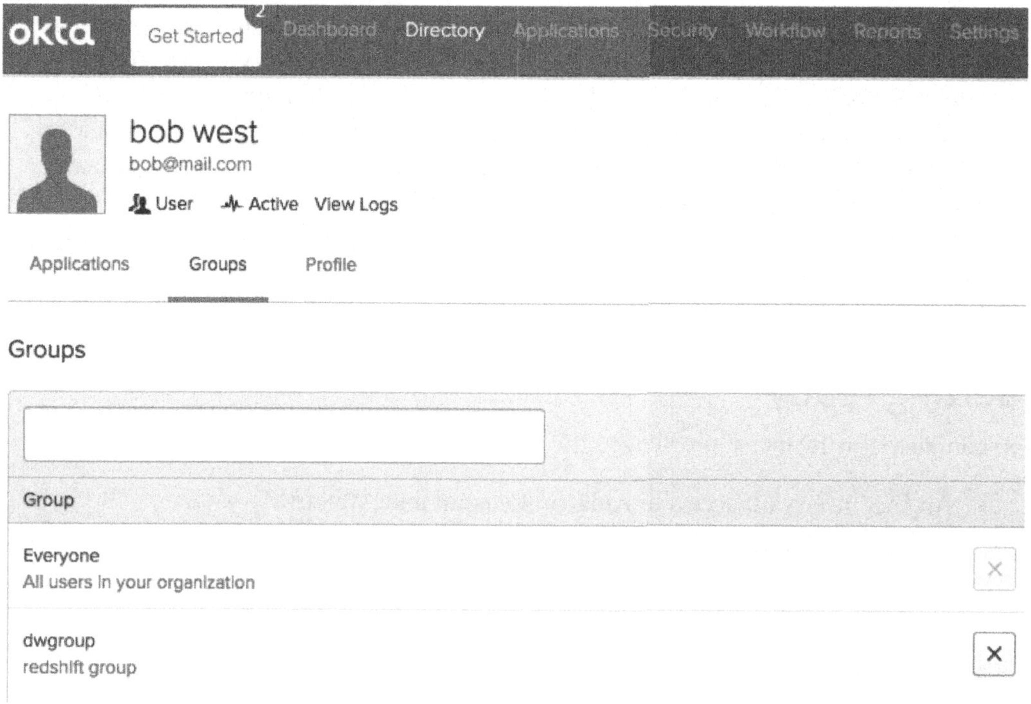

Figure 6.21 – Creating users and groups in Okta

3. Log in to Okta using the user `bob west`, reset the one-time password and note down the new password.

4. Navigate to the **Applications** tab, click on **Add application** and select **Amazon Web Services Redshift** as shown in the following screenshot:

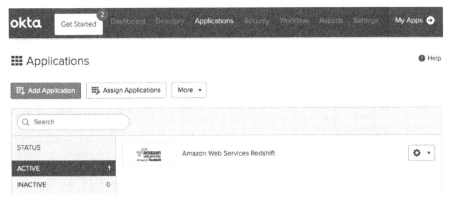

Figure 6.22 – Adding an Amazon Redshift application

5. Click on **Amazon Web Services Redshift** in **Applications** and navigate to the
    Sign on tab. Right-click on **IdP metadata** and save the file as `metadata.xml`.

6. Navigate to the AWS Management Console, navigate to the **AWS Identity and
    Access Management (IAM)** Console, and click on **idPs**.

7. Click on **Add provider** and type the provider's name as `okta` (or any meaningful
    name) and in the metadata document select the saved file `metadata.xml` as
    shown in the following screenshot:

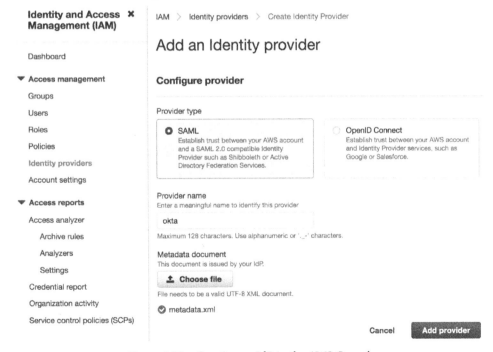

Figure 6.23 – Creating an IdP in the AWS Console

8. Navigate to the IAM Console, click on **Roles**, and choose a new **SAML 2.0 federation** role. Choose the **okta** IdP that you created in the previous step, select **Allow programmatic and AWS Management Console access** and click **Next: Permissions** as shown in the following screenshot:

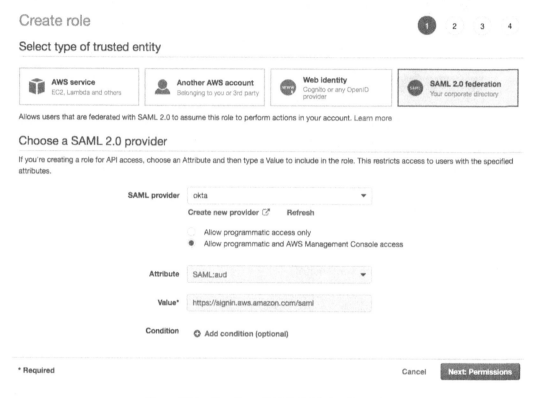

Figure 6.24 – Creating a SAML 2.0 federation role

9. Locate the **IdP** you just created by the **Provider Name** in the list of **IdPs**. Click on the name and make a copy of the **Provider ARN** value. This will be in the form `arn:aws:iam:[Your-AWS_Account_Id]:saml-provider/okta`.

10. Click on **Create policy**, create a policy with the name `redshiftaccess` (or any meaningful name), and copy and paste the following policy statement in the JSON table to allow access to the **Amazon Redshift cluster** replacing the [`Your-AWS_Region`] and [`Your-AWS_Account_Id`] with the values corresponding to your AWS account:

```
{
    "Version": "2012-10-17",
    "Statement": [{
```

```
        "Effect": "Allow",
            "Action": [
                "redshift:CreateClusterUser",
                "redshift:JoinGroup",
                "redshift:GetClusterCredentials",
                "redshift:DescribeClusters"
    ],
            "Resource": [
    "arn:aws:redshift:[Your-AWS_Region]:[Your-AWS_Account_
    Id]:cluster:*",

    "arn:aws:redshift:[Your-AWS_Region]:[Your-AWS_Account_
    Id]:dbuser:[cluster]/*",

    "arn:aws:redshift: [Your-AWS_Region]:[Your-AWS_Account_
    Id]:dbgroup:[cluster]/*"
    }]
    }
```

> **Note**
>
> In the preceding policy statement, the permissions allow connection to any Amazon Redshift cluster, dbuser, and dbgroups. Ideally, you can create different IAM policies to make them restrictive to the specific cluster/groups and users that you want to allow access to.

11. Once the **Role** is created, note down the **Role ARN** that will be in the form arn:aws:iam:[YOUR-AWS_ACCOUNT_Id]:role/redshiftacess.

12. Navigate back to Okta using the admin user and click on **Applications** -> **Amazon Webservices Redshift** → **Sign on** and then click **Edit**.

13. Paste the **Provider ARN** and **Role ARN** that you made a copy of earlier in this configuration, as comma-separated values, into corresponding fields as arn:aws:iam:[Your-AWS_Account_Id]:saml-provider/okta,arn:aws:iam:[Your-AWS_Account_Id]:role/redshiftacess.

14. **Session Duration**: Set the desired session duration for users in seconds, such as 3600.

15. In **Provide Redshift** related configuration, do the following:

- **DB User Format**: `${user.username}` (this is the default value).

- **Auto Create**: **AutoCreate Redshift property** (create a new database user if one does not exist) checked.

- **Allowed DB Groups**: This configuration determines which Okta groups (names) should be provided access to Redshift, for example `db_sales_grp`.

    Click **Save/Next**.

16. Now navigate to the SQL **Workbench/J** tool and choose the Amazon Redshift driver with AWS SDK. Use the following JDBC URL to connect to Amazon Redshift, by replacing the corresponding attributes that were set up in the Okta IDP:

```
jdbc:redshift:iam://[your-redshift-cluster-
connection-string]?plugin_name=com.amazon.redshift.
plugin.OktaCredentialsProvider&idp_host=[okta-
hostname]&preferred_role=[role-arn]&user=[okta-
user]&password=[okta-user-password]&app_id=[okta-
redhshift-app-id]
```

For [okta-redhshift-app-id] and [okta-hostname], refer to the URL for the application in your web browser:

```
https://[okta-hostname]-admin.okta.com/admin/app/amazon_
aws_redshift/instance/[okta-redhshift-app-id]
```

17. Click the **Test** button to verify whether Amazon Redshift is able to federate through the Okta IdP.

How it works

The following diagram shows how Amazon Redshift is able to authenticate the user through the IdP:

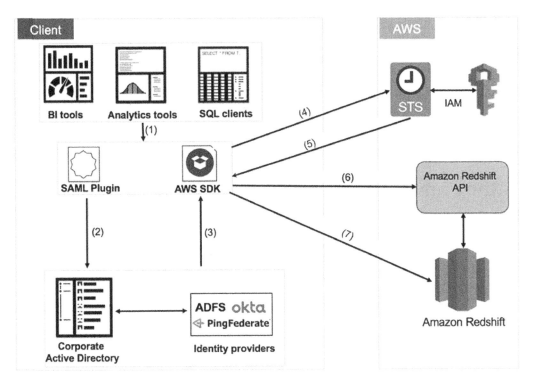

Figure 6.25 – Overall architecture for the integrated IdP

Here is the workflow for the federation with the IdP once integrated with Amazon Redshift:

1. Set up the JDBC/ODBC.

2. Authenticate using a corporate username/password.

3. The % IdP sends SAML assertion.

4. Call STS to assume role with SAML.

5. STS returns temporary credentials.

6. Use the temporary credentials to get the temporary cluster credentials.

7. Connect to Amazon Redshift using the temporary credentials.

Using IAM authentication to generate database user credentials

Amazon Redshift allows you to programmatically generate temporary database user credentials that can be used for automated scripts connect to the cluster. Using the `get-cluster-credentials` command in the **AWS Command Line Interface (AWS CLI)** and the `GetClusterCredentials` in the API, you can generate the temporary credentials that can then be used in the JDBC and ODBC options.

Getting ready

To complete this recipe, you will need the following setup:

- An IAM user with access to Amazon Redshift and AWS IAM

- An Amazon Redshift cluster deployed in AWS Region `eu-west-1`; we will reference the cluster ID as [Your-Redshift_Cluster]

- Amazon Redshift cluster masteruser credentials

- Access to any SQL interface such as a SQL client or the Amazon Redshift Query Editor

- The AWS CLI configured on your local client

How to do it

In this recipe, we will generate temporary credentials to connect to the Amazon Redshift cluster:

1. Open the command-line interface where the AWS CLI is installed. Type the following command to verify the AWS CLI installation; that should show the help manual:

   ```
   aws help
   ```

2. Execute the following command that will generate the temporary credentials for your Amazon Redshift cluster, replacing [Your-Redshift_Cluster] and [Your-Redshift_DB] with the respective values:

   ```
   aws redshift get-cluster-credentials --cluster-identifier
   [Your-Redshift_Cluster] --db-user temp_creds_user --db-
   name [Your-Redshift_DB] --duration-seconds 3600
   ```

The result of the preceding command will produce an output like the following:

```
{
    "DbUser": "IAM:temp_creds_user",
    "Expiration": "2020-12-08T21:12:53Z",
    "DbPassword":
"EXAMPLEjArE3hcnQj8zt4XQj9Xtma8oxYEM8OyxpDHwXVPyJYBDm/
gqX2Eeaq6P3DgTzgPg=="
}
```

3. Connect to the SQL client with the username and password credentials, using the preceding values to verify the connection.

> **Note**
> The credentials generated using the preceding command are temporary and will expire in 3,600 seconds.

Managing audit logs

Amazon Redshift allows you to log connection and user activities by using the audit logs. Audit logs are published into Amazon S3 asynchronously and provide a mechanism to allow you to monitor the requests to the cluster, which can be used to implement security requirements as well as for troubleshooting. For example, let's say on a particular day in the past, you want to find the user who might have truncated a particular table. The audit logs can query to uncover this information.

Getting ready

To complete this recipe, you will need the following setup:

- The IAM user with access to Amazon Redshift and AWS Glue
- An Amazon Redshift cluster deployed in AWS Region eu-west-1; we will reference the cluster ID as [Your-Redshift_Cluster]
- Amazon Redshift cluster masteruser credentials
- Access to any SQL interface such as a SQL client or the Amazon Redshift Query Editor
- An IAM role that can access Amazon S3; we will reference it in the recipes as [Your-Redshift_Role]
- Your AWS account number; we will reference it in recipes as [Your-AWS_Account_Id]

How to do it

In this recipe, we will illustrate how to turn on the audit logging in Amazon S3 (which is turned off by default) and easily query it:

1. Connect to the Amazon redshift console and navigate to **Amazon Redshift > Clusters > [YOUR_CLUSTER]**. Click on the **Maintenance and monitoring** tab and scroll down to the **Audit logging** option as shown in the following screenshot:

Audit logging   Edit

Audit logging logs information about connections and user activities in your database to monitor for security and troubleshooting purposes. The logs are stored in Amazon S3 buckets for convenient access.

Audit logging	S3 bucket	S3 key prefix	
Enabled			View logs in S3

Last log **2 hours ago** at 04:04 pm (UTC -06:00)   Log delivery to S3 was successful.

Figure 6.26 – Enabling Amazon Redshift audit logging

2. Click on the **Edit** button in **Audit logging** and set **Enable audit logging** to **Yes** and select (or create) an Amazon S3 bucket as shown in the following screenshot:

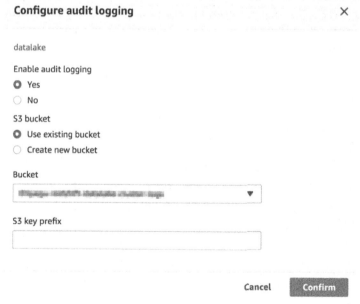

Figure 6.27 – Configuring the target S3 buckets for logging

The previous option turns on the connection logging that will start capturing the connection information such as client host IP, username, and so on, as detailed in `https://docs.aws.amazon.com/redshift/latest/mgmt/db-auditing.html#db-auditing-logs`. Logs will be delivered asynchronously, organized into hourly S3 prefix locations.

3. Once the user connections are made in the Amazon Redshift cluster, connection logs are delivered into previously specified target Amazon S3 location that can be verified used the AWS Console for Amazon S3 or the AWS CLI using the `aws s3 ls [AWS S3 Target bucket]` command.

    The log files are organized as `<AWS Account #>/redshift/<Region>/<Year>/<Month>/<Day>/<Hour>`.

4. Create a new crawler called `audit_crawl` with the database name `audit_logs_db` and the table name `auditawslogs` using the Amazon S3 location configured in the preceding step and choosing **Add crawler** under **Tutorials**. See *Chapter 9, Lake House Architecture,* for step-by-step instructions to configure the AWS Glue crawler.

5. Run `audit_crawl` and after the crawler has run, you should have a new table, `auditawslogs`, under **Data catalog** > **Databases** > **Tables** as shown in the following screenshot:

Figure 6.28 – AWS Glue

6. Connect to the SQL client using the superuser credentials and the `create audit_logs` schema pointing to the AWS Glue `audit_logs_db` database created previously:

```
create external schema audit_logs
from data catalog
database 'audit_logs_db'
iam_role 'arn:aws:iam::[Your-AWS_Account_Id]:role/[Your-Redshift_Role]'
create external database if not exists;
```

7. Use the following query to retrieve the audit information:

```
SELECT col0 AS event,
       col1 AS recordtime,
       col2 AS remotehost,
       col3 AS remoteport,
       col4 AS pid,
       col5 AS dbname,
       col6 AS username,
       col7 AS authmethod,
       col8 AS duration,
       col9 AS sslversion,
       col10 AS sslcipher,
       col11 AS mtu,
       col12 AS sslcompression,
       col13 AS sslexpansion,
       col14 AS iamauthguid,
       col15 AS application_name,
       col16 AS driver_version,
       col17 AS os_version,
       col18 AS plugin_name
FROM audit_logs.auditawslogs
WHERE partition_5 = 25
AND    partition_4 = 12
AND    partition_3 = 2020 LIMIT 10;
```

Here is the output of the preceding code:

```
event,recordtime,remotehost,remoteport,pid,dbname,
username,authmethod,duration,sslversion,sslcipher,
mtu,sslcompression,sslexpansion,iamauthguid,
application_name,driver_version,os_version,plugin_name

authenticated   Fri, 25 Dec 2020 09:02:04:228
[local]     49050 dev    rdsdb    Ident    0  0

initiating session Fri, 25 Dec 2020 09:02:04:228[local]
49050   dev    rdsdb Ident      0 0

disconnecting session   Fri, 25 Dec 2020 09:02:04:346
[local]   49050   dev   rdsdb    Ident       118856    0

authenticated Fri, 25 Dec 2020 09:02:40:156    [local]
49238 dev    rdsdb    Ident 0  0
```

As observed in the preceding output, all the session activity is logged as part of the audit trail and can be easily queried using a SQL query.

How it works

Audit logs are also available in system log tables, STL_USERLOG and STL_CONNECTION_LOG, but retention is limited in the system tables.

For longer retention and convenient sharing of the audit information, Amazon Redshift logs can be enabled that asynchronously send the logs into Amazon S3. The user activity log can be enabled by setting the enable_user_activity_logging parameter to **true** in the database parameter group in addition to the connection logs.

Monitoring Amazon Redshift

Monitoring the cluster performance metrics allows you to ensure the cluster is operating healthily. Amazon Redshift publishes metrics such as CPU, disk utilization, query workloads, and so on continuously. These metrics can be automatically monitored for anomalies to trigger notification events. Amazon Redshift publishes the cluster performance metrics to AWS CloudWatch as well, which allows you to monitor all your AWS services in a centralized location.

Getting ready

To complete this recipe, you will need the following setup:

- An IAM user with access to Amazon Redshift and Amazon SNS.

- An Amazon Redshift cluster deployed in AWS Region `eu-west-1`.

- Create an Amazon SNS topic (called `AmazonRedshiftHealthNotification`) to receive the alarm notifications using `https://docs.aws.amazon.com/sns/latest/dg/sns-create-topic.html`.

How to do it

In this recipe, we will illustrate how to watch the cluster and query monitoring metrics and also set up a health check alarm:

1. Connect to the Amazon redshift console and navigate to **Amazon Redshift** > **Clusters** > **[YOUR_CLUSTER]**. Click on **Cluster performance** to view the metrics such as CPU, disk utilization, and so on, as shown in the following screenshot:

Figure 6.29 – Monitoring cluster performance

2. Click on the **Query monitoring** tab, which shows the list of queries that have executing/completed queries, as shown in the following screenshot:

Figure 6.30 – Monitoring query execution history

Query monitoring also provides the ability to get insights into the overall workload in the cluster using the **Database performance** tab and also break down the time query spends into queue versus execution using the **Workload concurrency** tab.

3. Click on **Amazon Redshift** > **Alarms** > **Create alarm** and choose the following options to set up a health check alarm for the cluster:

- **Cluster identifier**: Choose the Amazon Redshift cluster for which you want to set up the alarm.

- **Alarm for metric**: Choose maximum for all nodes.

- **When metric value is**: Less than (<) 1.

- **If the alarm state is maintained for**: 10 consecutive periods of 5 minutes.

4. In the alarm details, choose the following options:

a. **Alarm name**: Any meaningful name for the health alarm

b. **Notification**: Enabled

c. **Notify SNS topic**: Select AmazonRedshiftHealthNotification

Click on **Create alarm** to complete the setup for the health check alarm.

How it works

The health check alarm is a binary value where 1 indicates a healthy cluster node, while 0 indicates an unhealthy node. The health check alarm is monitoring for any value that is less than 1 for 10 consecutive times for a duration of 5 minutes to notify through the SNS topic. Similarly, other performance metrics can be configured and notified when the thresholds are breached.

7
Performance Optimization

Amazon Redshift provides out-of-the-box capabilities for most workloads. Amazon Redshift defaults the table design choices, such as sort and distribution key, to AUTO and can learn from the query workloads to automatically set up the right structure. For more information, see *Working with automatic table optimization* (`https://docs.aws.amazon.com/redshift/latest/dg/t_Creating_tables.html`).

As a user of Amazon Redshift, it provides the necessary levers so that you can further optimize/pick a different choice when needed. The sort, distribution key, and table encoding choices have influential effects on the performance of queries, and in this chapter, we will discuss the optimization techniques we can use to improve these throughputs. Also, we will take a deep dive into analyzing queries to understand the rationale behind the tuning exercise.

In this chapter, we will cover the following recipes:

- Amazon Redshift Advisor
- Managing column compression
- Managing data distribution
- Managing sort keys

- Analyzing and improving queries

- Configuring **workload management (WLM)**

- Utilizing Concurrency Scaling

- Optimizing Spectrum queries

Technical requirements

You will need the following technical requirements to complete the recipes in this chapter:

- Access to the AWS Console.

- The AWS administrator should create an IAM user by following *Recipe 1 – Creating an IAM User*, in the *Appendix*. This IAM user will be used in some of the recipes in this chapter.

- The AWS administrator should create an IAM role by following *Recipe 3: Creating IAM Role for an AWS service*, in the *Appendix*. This IAM role will be used in some of the recipes in this chapter.

- The AWS administrator should deploy the AWS CloudFormation template (https://github.com/PacktPublishing/Amazon-Redshift-Cookbook/blob/master/Chapter07/chapter_7_CFN.yaml) and create two IAM policies:

  a. An IAM policy that's attached to the IAM user, which will give them access to Amazon Redshift, Amazon EC2, AWS Secrets Manager, AWS IAM, AWS CloudFormation, AWS KMS, AWS Glue, and Amazon S3.

  b. An IAM policy that's attached to the IAM role, which will allow the Amazon Redshift cluster to access Amazon S3.

- Attach the IAM role to the Amazon Redshift cluster by following *Recipe 4 – Attaching an IAM Role to the Amazon Redshift cluster*, in the *Appendix*. Take note of the IAM's role name. We will reference it in this chapter's recipes as [Your-Redshift_Role].

- An Amazon Redshift cluster deployed in AWS region eu-west-1.

- Amazon Redshift cluster master user credentials.

- Access to any SQL interface, such as a SQL client or the Amazon Redshift Query Editor.

- An AWS account number. We will reference it in this chapter's recipes as
  `[Your-AWS_Account_Id]`.
- This chapter's code files, which can be found in this book's GitHub repository:
  `https://github.com/PacktPublishing/Amazon-Redshift-Cookbook/tree/master/Chapter07`.

Amazon Redshift Advisor

Amazon Redshift Advisor was launched in mid 2018. It runs daily and continuously observes the workload's operational statistics on the cluster with its lens of best practices. Amazon Redshift Advisor uses sophisticated algorithms to provide tailored best practice recommendations, which allows us to get the best possible performance and cost savings. The recommendations are provided which is ranked by order of impact. Amazon Redshift Advisor eases administration. Some of the recommendations include the following:

- Optimization for the `COPY` command for optimal data ingestion
- Optimization for physical table design
- Optimization for manual workload management
- Cost optimization with a recommendation to delete a cluster after taking a snapshot, if the cluster is not being utilized

Along with the Advisor recommendation, the Automatic Table Optimization feature allows you to apply these recommendations via an auto-requiring administrator intervention, thereby creating a fully self-tuning system.

In this recipe, you will learn where to find Amazon Redshift Advisor so that you can view these recommendations.

Getting ready

To complete this recipe, you will need the following:

- An IAM user with access to Amazon Redshift
- An Amazon Redshift cluster deployed in AWS region `eu-west-1`

How to do it...

In this recipe, we will use the Amazon Redshift console to access the Advisor recommendation for your cluster. Let's get started:

1. Navigate to the AWS Management Console and select **Amazon Redshift**.

2. On the left-hand side, you will see **ADVISOR**. Click on it:

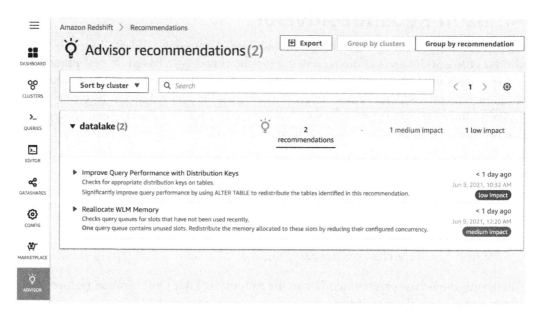

Figure 7.1 – Accessing the Advisor from the AWS Redshift console

3. If you have multiple clusters in a region, you can view the recommendations for all the clusters. You can group the recommendations by cluster or by category – cost, performance, security, or other:

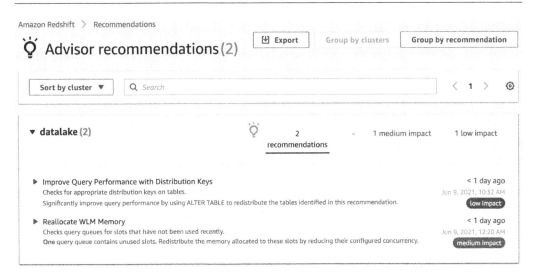

Figure 7.2 – Accessing Amazon Redshift Advisor

4. You can distribute the recommendations by exporting the recommendations
    from the console to a file. To export the recommendations from the **Advisor** page,
    select **Export**:

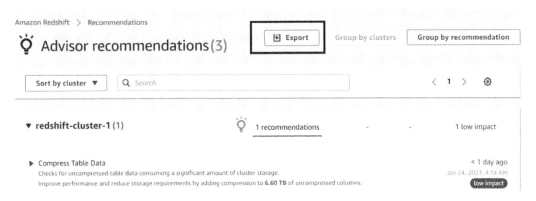

Figure 7.3 – Amazon Redshift Advisor recommendations

How it works...

Amazon Redshift builds recommendations by continuously analyzing the operational data of your cluster. The Advisor provides recommendations that have a significant impact on the performance of your cluster. The Advisor, alongside the Automatic Table Optimization feature, collects the query access patterns and analyzes them using a machine learning service to predict recommendations about the sort and distribution keys. These recommendations are then applied automatically to the target tables in the cluster. Advisor and Automatic Table Optimization execute during low workload intensity so that user queries are affected.

Managing column compression

Amazon Redshift's columnar architecture stores data columns upon columns on disk. Analytical queries select a subset of the columns and perform aggregation on millions to billions of records. The columnar architecture reduces the I/O by selecting a subset of the columns, thus improving query performance. When data is ingested into the Amazon Redshift table, it provides three to four times compression. This further reduces the storage footprint, which, in turn, reduces I/O and hence improves query performance. Reducing the storage footprint also saves you money. Amazon Redshift Advisor provides recommendations for compressing any uncompressed tables.

In this recipe, you will learn how Amazon Redshift automatically applies compression to new and existing tables. You will also learn how column-level compression can be modified for existing columns.

Getting ready

To complete this recipe, you will need the following:

- An IAM user with access to Amazon Redshift.
- An Amazon Redshift cluster deployed in AWS region eu-west-1.
- Amazon Redshift cluster master user credentials.
- Access to any SQL interface, such as a SQL client or the Amazon Redshift Query Editor.
- An IAM role attached to an Amazon Redshift cluster that can access Amazon S3. We will reference it in this recipe as [Your-Redshift_Role].
- An AWS account number. We will reference it in this recipe as [Your-AWS_Account_Id].

How to do it...

In this recipe, we will be analyzing the table-level compression that's applied by Amazon Redshift automatically. Let's get started:

1. Connect to the Amazon Redshift cluster using a SQL client or the Query Editor. Then, create the `customer` table using the following command:

```
drop table if exists customer;
CREATE TABLE customer
(
    C_CUSTKEY        BIGINT NOT NULL,
    C_NAME           VARCHAR(25),
    C_ADDRESS        VARCHAR(40),
    C_NATIONKEY      BIGINT,
    C_PHONE          VARCHAR(15),
    C_ACCTBAL        DECIMAL(18,4),
    C_MKTSEGMENT     VARCHAR(10),
    C_COMMENT        VARCHAR(117)
)
diststyle AUTO;
```

2. Now, let's analyze the compression types that have been applied to the columns. Execute the following command:

```
SELECT "column", type, encoding FROM pg_table_def
WHERE tablename = 'customer';
```

Here is the expected output:

column	type	encoding
c_custkey	bigint	az64
c_name	character varying(25)	lzo
c_address	character varying(40)	lzo
c_nationkey	bigint	az64
c_phone	character varying(15)	lzo
c_acctbal	numeric(18,4)	az64
c_mktsegment	character varying(10)	lzo
c_comment	character varying(117)	lzo

Amazon Redshift automatically applies a compression type of az64 for AZ64 for the INT, SMALLINT, BIGINT, TIMESTAMP, TIMESTAMPTZ, DATE, and NUMERIC column types. Az64 is Amazon's proprietary compression encoding algorithm, and it's designed to achieve a high compression ratio and improved query processing. The default encoding of lzo is applied to the varchar and character columns.

> **Reference to Different Encoding Types in Amazon Redshift**
> https://docs.aws.amazon.com/redshift/latest/dg/c_
> Compression_encodings.html

3. Now, let's recreate the customer table by encoding C_CUSTKEY as raw using the following SQL:

```
drop table if exists customer ;
CREATE TABLE customer
(
    C_CUSTKEY       BIGINT NOT NULL encode raw,
    C_NAME          VARCHAR(25),
    C_ADDRESS       VARCHAR(40),
    C_NATIONKEY     BIGINT,
    C_PHONE         VARCHAR(15),
    C_ACCTBAL       DECIMAL(18,4),
    C_MKTSEGMENT    VARCHAR(10),
    C_COMMENT       VARCHAR(117)
)
diststyle AUTO;
SELECT "column", type, encoding FROM pg_table_def
WHERE tablename = 'customer';
```

Here is the expected output:

column	type	encoding
c_custkey	bigint	az64
c_name	character varying(25)	lzo
c_address	character varying(40)	lzo
c_nationkey	bigint	az64
c_phone	character varying(15)	lzo
c_acctbal	numeric(18,4)	az64
c_mktsegment	character varying(10)	lzo
c_comment	character varying(117)	lzo

Figure 7.4 – Output of the preceding query

Notice that the c_custkey column has been encoded with a raw encoding (**none**).

4. Now, let's use COPY to load data from Amazon S3 using the following command, replacing [Your-AWS_Account_Id] and [Your-Redshift_Role] with their respective values:

```
COPY customer from 's3://packt-redshift-cookbook/
RetailSampleData/customer/' iam_role 'arn:aws:iam::[Your-AWS_
Account_Id]:role/[Your-Redshift_Role]'  CSV gzip COMPUPDATE
PRESET;
SELECT "column", type, encoding FROM pg_table_def
WHERE tablename = 'customer';
```

Here is the expected output:

column	type	encoding
c_custkey	bigint	none
c_name	character varying(25)	lzo
c_address	character varying(40)	lzo
c_nationkey	bigint	az64
c_phone	character varying(15)	lzo
c_acctbal	numeric(18,4)	az64
c_mktsegment	character varying(10)	lzo
c_comment	character varying(117)	lzo

Figure 7.5 – Output of the preceding query

> **Note**
>
> Amazon Redshift command with `compupdate` on determines the encoding for the columns for an empty table, even for columns set to raw; that is, no compression. Create the table with the `c_custkey` column set to encode raw. Then, run the `COPY` command with the `compupdate` preset option, which determines how the columns for empty tables are encoded. Then, we must verify the encodings of the columns and that the `c_custkey` column has an encoding type of `az64`.

How it works...

Amazon Redshift, by default, applies compression, which helps reduce the storage footprint and hence query performance due to a decrease in I/O. Each column can have different encoding types and columns that can grow and shrink independently. For an existing table, you can use the `ANALYZE COMPRESSION` command to determine the encoding type that results in storage savings. It is a built-in command that will find the optimal compression for each column. You can then apply the recommended compression to the table using the `alter` statement or by creating a new table with the new encoding types. Then, you can copy the data from the old table to the new table.

Managing data distribution

Distribution style is a table property that dictates how that table's data is distributed throughout the compute nodes. The goal of data distribution is to leverage the massively parallel processing of Amazon Redshift and reduce the I/O during query processing to improve performance. Amazon Redshift Advisor provides actionable recommendations on distribution style for the table via the `alter` statement. Using automatic table optimization allows you to self-manage the table distribution style based on workload patterns:

- **KEY**: The value is hashed. The same value goes to the same location (slice).
- **ALL**: The entirety of the table data goes to the first slice of every compute node.
- **EVEN**: Round robin data distribution is performed across the compute nodes and slices.
- **AUTO**: Combines the EVEN, ALL, and KEY distributions:

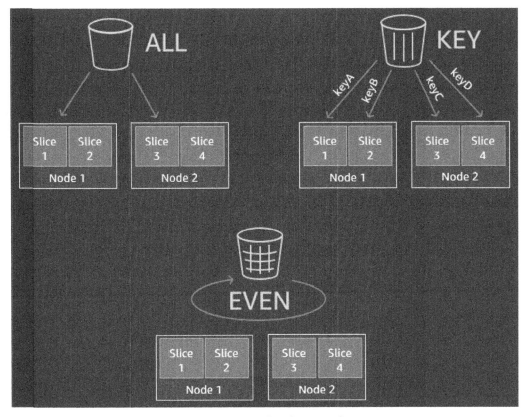

Figure 7.6 – Data distribution styles

In this recipe, you will learn how Amazon Redshift's automatic table style works and the benefits of different distribution styles.

Getting ready

To complete this recipe, you will need the following:

- An IAM user with access to Amazon Redshift.
- An Amazon Redshift cluster deployed in AWS region eu-west-1.
- Amazon Redshift cluster master user credentials.
- Access to any SQL interface, such as a SQL client or the Amazon Redshift Query Editor.

- An IAM role attached to an Amazon Redshift cluster that can access Amazon S3. We will reference it in this recipe as [Your-Redshift_Role].

- An AWS account number. We will reference it in this recipe as [Your-AWS_Account_Id].

How to do it...

In this recipe, we will create a customer table with different distribution keys and analyze their join effectiveness and data distribution:

1. Connect to the Amazon Redshift cluster using a SQL client or the Query Editor.

2. Create the dwdate table with the default auto-distribution style. Then, run the copy command, replacing [Your-AWS_Account_Id] and [Your-Redshift_Role] with the respective values:

```
DROP TABLE IF EXISTS dwdate;
CREATE TABLE dwdate
(
    d_datekey           INTEGER NOT NULL,
    d_date              VARCHAR(19) NOT NULL,
    d_dayofweek         VARCHAR(10) NOT NULL,
    d_month             VARCHAR(10) NOT NULL,
    d_year              INTEGER NOT NULL,
    d_yearmonthnum      INTEGER NOT NULL,
    d_yearmonth         VARCHAR(8) NOT NULL,
    d_daynuminweek      INTEGER NOT NULL,
    d_daynuminmonth     INTEGER NOT NULL,
    d_daynuminyear      INTEGER NOT NULL,
    d_monthnuminyear    INTEGER NOT NULL,
    d_weeknuminyear     INTEGER NOT NULL,
    d_sellingseason     VARCHAR(13) NOT NULL,
    d_lastdayinweekfl   VARCHAR(1) NOT NULL,
    d_lastdayinmonthfl  VARCHAR(1) NOT NULL,
    d_holidayfl         VARCHAR(1) NOT NULL,
    d_weekdayfl         VARCHAR(1) NOT NULL
);
COPY public.dwdate from 's3://packt-redshift-cookbook/
dwdate/' iam_role 'arn:aws:iam::[Your-AWS_Account_
```

```
Id]:role/[Your-Redshift_Role]'  CSV gzip COMPUPDATE
PRESET dateformat 'auto';
```

To verify the distribution style of the dwdate table, execute the preceding command.

Here is the expected output:

schema	table	diststyle	skew_rows
public	dwdate	AUTO(ALL)	

Figure 7.7 – Output of the preceding query

Amazon Redshift, by default, sets the distribution style to AUTO(ALL). Amazon Redshift automatically manages the distribution style for the table, and for small tables, it creates a distribution style of ALL. With the ALL distribution style, the data for this table is stored on every compute node slice as 0. The distribution style of ALL is well-suited for small dimension tables, which enables join performance optimization for large tables with smaller dimension tables.

Let's create the customer table with the default auto-distribution style using the following code, replacing [Your-AWS_Account_Id] and [Your-Redshift_Role].

3. Now, let's modify the distribution style of the customer table using the c_nationkey column by executing the following query:

```
alter table customer alter distkey C_NATIONKEY;
```

4. Now, let's verify the distribution style of the customer table by executing the following query:

```
select "schema", "table", "diststyle", skew_rows
from svv_table_info
where "table" = 'customer';
```

Here is the expected output:

schema	table	diststyle	skew_rows
public	customer	KEY(c_nationkey)	100.00

Figure 7.8 – Output of the preceding query

c_nationkey causes the skewness in the distribution, as shown by the skew_row column, since it has less distinct values (low cardinality). Ideally, skew_row should be less than 5. When data is skewed, some compute nodes will do more work compared to others. The performance of the query is affected by the compute node that contains more data.

5. Now, let's alter the distribution key for the customer table using the high cardinality column; that is, c_custkey. Execute the following query and verify the table skew:

```
alter table customer alter distkey c_custkey;
select "schema", "table", "diststyle", skew_rows
from svv_table_info
where "table" = 'customer';
---output----
```

schema	table	diststyle	skew_rows
public	customer	KEY(c_custkey)	1.00

Now, the customer table has low skew_rows, which will ensure all the compute nodes can perform equal work when processing the query.

How it works...

Amazon Redshift data distribution is a physical table property. It determines how the data is distributed across the compute nodes. The purpose of data distribution is to have every compute node work in parallel to execute the workload and reduce the I/O during join performance, to optimize performance. Amazon Redshift's automatic table optimizations enable you to achieve this. You also have the option to select your distribution style to fine-tune your most demanding workloads to achieve significant performance. Creating a Redshift table with auto-table optimization will automatically change the distribution style based on your workload pattern. You can review the alter table recommendations in the svv_alter_table_recommendations view, and the actions that have been applied by automatic table optimization in the svl_auto_worker_action view.

Managing sort keys

Data sorting in Amazon Redshift is a concept regarding how data is physically sorted on the disk. Data sorting is determined by the `sortkey` property defined in the table. Amazon Redshift automatically creates in-memory metadata called zone maps. Zone maps contain the minimum and maximum values for each block. Zone maps automatically enable you to eliminate I/O from scanning blocks that do not contain data for queries. Sort keys make zone maps more efficient.

`sortkey` can be defined on one or more columns. The columns that are defined in the sort keys are based on your query pattern. Most frequently, filtered columns are good candidates for the sort key. The sort key column's order is defined from low to high cardinality. Sort keys enable range-restricted scans to prune blocks, eliminating I/O and hence optimizing query performance. Redshift Advisor provides recommendations on optimal sort keys, and automatic table optimization handles the sort key changes based on our query pattern.

In this recipe, you will learn how Amazon Redshift compound sort keys work.

Getting ready

To complete this recipe, you will need the following:

- An IAM user with access to Amazon Redshift.

- An Amazon Redshift cluster deployed in AWS region eu-west-1.

- Amazon Redshift cluster master user credentials.

- Access to any SQL interface, such as a SQL client or the Amazon Redshift Query Editor.

- An IAM role attached to an Amazon Redshift cluster that can access Amazon S3. We will reference it in this recipe as [Your-Redshift_Role].

- An AWS account number. We will reference it in this recipe as [Your-AWS_Account_Id].

How to do it...

In this recipe, we will use the lineitem table with sort keys and analyze the performance queries. Let's get started:

1. Connect to the Amazon Redshift cluster using a SQL client or the Query Editor.

2. Let's create the lineitem table with the default auto sortkey using the following code. Remember to replace [Your-AWS_Account_Id] and [Your-Redshift_Role] with their respective values:

```
drop table if exists lineitem;
CREATE TABLE lineitem
(
    L_ORDERKEY          BIGINT NOT NULL,
    L_PARTKEY           BIGINT,
    L_SUPPKEY           BIGINT,
    L_LINENUMBER        INTEGER NOT NULL,
    L_QUANTITY          DECIMAL(18,4),
    L_EXTENDEDPRICE     DECIMAL(18,4),
    L_DISCOUNT          DECIMAL(18,4),
    L_TAX               DECIMAL(18,4),
    L_RETURNFLAG        VARCHAR(1),
    L_LINESTATUS        VARCHAR(1),
    L_SHIPDATE          DATE,
    L_COMMITDATE        DATE,
    L_RECEIPTDATE       DATE,
    L_SHIPINSTRUCT      VARCHAR(25),
    L_SHIPMODE          VARCHAR(10),
    L_COMMENT           VARCHAR(44)
)
distkey (L_ORDERKEY) ;
COPY lineitem from 's3://packt-redshift-cookbook/
lineitem/' iam_role 'arn:aws:iam::[Your-AWS_Account_
Id]:role/[Your- Redshift_Role]'  CSV gzip COMPUPDATE
PRESET;
```

> **Note**
>
> Depending on the size of the cluster, the COPY command will take around 15 minutes to complete due to the size of the data.

3. Let's verify the sort key of the `lineitem` table with the default auto `sortkey` using the following query:

```
select "schema", "table", "diststyle", skew_rows,
sortkey1, unsorted
from svv_table_info
where "table" = 'lineitem';
```

Here is the expected output:

schema	table	diststyle	skew_rows	sortkey1	unsorted
public	lineitem	KEY(l_orderkey)	1.00	AUTO(SORTKEY)	

Figure 7.9 – Output of the preceding query

As shown in the preceding output, the `lineitem` table has been set with `AUTO(sortkey)`. Amazon Redshift Advisor, based on your workload pattern, will make recommendations and the automatic table optimization will alter the table with an optimal sort key.

4. To see the effectiveness of block pruning using the sort key, execute the following query and take note of `query_id`:

```
SELECT
     l_returnflag,
     l_linestatus,
     sum(l_quantity) as sum_qty,
     sum(l_extendedprice) as sum_base_price,
     sum(l_extendedprice * (1 - l_discount)) as sum_disc_
price,
     count(*) as count_order
FROM
    lineitem
WHERE
     l_shipdate = '1992-01-10'
GROUP BY
     l_returnflag,
     l_linestatus
ORDER BY
     l_returnflag,
     l_linestatus;
select PG_LAST_QUERY_ID() as query_id;
```

Here is the expected output:

```
query_id
1240454
```

> **Note**
>
> Amazon Redshift captures the operational statistics of each query step in system tables. Details about `Svl_query_summary` can be found at `https://docs.aws.amazon.com/redshift/latest/dg/r_SVL_QUERY_SUMMARY.html`.

5. Execute the following query to measure the effectiveness of the sort key for the preceding query, replacing `[query_id]` with the output from the preceding step:

```
SELECT query, step, label, is_rrscan, rows, rows_pre_filter, is_diskbased
from svl_query_summary where query in ([query_id])
and label like '%lineitem%'
order by query,step;
```

Here is the expected output:

query	step	label	is_rrscan	rows	rows_pre_filter	is_diskbased
29369379	0	scan tbl=1620612 name=lineitem	t	18385	345590852	f

`rows_pre_filter` indicates that Amazon Redshift was effectively able to use the sort key to `rows_pre_filtered` 4,066,288 down to 18,385. `is_rrscan` is true for these range scans. Amazon Redshift automatically leverages zone maps to prune out the blocks that do not match the filter criteria of the query.

6. Let's alter the `lineitem` table and add the `l_shipdate` column as our `sortkey`. Most of the queries we will run will use `l_shipdate` as the filter. L_shipdate is a low cardinality column:

```
alter table lineitem alter sortkey (L_SHIPDATE);
```

> **Note**
>
> Depending on the size of the cluster, the ALTER statement will take at around 15 minutes to complete due to the size of the data.

To see the effectiveness of `sortkey`, execute the following query and capture the query ID:

```
query_id_1
```

Here is the expected output:

```
1240216
```

7. Now, let's modify the query so that it purposely casts the `l_shipdate` column as a `varchar` data type and then applies the filter. Execute the following modified query and capture the output of `query_id`:

```
set enable_result_cache_for_session = off;

SELECT
    l_returnflag,
    l_linestatus,
    sum(l_quantity) as sum_qty,
    sum(l_extendedprice) as sum_base_price,
    sum(l_extendedprice * (1 - l_discount)) as sum_disc_
price,
    count(*) as count_order
FROM
    lineitem
WHERE
    cast(l_shipdate as varchar(10) ) = '1992-01-10'
GROUP BY
    l_returnflag,
    l_linestatus
ORDER BY
    l_returnflag,
    l_linestatus;

select PG_LAST_QUERY_ID() as query_id_2;
---expected sample output---
query_id_2
1240218
```

8. Now, let's execute the following query to analyze the effectiveness of the sort key columns, replacing [query_id_1] and [query_id_2] shown in the preceding steps:

```
SELECT query, step,    label, is_rrscan, rows, rows_pre_
filter, is_diskbased
```

```
from svl_query_summary where query in ([query_id_1],[
query_id_2])
```

```
and label like '%lineitem%'
```

```
order by query,step;
```

Here is the expected output:

query	step	label	is_rrscan	rows	rows_pre_filter	is_diskbased
29369379	0	scan tbl=1620612 name=lineitem t		18385	345590852	f
29369439	0	scan tbl=1620612 name=lineitem f		18385	599037902	f

Figure 7.10 – Output of the preceding query

[query_id_1], which used l_shipdate to filter rows_pre_filter, is 4066288 versus [query_id_2], which was cast to rows_pre_filter and is 599037902. This means that a full table scan was performed. As a best practice, to make your sort keys effective, avoid applying functions or casting to sort key columns.

How it works...

Using sort keys when creating a table allows you to perform efficient range-restricted scans of the data, when the sort key is referenced in the where conditions. Amazon Redshift automatically leverages the in-memory metadata to prune out the blocks. The sort keys make the zone maps more pristine. Applying sort keys to the most commonly used columns as filters in a query can significantly reduce the I/O, and hence optimize query performance for any workload. You can learn more about sort keys at https://docs.aws.amazon.com/redshift/latest/dg/t_Sorting_data.html.

Analyzing and improving queries

Amazon Redshift defaults the table sort key and distribution key to AUTO. Amazon Redshift can learn from the workloads and automatically set the right sort and distribution style, the two big levers that dictate the table's design and optimization. Amazon Redshift also provides insights into the query plan, which helps optimize the queries when authoring them. This plan contains detailed steps about how to fetch the data.

Getting ready

To complete this recipe, you will need the following:

- An IAM user with access to Amazon Redshift.

- An Amazon Redshift cluster deployed in AWS region eu-west-1.

- Amazon Redshift cluster master user credentials.

- Access to any SQL interface, such as a SQL client or the Amazon Redshift Query Editor.

- An IAM role attached to an Amazon Redshift cluster that can access Amazon S3. We will reference it in this recipe as [Your-Redshift_Role].

- An AWS account number. We will reference it in this recipe as [Your-AWS_Account_Id].

How to do it...

In the recipe, we will use the Retail System Dataset from *Chapter 3, Loading and Unloading Data*, to perform analytical queries and optimize them:

1. Connect to the Amazon Redshift cluster using any SQL interface, such as a SQL client or the Query Editor, and execute EXPLAIN on a query:

```
explain
SELECT o_orderstatus,
       COUNT(o_orderkey) AS orders_count,
       SUM(l_quantity) AS quantity,
       MAX(l_extendedprice) AS extendedprice
FROM lineitem
   JOIN orders ON l_orderkey = o_orderkey
WHERE
   L_SHIPDATE = '1992-01-29'
GROUP BY o_orderstatus;
```

Here is the expected output:

```
QUERY PLAN
-----------------------------------------------------------------
--------------
  XN HashAggregate    (cost=97529596065.20..97529596065.22
rows=3 width=36)
```

```
    -> XN Hash Join DS_BCAST_INNER
(cost=3657.20..97529594861.20 rows=120400 width=36)
        Hash Cond: ("outer".o_orderkey = "inner".l_
orderkey)
            -> XN Seq Scan on orders  (cost=0.00..760000.00
rows=76000000 width=13)
            -> XN Hash  (cost=3047.67..3047.67 rows=243814
width=31)
                -> XN Seq Scan on lineitem
(cost=0.00..3047.67 rows=243814 width=31)
                    Filter: (l_shipdate = '1992-01-
29'::date)
```

As shown in the preceding output, the `explain` command provides insights into the steps that were performed by the query. As we can see, `lineitem` and the `orders` table have been joined using a hash join. Each step also provides the relative cost of comparing the expensive steps in the query for optimization purposes.

> **Note**
>
> Please also see `https://docs.aws.amazon.com/redshift/latest/dg/c-query-planning.html` for a step-by-step illustration of the query planning and execution steps.

2. Now, execute the analytical query using the following command to capture `query_id` for analysis:

```
SELECT o_orderstatus,
       COUNT(o_orderkey) AS orders_count,
       SUM(l_quantity) AS quantity,
       MAX(l_extendedprice) AS extendedprice
FROM lineitem
  JOIN orders ON l_orderkey = o_orderkey
WHERE L_SHIPDATE = '1992-01-29'
GROUP BY o_orderstatus;
select
PG_LAST_QUERY_ID() as query_id;
```

Here is the expected output:

```
query_id

24580051
```

Note that this query_id that will be used later to analyze the query.

3. Execute the following command to analyze the effectiveness of the sort key column on the lineitem table by replacing [query_id] from the preceding step:

```
SELECT step, label, is_rrscan, rows, rows_pre_filter, is_
diskbased

from svl_query_summary where query = [query_id]

order by step;
```

Here is the expected output:

```
step |                       label                      | is_
rrscan |   rows  | rows_pre_filter | is_diskbased

------+---------------------------------------------+------
-----+--------+-----------------+------------

    0 | scan    tbl=1450056 name=lineitem               | t
| 57856 |         599037902 | f

    0 | scan    tbl=361382 name=Internal Worktable | f
|      1 |                 0 | f

    0 | scan    tbl=1449979 name=orders                | t
| 79119 |         76000000 | f

    0 | scan    tbl=361380 name=Internal Worktable | f
| 173568 |                 0 | f

    0 | scan    tbl=361381 name=Internal Worktable | f
|     32 |                 0 | f
```

As we can see, the query optimizer can effectively make use of the range restricted scan (is_rrscan) on the l_shipdate column in the lineitem table, to filter out the rows from 599037902 rows to 57856. This can be compared to the rows_pre_filter and rows columns in the preceding output. Also, none of the steps spill to disk, as indicated by is_diskbased = f.

4. Now, let's execute the following command to analyze the effectiveness of our data distribution:

```
SELECT step,
       label,
       slice,
       ROWS,
       bytes
FROM SVL_QUERY_REPORT
WHERE query IN (24580051)
ORDER BY step;
```

Here is the expected output:

```
|                           label                         | slice
| rows  |  bytes
-------+---------------------------------------------------+------
-+-------+---------
     0 | scan    tbl=1450056 name=lineitem                 |     2
| 1780  |   56960
     0 | scan    tbl=1450056 name=lineitem                 |    27
| 1859  |   59488
     0 | scan    tbl=1450056 name=lineitem                 |     5
| 1778  |   56896
     0 | scan    tbl=1450056 name=lineitem                 |    12
| 1755  |   56160
     0 | scan    tbl=1450056 name=lineitem                 |     6
| 1833  |   58656
     0 | scan    tbl=1450056 name=lineitem                 |    28
| 1874  |   59968
```

Notice that all the slices are processing approximately the same number of rows. That indicates good data distribution.

5. Amazon Redshift provides consolidated alerts from the query execution to prioritize the analysis effort. You can execute the following query to view the alerts from the query's execution:

```
select event, solution
from stl_alert_event_log
where query in (24580051);
```

Here is the expected output:

```
Very selective query filter:ratio=rows(2470)/rows_pre_
user_filter(2375000)=0.001040
```

```
Review the choice of sort key to enable range restricted
scans, or run the VACUUM command to ensure the table is
sorted
```

In the preceding query output, since we've already confirmed that the sort keys are effectively being used, using VACUUM will ensure that the data is sorted and that range restricted scans can be more effective.

6. Another alert that you can view from stl_alert_event_log is *"Statistics for the tables in the query are missing or out of date."* To fix this issue, you can execute the Analyze query, as follows:

```
analyze lineitem;
```

Here is the expected output:

```
ANALYZE executed successfully
```

Here, lineitem has been updated with the current statistics, which will enable the optimizer to pick an optimal plan.

How it works...

Amazon Redshift automates performance tuning as part of its managed service. This includes automatic vacuum delete, automatic table sort, automatic analyze, and Amazon Redshift Advisor for actionable insights into optimizing cost and performance. These capabilities are enabled through a **machine learning** (**ML**) model that can learn from your workloads to generate and apply precise, high-value optimizations. You can read more about automatic table optimization here: https://aws.amazon.com/blogs/big-data/optimizing-tables-in-amazon-redshift-using-automatic-table-optimization/.

Configuring workload management (WLM)

Amazon Redshift **workload management (WLM)** enables you to set up query priorities in a cluster. WLM helps you create query queues that can be defined based on different parameters such as memory allotment, priority, user groups, query groups, and query monitoring rules. Users generally use WLM to set priorities for different query types, such as long-running versus short running or ETL versus Reporting, and so on. In this recipe, we will demonstrate how to configure WLM within a Redshift cluster. By doing this, you can manage multiple workloads running on the same cluster, and each of them can be assigned different priorities based on your business needs.

Getting ready

To complete this recipe, you will need the following:

- An IAM user with access to Amazon Redshift
- An Amazon Redshift cluster deployed in AWS region eu-west-1

How to do it...

In this recipe, we will configure WLM for your cluster using the AWS Console:

1. Open the Amazon Redshift console at `https://console.aws.amazon.com/redshiftv2/home`.

2. From the left-hand tool bar, browse to **CONFIG** and select **Workload Management**:

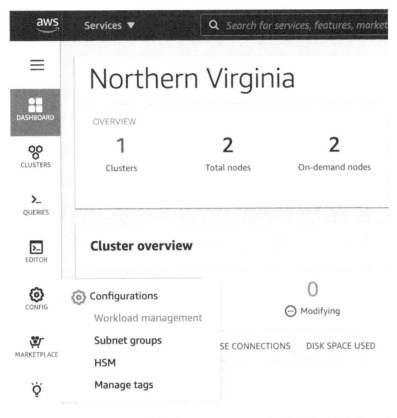

Figure 7.11 – Navigating Workload Management on the AWS Redshift Console

3. On the **Workload management** page, we will need to create a new parameter group by clicking the **Create** button:

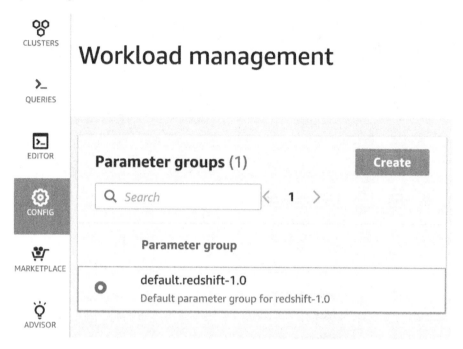

Figure 7.12 – Configuring a new parameter group

4. A **Create parameter group** pop-up will open. Enter a **Parameter group name** and **Description**. Click on **Create** to finish creating a new parameter group:

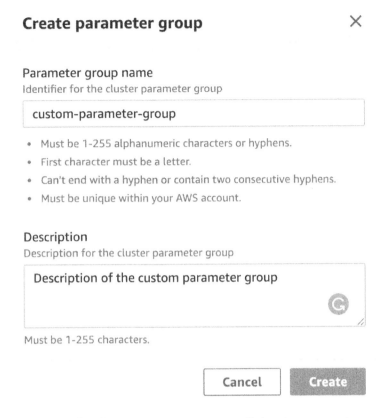

Figure 7.13 – Creating a new parameter group called custom-parameter-group

5. By default, **Automatic WLM** is configured under **Workload Management**. Automatic WLM is recommended, and it calculates the optimal memory and concurrency for query queues.

6. To create a new queue, click on **Edit workload queues** in the **Workload queues** section. On the **Modify workload queues: custom-parameter-group** page, click on **Add queue**.

7. You can configure the queue name by replacing the **Queue 1** string and configuring other settings, such as **Concurrency scaling mode** between **auto** and **off** and **Query priority** between 5 levels ranging from lowest to highest. Additionally, you can include **User groups** or **Query groups** that need to be routed to this specific queue.

For example, we created an `ETL` queue with concurrency scaling disabled and query priority set to **Normal**. The user groups for `data_engineers` and query groups for `load` and `transform` will be routed to this queue:

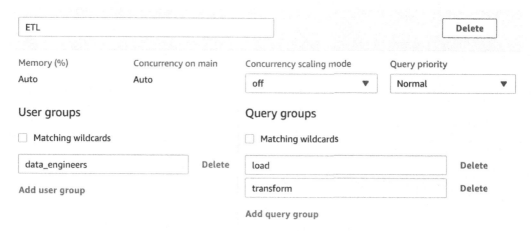

Figure 7.14 – Configuring the ETL queue on the parameter group

8. You can repeat *step 7* to create a total of 8 queues.

9. You can create **Query monitoring rules** by either selecting **Add rule from template** or **Add custom rule**. This allows you to perform the log, abort, or change query priority action based on the predicates for the given query monitoring metrics.

For example, here, we created a rule to abort the query if it returns more than 100 million rows:

Figure 7.15 – Configuring a query monitoring rule

10. To finish configuring the WLM settings, browse to the bottom of the page and click **Save**.

11. To apply the new WLM settings to the cluster, browse to **CLUSTERS** and click the checkbox besides the Amazon Redshift cluster that you want to apply the new WLM settings to. Go to **Actions** and select **Modify**:

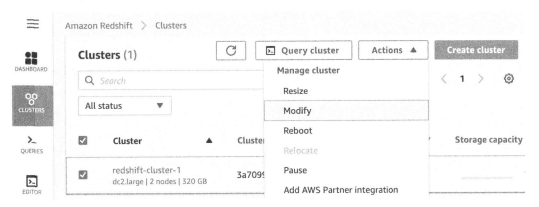

Figure 7.16 – Applying custom-parameter-group to your cluster

12. Under the **Modify cluster** page, browse to the second set of **Database configurations**. Click the **Parameter groups** dropdown and select the newly created parameter group.

13. Go to the bottom of the page and select **Modify cluster**. The changes are in the queue and applied once the cluster is rebooted.

14. To reboot the cluster at an appropriate time that suits the business, click the checkbox besides the Amazon Redshift cluster, go to **Actions**, and select **Reboot**. A pop-up will appear to confirm the reboot. Select **Reboot cluster**.

How it works...

Amazon WLM's settings allows you to set up workload priorities and the concurrency of different types of workloads that run on an Amazon Redshift cluster. In addition, we have Auto WLM (recommended), which manages short query acceleration, memory allotment, and concurrency automatically. Using manual WLM, you can configure the memory and concurrency values for your workloads, if needed (not recommended).

Utilizing Concurrency Scaling

The Concurrency Scaling feature provided by Amazon Redshift allows you to support concurrent users and queries for steady query performance. Amazon Redshift utilizes resources that are available in a cluster to maximize throughput for analytical queries. Hence, when multiple queries are to be executed at the same time, Amazon Redshift will utilize **workload management (WLM)** to execute a few queries at a time so that they complete as soon as possible and don't take up the rest of the queries. This is done instead of you having to run all the queries for longer.

When the Concurrency Scaling feature is turned on, Amazon Redshift can instantly bring up additional redundant clusters to execute the queued-up queries and support burst traffic in the data warehouse. The redundant clusters are automatically shut down once the queries complete/there are no more queries waiting in the queue.

Getting ready

To complete this recipe, you will need the following:

- An Amazon Redshift cluster deployed in AWS region eu-west-1. You will also need the retail system dataset from the *Loading data from Amazon S3 using COPY* recipe in *Chapter 3, Loading and Unloading Data*.

- Amazon Redshift cluster master user credentials.

- Access to any SQL interface, such as a SQL client or the Amazon Redshift Query Editor.

- Install the par_psql client tool (`https://github.com/gbb/par_psql`) and psql `https://docs.aws.amazon.com/redshift/latest/mgmt/connecting-from-psql.html` on a Linux machine that can connect to an Amazon Redshift cluster.

How to do it...

In this recipe, we will be using the par_psql (`https://github.com/gbb/par_psql`) tool to execute parallel queries on Amazon Redshift to simulate concurrent workloads. Let's get started:

1. Navigate to the AWS Amazon Redshift console and go to **Amazon Redshift** > **Clusters** > your Amazon Redshift Cluster. Click on the **Properties** tab and scroll down to **Database configurations**, as shown in the following screenshot:

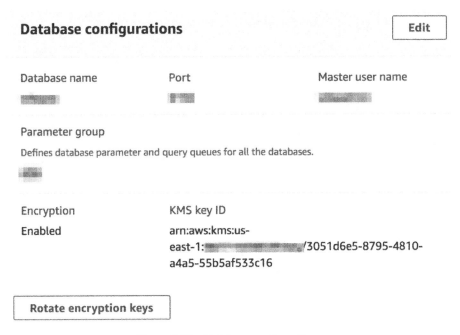

Figure 7.17 – Database configurations

2.   Select the **Parameter group** property associated with the Amazon Redshift cluster.

3.   Click on the **Parameter group** property associated with the cluster.

4.   Verify that **max_concurrency_scaling_clusters** has been set to > =1 and that **Workload queues** has **Concurrency scaling mode** set to **auto**, as shown here:

Workload queues

Edit workload queues

Short query acceleration is enabled for queries whose maximum runtime is dynamic. Learn more ⬈

Default queue

This is the default queue.

Memory (%)	Concurrency on main	Concurrency scaling mode	Query priority
Auto	Auto	auto	Normal

▶ **Query monitoring rules (0)**

Figure 7.18 – Workload queues

5. Update **Concurrency scaling mode** to auto in **Workload Queues**.

    For a step-by-step guide to setting up the Concurrency Scaling feature, please refer to the *Managing workload management (WLM)* recipe of this chapter.

6. Download the `par_psql` script from `https://github.com/PacktPublishing/Amazon-Redshift-Cookbook/blob/master/Chapter07/conc_scaling.sql` and copy it into the path where `par_psql` has been installed. This script uses the retail system dataset, which we mentioned in the *Getting started* section.

7. Execute the following command using the SQL client to capture the test's `starttime`:

    ```
    select sysdate as starttime
    ```

    Here is the expected output:

    ```
    starttime
    2020-12-04 16:10:43
    ```

8. Execute the following command on the Linux box to simulate 100 concurrent query runs:

    ```
    export PGPASSWORD=[PASSWORD]
    ./par_psql --file=conc_scaling.sql -h [YOUR AMAZON
    REDSHIFT HOST] -p [PORT] -d [DATABASE_NAME] -U [USER_
    NAME]
    ```

9. Wait until all the queries have completed. Execute the following query to analyze the query execution. Do this by replacing `[starttime]` with the value corresponding to the datetime at the start of the script's execution, before the following query:

    ```
    SELECT w.service_class AS queue
         , case when q.concurrency_scaling_status = 1 then
    'Y' else 'N' end as conc_scaled
         , COUNT( * ) AS queries
         , SUM( q.aborted )  AS aborted
         , SUM( ROUND( total_queue_time::NUMERIC / 1000000,2
    ) ) AS queue_secs
         , SUM( ROUND( total_exec_time::NUMERIC / 1000000,2 )
    )  AS exec_secs
    FROM stl_query q
         JOIN stl_wlm_query w
    ```

```
             USING (userid,query)
WHERE q.userid > 1
   AND q.starttime > '[starttime]'
GROUP BY 1,2
ORDER BY 1,2;
```

Here is the expected output:

```
queue | conc_scaled | queries | aborted | queue_secs |
exec_secs
-------+-------------+---------+---------+------------+--
---------
     9 | N           |      75 |       0 |    3569.83 |
31.24
     9 | Y           |      25 |       0 |       0.0|
10.97
```

As we can see, Amazon Redshift was able to take advantage of the Concurrency Scaling feature to execute 25% of the queries on the burst cluster.

How it works...

Concurrency Scaling allows users see the most current data, independent of whether the queries execute the main cluster or a Concurrency Scaling cluster. When Concurrency Scaling is used for peak workloads, you will be charged additional cluster time, but only for when they're used. Concurrency Scaling is enabled at a WLM queue, and eligible queries are sent to perform Concurrency Scaling when the concurrency in the queue exceeds the defined values, to ensure the queries do not wait. You can find more details about the queries that are eligible for Concurrency Scaling here: https://docs.aws. amazon.com/redshift/latest/dg/concurrency-scaling.html.

Optimizing Spectrum queries

Amazon Redshift Spectrum allows you to extend your Amazon Redshift data warehouse so that it can use SQL queries on data that is stored in Amazon S3. Optimizing Amazon Redshift Spectrum queries allows you to gain optimal throughput for SQL queries, as well as saving costs associated with them. In this recipe, we will learn how to gain insights into the performance of Spectrum-based queries and optimize them.

Getting ready

To complete this recipe, you will need the following:

- An IAM user with access to Amazon Redshift and Amazon S3.

- An Amazon Redshift cluster deployed in AWS region eu-west-1.

- Amazon Redshift cluster master user credentials.

- Access to any SQL interface, such as a SQL client or the Amazon Redshift Query Editor.

- An IAM role attached to an Amazon Redshift cluster that can access Amazon S3. We will reference it in this recipe as [Your-Redshift_Role].

- An AWS account number. We will reference it in this recipe as [Your-AWS_Account_Id].

How to do it...

In this recipe, we will use the Amazon.com customer product reviews dataset (refer to *Chapter 3*, *Loading and Unloading Data*) to demonstrate how to gain insight into Spectrum's SQL performance and tune it:

1. Open any SQL client tool and connect to the Amazon Redshift cluster. Create a schema that points to the reviews dataset by using the following command, remembering to replace the [Your-AWS_Account_Id] and [Your-Redshift_Role] values with your own:

```
CREATE external SCHEMA reviews_ext_schema
FROM data catalog DATABASE 'reviews_ext_schema'
iam_role 'arn:aws:iam::[Your-AWS_Account_Id]:role/[Your-Redshift_Role]'
CREATE external DATABASE if not exists;
```

2. Using the reviews dataset, create a parquet version of the external tables by using the following command:

```
CREATE external TABLE reviews_ext_schema.amazon_product_reviews_parquet(
    marketplace varchar(2),
    customer_id varchar(32),
    review_id varchar(24),
    product_id varchar(24),
```

```
    product_parent varchar(32),
    product_title varchar(512),
    star_rating int,
    helpful_votes int,
    total_votes int,
    vine char(1),
    verified_purchase char(1),
    review_headline varchar(256),
    review_body varchar(max),
    review_date date,
    year int)
stored as parquet
location 's3://packt-redshift-cookbook/reviews_parquet/';
```

3. Using the `reviews` dataset, create a plain text file (tab-delimited) version of the external tables by using the following command:

```
CREATE external TABLE reviews_ext_schema.amazon_product_
reviews_tsv(
    marketplace varchar(2),
    customer_id varchar(32),
    review_id varchar(24),
    product_id varchar(24),
    product_parent varchar(32),
    product_title varchar(512),
    star_rating int,
    helpful_votes int,
    total_votes int,
    vine char(1),
    verified_purchase char(1),
    review_headline varchar(256),
    review_body varchar(max),
    review_date date,
    year int)
row format delimited
fields terminated by '\t'
stored as textfile
location 's3://packt-redshift-cookbook/reviews_tsv/';
```

4. Execute the following analytical queries to calibrate the throughputs. Take note of the `parquet_query_id` and `tsv_query_id` outputs:

```
SELECT verified_purchase,
       SUM(total_votes) total_votes,
       avg(helpful_votes) avg_helpful_votes,
       count(customer_id) total_customers
FROM reviews_ext_schema.amazon_product_reviews_parquet
WHERE review_headline = 'Y'
GROUP BY verified_purchase;


select PG_LAST_QUERY_ID() as parquet_query_id;


SELECT verified_purchase,
       SUM(total_votes) total_votes,
       avg(helpful_votes) avg_helpful_votes,
       count(customer_id) total_customers
FROM reviews_ext_schema.amazon_product_reviews_tsv
WHERE review_headline = 'Y'
GROUP BY verified_purchase;


select PG_LAST_QUERY_ID() as tsv_query_id;
```

5. Analyze the performance of both these queries by using the following command, substituting [parquet_query_id] and [tsv_query_id] from the previous step:

```
select query, segment, elapsed as elapsed_ms, s3_scanned_
rows, s3_scanned_bytes, s3query_returned_rows, s3query_
returned_bytes, files
from svl_s3query_summary
where query in ([parquet_query_id], [tsv_query_id])
order by query,segment ;
```

Here is the expected output:

```
query,elapsed_ms,s3_scanned_rows,s3_scanned_
bytes,s3query_returned_rows,s3query_returned_bytes,files
parquet_query_id  3000554    5906460    142428017    4
1917    10
```

```
tsv_query_id    9182604   5906460    2001945218    4
5222         10
```

As we can see, the `.tsv` version of the dataset took 9 seconds versus 3 seconds in parquet since it has to scan 2 GB of data; only 0.14 MB of the data has to be scanned when it's in parquet format, even though the content of the files was the same.

Having the data in a columnar format such as parquet improves the query's throughput. It also reduces the cost that's incurred with the query due to an optimal scan being performed on the dataset.

How it works...

Optimizing Amazon Redshift Spectrum queries works on the principle of reducing the Amazon S3 scan and pushed down operations as much as possible into the infinitely scalable Spectrum engine. This can be achieved by using the following techniques:

- Amazon Redshift Spectrum supports structured and semi-structured data formats such as AVRO, PARQUET, ORC, TEXTFILE, JSON, and so on, and using a columnar file format such as parquet or ORC can reduce I/O by reading only the needed columns.

- Compress the row format file, such as a textfile, with compression file such as `.gzip`, snappy or `.bzip` to save costs and gain faster performance.

- Use an optimal file size:

  a. Avoid excessively small files (less than 1 MB).

  b. Avoid large files (1 GB or more) if the file format can't be split; for example, `.gzip`/snappy compressed text files.

- Organize the files as partitions. Take advantage of partition pruning and saving costs with the query.

You can read more about optimization techniques here: `https://aws.amazon.com/blogs/big-data/10-best-practices-for-amazon-redshift-spectrum/`.

8
Cost Optimization

Amazon Redshift allows you to operate your data warehouse from a few gigabytes to a petabyte in size so that is simple to manage and is cost-effective. The cost is predictable, even with unpredictable workloads, and provides up to 3x better price performance than any other data warehouse with just $1,000 per terabyte per year.

Amazon Redshift provides flexible pricing options, both on-demand and reserved. With reserved instance pricing, you can save up to 75% by committing to a 1-year or 3-year term. There are a number of best practices you can follow to ensure you're getting the best value with Amazon Redshift. This chapter will discuss some of the common cost optimization methods that you can adopt to get the best cost performance.

The following recipes will be covered in this chapter:

- AWS Trusted Advisor
- Amazon Redshift Reserved Instance pricing
- Configuring pause and resume for an Amazon Redshift cluster
- Scheduling pause and resume
- Configuring elastic resize for an Amazon Redshift cluster
- Scheduling elastic resize
- Using cost controls to set actions for Redshift Spectrum
- Using cost controls to set actions for Concurrency Scaling

Technical requirements

To complete the recipes in this chapter, you will need to consult the following technical requirements:

- Access to the AWS Console.

- An AWS administrator should create an IAM user by following *Recipe 1 – Creating an IAM user,* in the *Appendix.* This IAM user will be used to some of the recipes in this chapter.

- An AWS administrator should deploy the AWS CloudFormation template (`https://github.com/PacktPublishing/Amazon-Redshift-Cookbook/blob/master/Chapter08/chapter_8_CFN.yaml`) and create one IAM policy and one IAM role:

  a. An IAM policy attached to the IAM user, which will give them access to Amazon Redshift, AWS Secrets Manager, Amazon CloudWatch, Amazon CloudWatch Logs, AWS KMS, AWS Glue, Amazon EC2, AWS Trusted Advisor, AWS Billing, AWS Cost Explorer, and Amazon S3.

  b. An IAM role with access to schedule pause and resume and elastic resizing for a Redshift cluster. We will reference this as `Chapter8RedshiftSchedulerRole`.

- An Amazon Redshift cluster deployed in AWS Region eu-west-1.

AWS Trusted Advisor

AWS Trusted Advisor provides you with a summarized dashboard and detailed real-time guidance to help you provision your resources while following AWS best practices. Trusted Advisor checks help you optimize your AWS infrastructure, reduce your overall costs, increase security and performance, and monitor your service limits.

AWS Trusted Advisor provides cost optimization checks for unutilized Amazon Redshift clusters. It also provides cost optimization checks for the on-demand Amazon Redshift clusters that can benefit from Reserved Instance cost pricing, thus providing you with significant cost savings.

Getting ready

To complete this recipe, you will need the following:

- An IAM user with access to Amazon Redshift and AWS Trusted Advisor

- An Amazon Redshift cluster deployed in AWS Region eu-west-1

How to do it...

In this recipe, we will use AWS Trusted Advisor to identify opportunities for potential savings:

1. Navigate to the AWS Management Console and select **AWS Trusted Advisor**.

2. On the **Trusted Advisor Dashboard** page, you will see a summary of checks for cost optimization, along with potential monthly savings:

Trusted Advisor Dashboard

Figure 8.1 – AWS Trusted Advisor Dashboard

3. To drill down into the details of cost optimization, select **Cost Optimization** from the left pane. If the Amazon Redshift clusters are underutilized, it will list these clusters and their corresponding costs. You can choose to pause or delete the clusters to reduce costs on on-demand clusters:

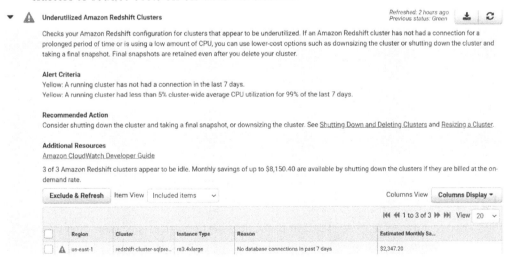

Figure 8.2 – Cost optimization recommendations

4. The cost optimization recommendations show the potential savings you could make, along with Reserved Instances, for on-demand clusters. This is based on their usage over the past 30 days:

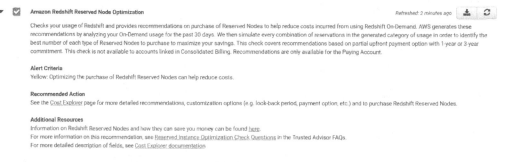

Figure 8.3 – Amazon Redshift cost optimization opportunities

5. To view these potential cost savings, navigate to **Cost Explorer** from the Management Console. Choose **recommendations** under **Reservations**. The recommendations are to use Reserved Instances instead of on-demand ones, which results in potential savings of 34% compared to on-demand. We will dive deeper into potential savings with Reserved Instance pricing in the next recipe:

Figure 8.4 – Amazon Redshift cost optimization recommendations

How it works...

AWS Trusted Advisor is an application that infers best practices based on operational data that's been derived from thousands of AWS customers. These checks are fall into different categories, such as cost optimization, security, fault tolerance, performance, and service limits. For a full list of checks, go to https://aws.amazon.com/premiumsupport/technology/trusted-advisor/best-practice-checklist/.

Amazon Redshift Reserved Instance pricing

Amazon Redshift Reserved Instance pricing is a billing construct that results in significant savings for on-demand clusters that are utilized 24x7. To get large discounts on the clusters for your data warehouse workload, you can reserve your instances. Once you have determined the size and number of clusters for your workload, you can purchase **Reserved Instances (RIs)** for discounts from 34% to 75% compared to on-demand pricing.

RIs can be purchased using full upfront, partial upfront, or sometimes no upfront payment plans. RIs can be purchased for up to 1 or 3 years. They are not tied to a particular cluster; they can be pooled across clusters in your account. The following representative chart shows the significant cost optimization you can get by using RI pricing for 1 year or 3 years for different instances:

Instance Type	Storage/Node	Memory	CPUs	Disk Type	RI Discount*	
					1 Year	3 Years
RA3 4xlarge	Scales to 64 TB	96 GB	12	RMS (SSD+S3)	34%	63%
RA3 16xlarge	Scales to 64 TB	384 GB	48	RMS (SSD+S3)	34%	63%
DC2 large	160 GB	16 GB	2	SSD	37%	62%
DC2 8xlarge	2.56 TB	244 GB	32	SSD	34%	69%

Figure 8.5 – Representative RI savings

Please see https://aws.amazon.com/redshift/pricing/ for the latest pricing and savings recommendations.

Getting ready

To complete this recipe, you will need the following:

- An IAM user with access to Amazon Redshift, AWS Billing, and AWS Cost Explorer
- An Amazon Redshift cluster deployed in AWS Region eu-west-1

How to do it...

In this recipe, we will use Cost Explorer to see the significant cost savings we can gain by using RIs for an existing on-demand cluster. Then, using the Amazon Redshift console, we will dive into how to purchase reserved nodes. Let's get started:

1. Navigate to the AWS Management Console and select **Cost Explorer**.

2. On the left-hand side, choose **Recommendations** under **Reservation**. By selecting **1 year** for **RI term** with **All upfront** as your **Payment option**, the pricing will result in 34% savings compared to using on-demand clusters:

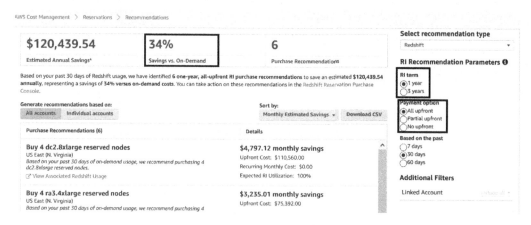

Figure 8.6 – AWS cost optimization recommendations

3. Now, let's see the benefits of cost savings when setting **RI term** to **3 years**. Here, the upfront results in significant cost savings of 65% compared to on-demand pricing:

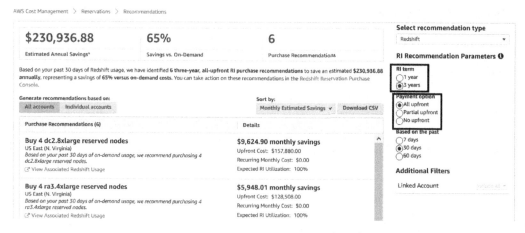

Figure 8.7 – AWS cost optimization benefits

4. To purchase the reserved nodes, navigate to the Amazon Redshift console. Choose **Clusters** and then select **Reserved nodes**:

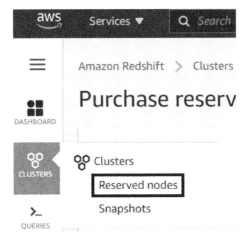

Figure 8.8 – Purchasing RIs

5. Choose the instance types you want to use and the RI term, which will either be **1 year** or **3 years**:

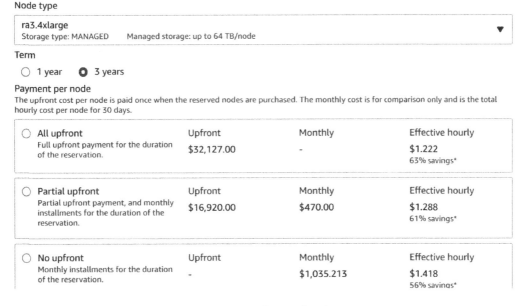

Figure 8.9 – RI plans and savings

6. Enter the number of nodes you need, check the acknowledgement checkbox, and select **Purchase reserved nodes**. Once you have purchased these reserved nodes, your billing will reflect your cost savings:

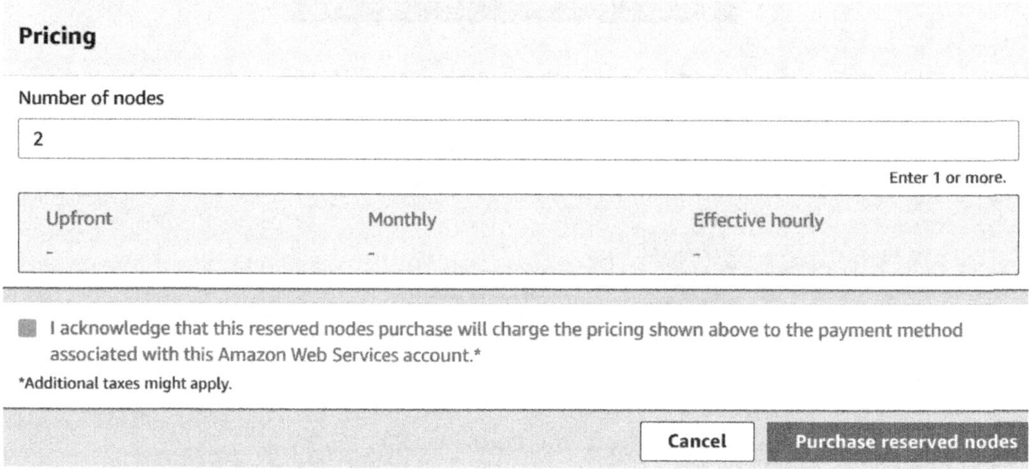

Pricing

Number of nodes

2

Enter 1 or more.

Upfront	Monthly	Effective hourly
–	–	–

☐ I acknowledge that this reserved nodes purchase will charge the pricing shown above to the payment method associated with this Amazon Web Services account.*

*Additional taxes might apply.

Cancel   **Purchase reserved nodes**

Figure 8.10 – Purchase reserved nodes

> **Note**
> You can refer to the different RI pricing options for Amazon Redshift at the following links:
>
> https://docs.aws.amazon.com/redshift/latest/mgmt/purchase-reserved-node-instance.html
>
> https://aws.amazon.com/redshift/pricing/

Configuring pause and resume for an Amazon Redshift cluster

Customers generally have a set of development, test, and production workloads. Here, production workloads must be up and running 24x7. The same can't be said for the development and test workloads. To make cost-conscious decisions, customers can use the pause and resume feature within Amazon Redshift to only resume for the development and test clusters when they are in use, and then pause them when they're not in use. Customers can perform this action on-demand or even schedule this for a specific interval.

Getting ready

To complete this recipe, you will need the following:

- An IAM user with access to Amazon Redshift

- An Amazon Redshift cluster deployed in AWS Region eu-west-1

How to do it...

In this recipe, you will learn how to pause and resume the Amazon Redshift cluster using the AWS Console. Let's get started:

1. Open the Amazon Redshift console: `https://console.aws.amazon.com/redshiftv2/home`.

2. Select the cluster that you would like to pause. Then, click on **Actions** and select **Pause**, as shown in the following screenshot:

Figure 8.11 – Selecting your cluster from the Amazon Redshift console

3. In the **Pause cluster** window, you have multiple options:

- **Pause now**: This option allows you to perform the pause operation on-demand.

- **Pause later**: This option allows you to perform the pause operation at a particular date and time.

- **Pause and resume on schedule**: This option allows you to perform the pause and resume operations on a given schedule.

We will review pausing the cluster on-demand here. Select the **Pause now** category and click on the **Pause now** button to start the pause operation:

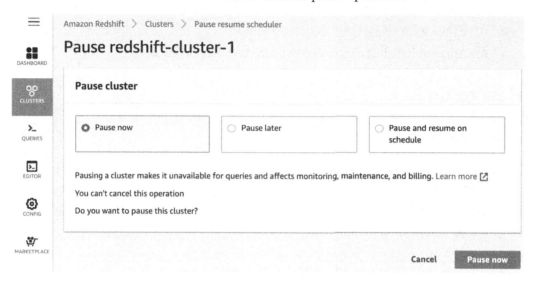

Figure 8.12 – Pausing the cluster

4. To verify that the cluster was paused successfully, go to the **CLUSTERs** tab and review the **Status** details provided:

Figure 8.13 – Verifying that the cluster has been paused

5. Select the cluster that you would like to pause, click on **Actions**, and select **Resume**:

Figure 8.14 – Resuming the cluster

6. In the **Resume cluster** window, you have multiple options:

-   **Resume now**: This option allows you to perform the resume operation on-demand.

-   **Resume later**: This option allows you to perform the resume operation at
    a particular date and time.

-   **Resume and pause on schedule**: This option allows you to perform the pause and
    resume operations on a given schedule.

    We will review resuming the cluster on-demand here. Select the **Resume now**
    category and click on the **Resume now** button to start the resume operation:

Amazon Redshift > Clusters > Pause resume scheduler

Resume redshift-cluster-1

Resume cluster

| ● Resume now | ○ Resume later | ○ Resume and pause on schedule |

Are you sure you want to resume the cluster redshift-cluster-1?

Cancel   **Resume now**

Figure 8.15 – Resuming the cluster

7. To verify that the cluster is resumed successfully, go to the **CLUSTER** tab and review the **Status** details provided:

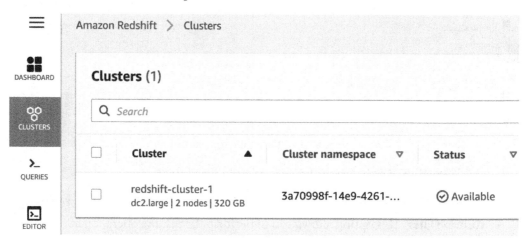

Figure 8.16 – Verifying that the cluster has been resumed (available)

> **Note**
>
> The pause and resume operations can also be performed using the Redshift API or SDK (`https://docs.aws.amazon.com/redshift/latest/APIReference/API_Operations.html`). This allows you to automate your operational tasks easily. For example, you can pause your development/test cluster when it's not in use during non-business hours.

Scheduling pause and resume

Using the Amazon Redshift console, customers can schedule when the cluster will be paused and resumed. For example, you can ensure that the cluster is only used for development during normal business hours.

Getting ready

To complete this recipe, you will need the following:

- An IAM user with access to Amazon Redshift.

- An IAM role, `Chapter8RedshiftSchedulerRole`, that can schedule the pause and resume operations for a Redshift cluster.

- An Amazon Redshift cluster deployed in AWS Region eu-west-1.

How to do it...

In the recipe, you will learn how to pause and resume the Amazon Redshift cluster on a schedule. Let's get started:

1. Open the Amazon Redshift console: `https://console.aws.amazon.com/redshiftv2/home`.

2. Select the cluster that you would like to pause. Then, click on **Actions** and select **Pause**, as shown in the following screenshot:

Figure 8.17 – Selecting your cluster from the Amazon Redshift console

3. To create a schedule for pause and resume, in the **Pause cluster** window, select **Pause and resume on schedule**. Provide a **Schedule name** and **Description**:

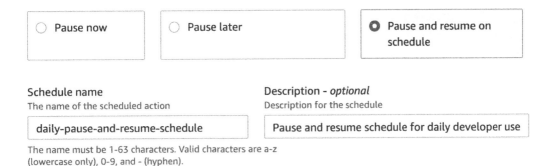

Figure 8.18 – Creating a schedule for pause and resume

4. For this schedule, the **Starts on** and **Ends on** dates that should be applied. In the **Editor** window, you can choose **Week**, **Day**, or **Month** for the pause and resume schedule:

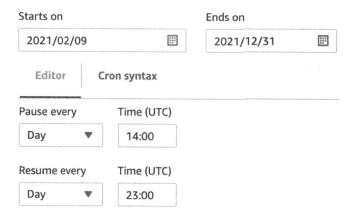

Figure 8.19 – Picking a time to pause and resume

5. In the **Scheduler permissions** section, you will need to select the pre-created **IAM role** from the dropdown. We can use this to perform the modify operation on the Redshift cluster and call the Redshift scheduler. Finally, click on the **Schedule recurring pause and resume** button to schedule the operation:

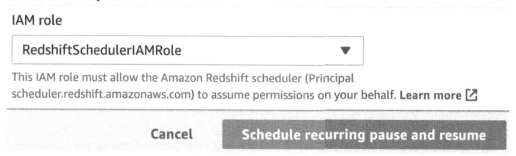

Figure 8.20 – Providing permissions to perform the pause and resume operation

How it works...

When you pause a cluster, a snapshot is created, queries are terminated, and the cluster enters the paused state. From a pricing perspective, on-demand billing is suspended for that cluster, and only the storage incurs charges. When you resume the cluster, it creates a cluster from the snapshot that was taken during the pause operation.

Configuring Elastic Resize for an Amazon Redshift cluster

The analytics workload requirements for enterprises change over time. Resizing makes it easy to scale the workload up or down, and even change to newer instance classes with a few clicks. Elastic Resize is a mechanism that's used to add nodes, remove nodes, and change node types for an existing Amazon Redshift cluster.

Getting ready

To complete this recipe, you will need the following:

- An IAM user with access to Amazon Redshift
- An Amazon Redshift cluster deployed in AWS Region eu-west-1

How to do it...

In this recipe, you will learn how to scale an existing Redshift cluster on demand. Let's get started:

1. Open the Amazon Redshift console: `https://console.aws.amazon.com/redshiftv2/home`.

2. Select **redshift-cluster-1**, click **Actions**, and select **Resize**:

Figure 8.21 – Cluster management for the Resize option

3. In the **Resize cluster** window, you can select **Elastic Resize** or **Classic Resize**. Here, we will select **Elastic Resize**:

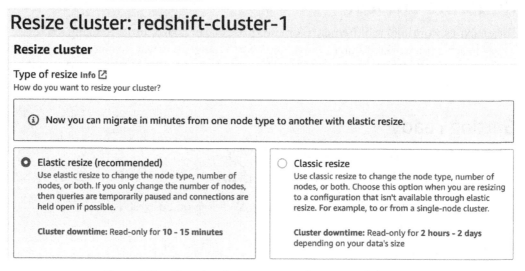

Figure 8.22 – Choosing the Elastic resize (recommended) option

4. On the same page, you can view your **Current cluster configuration** and what your **New cluster configuration** will be. Select a new node type from the **Node type** dropdown and selecting the number of nodes from the **Nodes** dropdown.

    Here, we are moving from our 2-node `dc.large` existing cluster to a 2-node `ra3.xlplus` cluster:

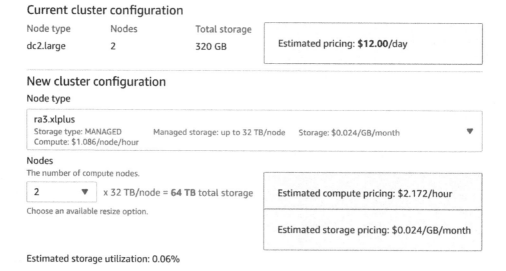

Figure 8.23 – Verifying the current and target sizing options

5. For the resize options, you can choose **Resize the cluster now**, **Schedule resize at a later time** or **Schedule recurring resize events**. For on-demand resizing, select **Resize the cluster now** and click the **Resize cluster now** button. This will start the resize operation immediately:

Figure 8.24 – Initiating the elastic resize operation

6. To monitor the resize operation, go to the **EVENTS** tab on the Redshift home screen: `https://console.aws.amazon.com/redshiftv2/home?#events`. This page will show the steps that were taken to resize the cluster:

Figure 8.25 – Monitoring the elastic resizing

7. To validate the new configuration, go to the **CLUSTER** tab and review the cluster details:

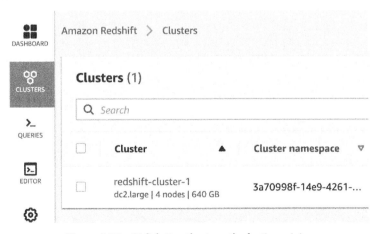

Figure 8.26 – Validating the target's elastic resizing

Scheduling Elastic Resizing

Although we've reviewed the on-demand resize operations that satisfy most use cases, there are times when customers are interested in scheduling a resize operation based on their business requirements. For example, you might want to upsize your cluster before starting your scheduled extract, transform and load process to satisfy any SLA needs.

Getting ready

To complete this recipe, you will need the following:

- An IAM user with access to Amazon Redshift
- An IAM role, `Chapter8RedshiftSchedulerRole`, that can schedule elastic resizing for a Redshift cluster
- An Amazon Redshift cluster deployed in AWS Region eu-west-1

How to do it...

In this recipe, you will learn how to elastic resize the existing Redshift cluster using a schedule:

1. Open the Amazon Redshift console: `https://console.aws.amazon.com/redshiftv2/home`.

2. Select the cluster, click **Actions**, and select **Resize**:

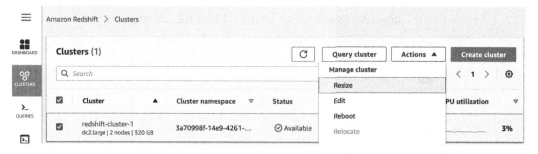

Figure 8.27 – Cluster management

3. Select the **Schedule recurring resize events** option to repeat the upsize/downsize operation based on a schedule:

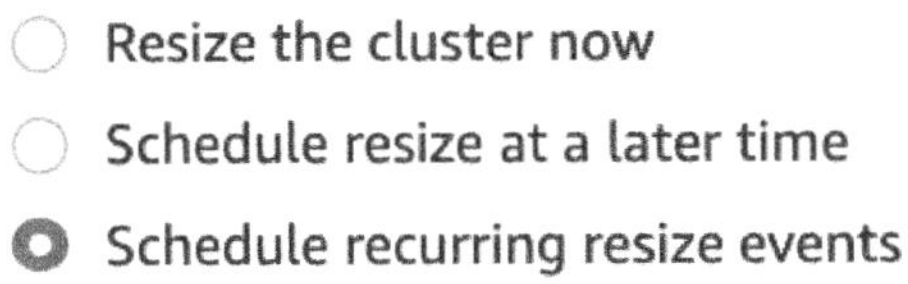

○ Resize the cluster now

○ Schedule resize at a later time

◉ Schedule recurring resize events

Figure 8.28 – Creating a recurring resize event

4. Under the **Schedule resize** section, enter the name of the schedule under **Schedule name**. Then, enter the dates when this schedule needs to start and stop by entering them into **Starts on** and **Ends on**. Now, you can select when and how the cluster configuration needs to change by selecting a **Node type**, **Number of nodes**, and editing the **Increase size every** section.

For example, here, we want to scale the workload up to **4** nodes on day of 25 of every month to manage the end of month reporting workload. Then, we want to scale it back down to **2** nodes at the start of every month:

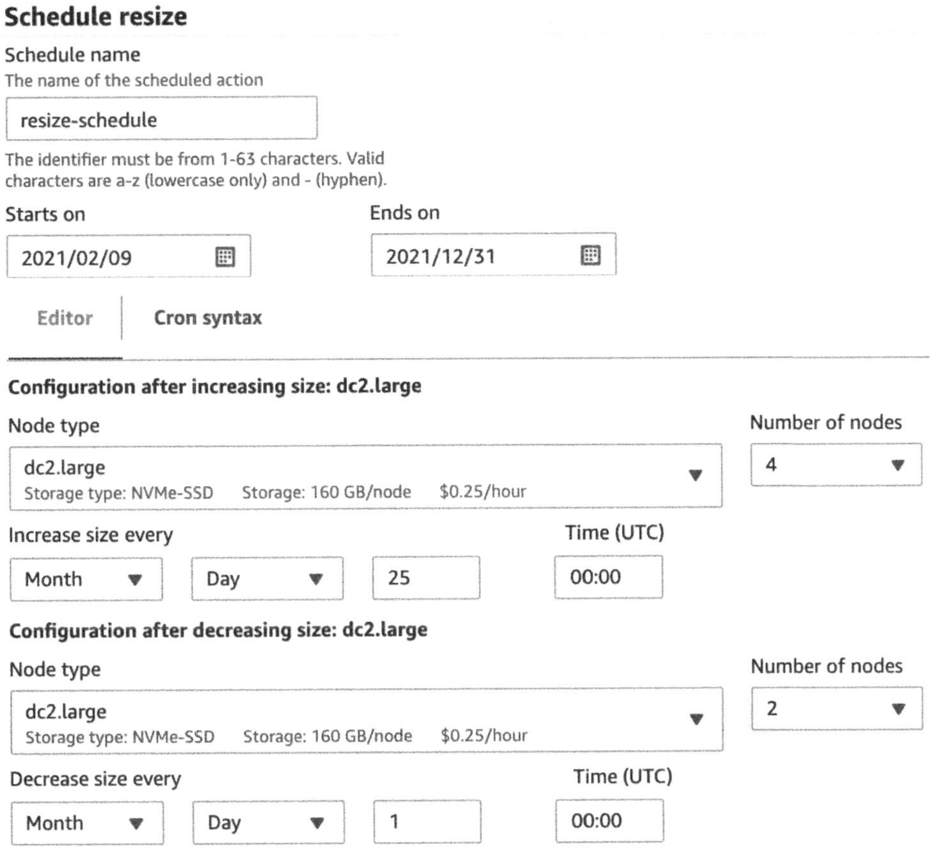

Schedule resize

Schedule name
The name of the scheduled action

    resize-schedule

The identifier must be from 1-63 characters. Valid characters are a-z (lowercase only) and - (hyphen).

Starts on

    2021/02/09

Ends on

    2021/12/31

Editor | **Cron syntax**

Configuration after increasing size: dc2.large

Node type

    dc2.large
    Storage type: NVMe-SSD   Storage: 160 GB/node $0.25/hour

Number of nodes

    4

Increase size every

    Month   Day   25

Time (UTC)

    00:00

Configuration after decreasing size: dc2.large

Node type

    dc2.large
    Storage type: NVMe-SSD   Storage: 160 GB/node $0.25/hour

Number of nodes

    2

Decrease size every

    Month   Day   1

Time (UTC)

    00:00

Figure 8.29 – Creating an elastic resize (upsize and downsize) schedule

5. In the **Scheduler permissions** section, select the pre-created IAM role from the dropdown. Here, you can resize on the Redshift cluster and call the Redshift scheduler. Finally, click the **Schedule resize** button to schedule the elastic resize operation.

   Here, we are selecting an IAM role from the dropdown called **RedshiftSchedulerIAMRole**, which was pre-created with the correct access:

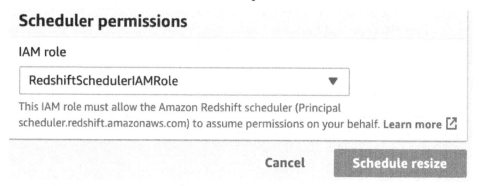

Figure 8.30 – Selecting RedshiftSchedularIAMRole for scheduling the elastic resize operation

6. Validate that the resize operation has been created by clicking on your cluster from the main **CLUSTER** option and selecting the **Schedule** tab. The resize operations will be listed under the **Resize schedule** section:

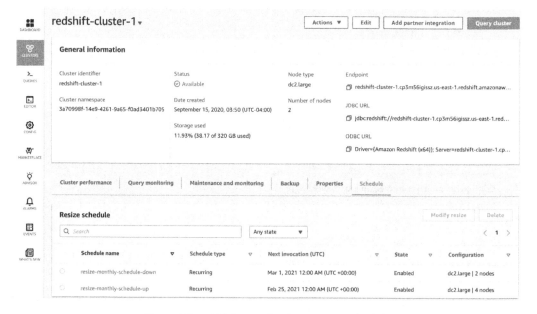

Figure 8.31 – Validating the elastic resize schedule

How it works...

Amazon Elastic Resize takes around 10-15 minutes to complete. During this time, the cluster is in read-only mode. When changing the node count but keeping the node type the same, the data gets redistributed at the backend, the queries are momentarily paused, and any connections are held open. When changing the node type, the operation creates a new cluster from a snapshot, and the open connections are terminated.

Using cost controls to set actions for Redshift Spectrum

Amazon Redshift allows you to extend your data warehouse to a data lake by performing SQL queries directly on data on Amazon S3. You will be charged based on the number of bytes that's scanned by Redshift Spectrum, rounded up to the next megabyte, with a 10 MB minimum per query (`https://aws.amazon.com/redshift/pricing/#Redshift_Spectrum_pricing`). There are no charges for **Data Definition Language** (**DDL**) statements such as CREATE/ALTER/DROP TABLE for managing partitions and failed queries.

In this recipe, you will learn how to use cost controls when using Amazon Redshift Spectrum.

Getting ready

To complete this recipe, you will need the following:

- An IAM user with access to Amazon Redshift
- An Amazon Redshift cluster deployed in AWS Region eu-west-1

How to do it...

In this recipe, you will set up controls for Amazon Redshift Spectrum usage to prevent any accidental scans being performed by a monstrous query. Let's get started:

1. Navigate to the AWS Amazon Redshift console and navigate to **Amazon Redshift > Clusters** > *your Amazon Redshift cluster*. Click on the **Properties** tab and scroll down to **Database configurations**, as shown in the following screenshot:

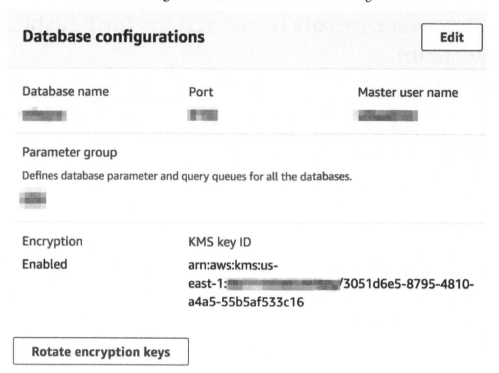

Figure 8.32 – Selecting the parameter group associated with the Amazon Redshift cluster

Click on the parameter group associated with the cluster.

2. Click on **Edit workload queues** and then **Add custom rule**, as shown in the following screenshot:

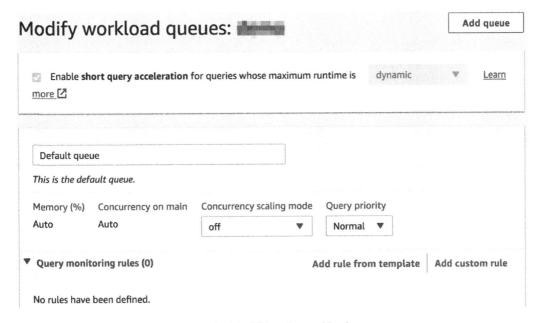

Figure 8.33 – Modifying the workload queues

For a step-by-step guide on setting up workload management, please refer to the *Managing workload management (WLM)* recipe in *Chapter 7, Performance Optimization*. You cannot edit the default parameter groups, so you must create a custom parameter group to edit the queues and monitoring rules associated with your cluster.

3. Type in any rule names (any user-friendly names) and the dropdown next to the predicates and select **Spectrum scan (MB)**. Select > from the next dropdown and **100,000,000** as the value. Then, for **Actions**, select **abort** and press **Save**:

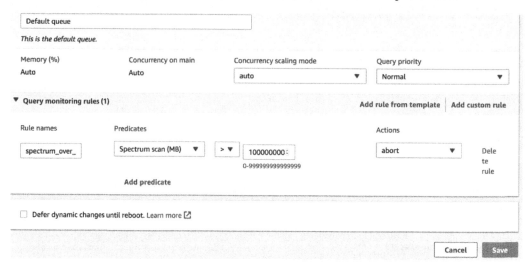

Figure 8.34 – Adding a custom query monitoring rule for Spectrum

Amazon Redshift will now abort any query that scans data that's over 100 TB in size, and you will not be charged for any queries that were aborted. This prevents any user from accidentally scanning a large amount of data from your data warehouse.

4. Now, let's create some cost controls at the Amazon Redshift cluster level. Navigate to **Amazon Redshift** > **Clusters** > your cluster, as shown in the following screenshot, and click on **Edit**:

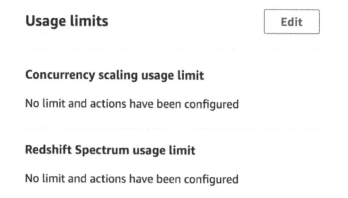

Figure 8.35 – Configuring your Redshift Spectrum usage limit

5. Click on **Configure usage limit**. It should correspond with your **Redshift Spectrum usage limit**, as shown in the following screenshot:

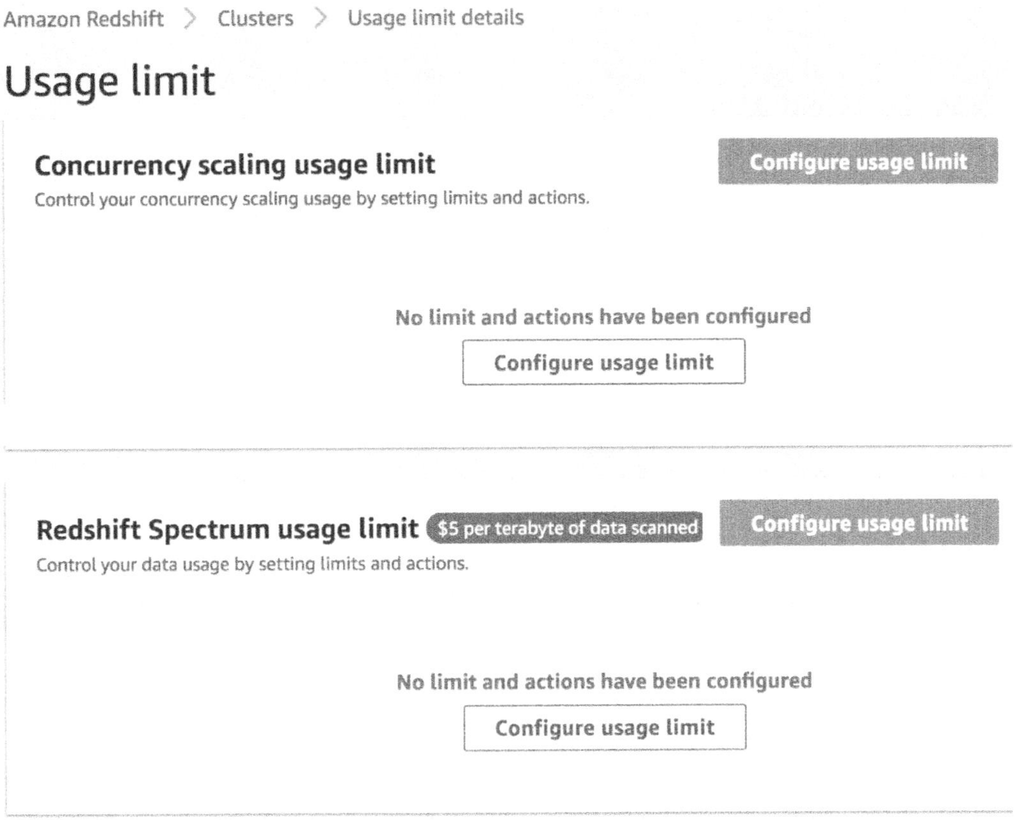

Amazon Redshift > Clusters > Usage limit details

Usage limit

Concurrency scaling usage limit
Control your concurrency scaling usage by setting limits and actions.

Configure usage limit

No limit and actions have been configured

Configure usage limit

Redshift Spectrum usage limit $5 per terabyte of data scanned
Control your data usage by setting limits and actions.

Configure usage limit

No limit and actions have been configured

Configure usage limit

Figure 8.36 – Configuring your limits and actions for Spectrum

7. For **Time period**, select **Monthly** and for **Usage limit (TB)**, enter 1000, as follows:

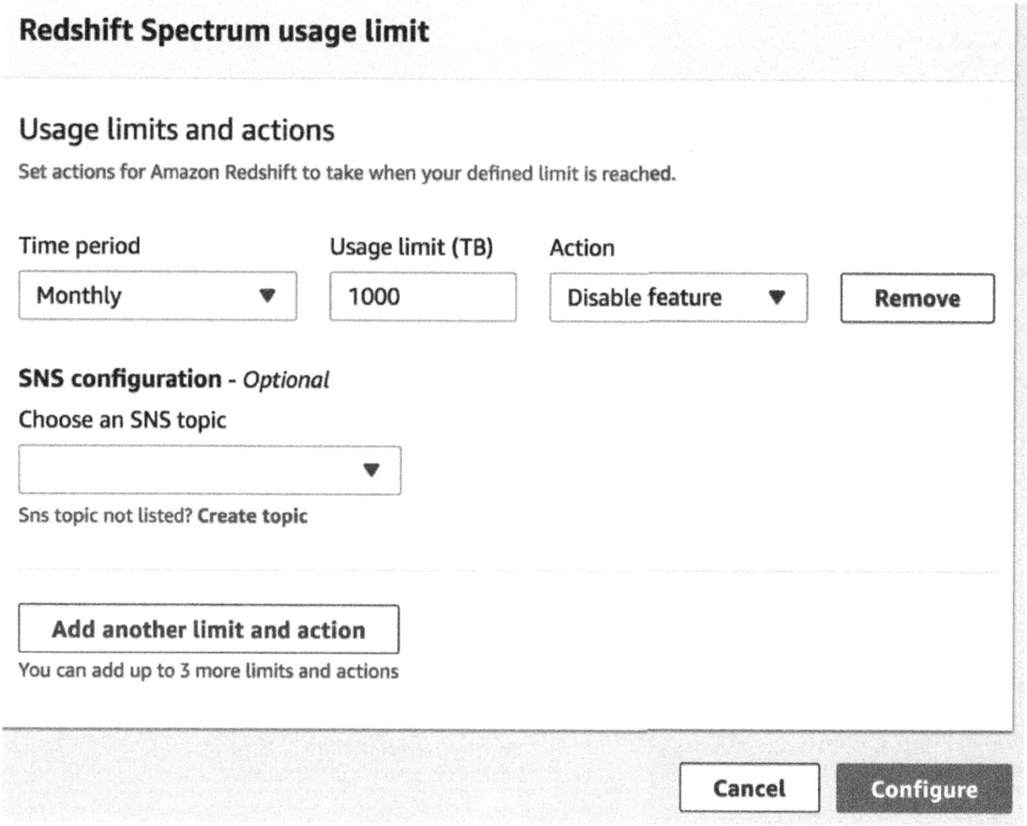

Redshift Spectrum usage limit

Usage limits and actions

Set actions for Amazon Redshift to take when your defined limit is reached.

Time period	Usage limit (TB)	Action	
Monthly ▼	1000	Disable feature ▼	Remove

SNS configuration - *Optional*

Choose an SNS topic

[▼]

Sns topic not listed? **Create topic**

[**Add another limit and action**]

You can add up to 3 more limits and actions

Cancel   Configure

Figure 8.37 – Setting up monthly limits for Spectrum usage

Now, the Amazon Redshift Spectrum feature is disabled when the monthly limit of 1,000 TB of data scanned is exceeded.

Using cost controls to set actions for Concurrency Scaling

Amazon Redshift Concurrency Scaling adds transient clusters to support concurrent user queries. Concurrency Scaling is charged at a per-second, on-demand rate for a Concurrency Scaling cluster in excess of the free credits that have been applied, but only when it's serving your queries. It provides a 1-minute minimum charge each time a Concurrency Scaling cluster is activated. You can accumulate 1 hour of Concurrency Scaling cluster credits every 24 hours while your main cluster is running, which expires every month. In this recipe, we will learn how to manage costs for Concurrency Scaling to avoid any unexpected surprises. Please also see `https://aws.amazon.com/redshift/pricing/#Concurrency_Scaling_pricing` for more details.

Getting ready

To complete this recipe, you will need the following:

- An IAM user with access to Amazon Redshift
- An Amazon Redshift cluster deployed in AWS Region eu-west-1

How to do it...

In the recipe, you will set up controls for Concurrency Scaling usage on your Amazon Redshift cluster. Let's get started:

1. Navigate to **Amazon Redshift** > **Clusters** > *your cluster*, as shown here. Then, click on **Edit** next to **Usage limits**:

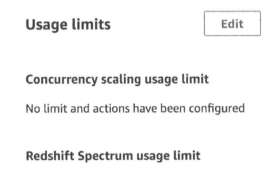

Figure 8.38 – Configuring your Redshift Spectrum usage limit

2. Click on **Configure usage limit** to edit it so that it corresponds to your **Concurrent scaling usage limit**, as shown in the following screenshot:

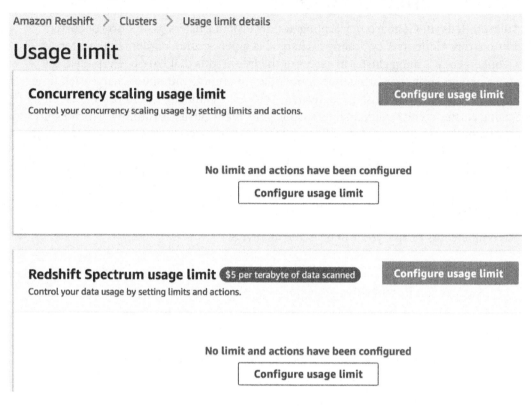

Figure 8.39 – Configuring the limits and actions for Spectrum

3. For **Time period**, select **Monthly** and for **Usage Limit (hh:mm)**, enter 3 0, as follows:

Amazon Redshift > Clusters > Configure usage limit

Configure usage limit

Configure usage

☑ Concurrency scaling   ☐ Redshift Spectrum

Concurrency scaling usage limit

ⓘ You can accumulate **one hour** of concurrency scaling cluster credits every 24 hours while your cluster is running

Usage limits and actions

Set actions for Amazon Redshift to take when your defined limit is reached.

Time period	Usage limit (hh:mm)	Action	
Monthly ▼	30	0	Disable feature ▼	Remove

SNS configuration - *Optional*

Choose an SNS topic

| ▼ |

Sns topic not listed? **Create topic**

| **Add another limit and action** |

You can add up to 3 more limits and actions

| Cancel | Configure |

Figure 8.40 – Setting up monthly limits for Concurrency Scaling usage

Now, the Amazon Redshift Concurrency Scaling feature will be disabled when the monthly limit is in excess of 30 hours.

In addition to disabling Concurrency Scaling when exceeding limits on your cluster, you can also limit the number of concurrent clusters that are spun up using the max_concurrency_scaling_clusters parameter, which we covered in *Chapter 7, Performance Optimization*.

9
Lake House Architecture

The lake house is an architectural pattern that makes data easily accessible across customers' analytics solutions, thereby preventing data silos. **Amazon Redshift** is the backbone of the lake house architecture—it allows enterprise customers to query data across data lakes, operational databases, and multiple data warehouses to build an analytics solution without having to move data in and out of these different systems. In this chapter, you will learn how you can leverage the lake house architecture to extend the data warehouse to services outside Amazon Redshift to build your solution, while taking advantage of the built-in integration. For example, you can use the Federated Query capability to join the operational data in your relational systems to historical data in Amazon Redshift to analyze a promotional trend.

The following recipes are discussed in this chapter:

- Building a data lake catalog using **Amazon Web Services** (**AWS**) Lake Formation
- Exporting a data lake from Amazon Redshift
- Extending a data warehouse using Amazon Redshift Spectrum
- Data sharing across multiple Amazon Redshift clusters
- Querying operational sources using Federated Query

Technical requirements

Here are the technical requirements in order to complete the recipes in this chapter:

- Access to the AWS Management Console.

- AWS administrators should create an **Identity and Access Management (IAM)** user by following *Recipe 1 – Creating an IAM user* in the *Appendix*. This IAM user will be deployed to perform some of the recipes in this chapter.

- AWS administrators should create an IAM role by following *Recipe 3 – Creating an IAM Role for an AWS service* in the *Appendix*. This IAM role will be deployed to perform some of the recipes in this chapter.

- AWS administrators should deploy the AWS CloudFormation template (`https://github.com/PacktPublishing/Amazon-Redshift-Cookbook/blob/master/Chapter09/chapter_9_CFN.yaml`) to create two IAM policies:

  a. An IAM policy attached to the IAM user that will give them access to Amazon Redshift, **Amazon Elastic Compute Cloud (Amazon EC2)**, **Amazon Simple Storage Service (Amazon S3)**, **Amazon Simple Notification Service (Amazon SNS)**, Amazon CloudWatch, Amazon CloudWatch Logs, **AWS Key Management Service (AWS KMS)**, AWS IAM, AWS CloudFormation, AWS CloudTrail, **Amazon Relational Database Service (Amazon RDS)**, AWS Lake Formation, AWS Secrets Manager, and AWS Glue

  b. An IAM policy attached to the IAM role that will allow the Amazon Redshift cluster to access Amazon S3, Amazon RDS, and AWS Glue

- Attach an IAM role to the Amazon Redshift cluster by following *Recipe 4 – Attaching an IAM Role to the Amazon Redshift cluster* in the *Appendix*. Make a note of the IAM role name—we will refer to this in the recipes as `[Your-Redshift_Role]`.

- An Amazon Redshift cluster deployed in the `eu-west-1` AWS Region.

- Amazon Redshift cluster masteruser credentials.

- Access to any **Structured Query Language (SQL)** interface such as a SQL client or the Amazon Redshift Query Editor.

- An AWS account number—we will refer to this in the recipes as `[Your-AWS_Account_Id]`.

- An Amazon S3 bucket created in the eu-west-1 Region. We will refer to this in the recipes as `[Your-Amazon_S3_Bucket]`.

- The code files are referenced in the GitHub repository at `https://github.com/PacktPublishing/Amazon-Redshift-Cookbook/tree/master/Chapter09`.

Building a data lake catalog using AWS Lake Formation

The data lake design pattern has been widely adopted in the industry. Data lakes help to break data silos by allowing you to store all of your data in a single, unified place. You can collect the data from different sources and data can arrive at different frequencies—for example, clickstream data. The data format can be structured, unstructured, or semi-structured. Analyzing a unified view of the data allows you to derive more value and helps to derive more insight from the data to drive business value.

Your data lake should be secure and should meet your compliance requirements, with a centralized catalog that allows you to search and easily find data that is stored in the lake. One of the advantages of data lakes is that you can run a variety of analytical tools against them. You may also want to do new types of analysis on your data. For example, you may want to move from answering questions on what happened in the past to what is happening in real time, and using statistical models and forecasting techniques to understand and answer what could happen in the future. To do this, you need to incorporate **machine learning** (**ML**), big data processing, and real-time analytics. The pattern that allows you to integrate your analytics into a data lake is the lake house architecture. Amazon S3 object storage is used for centralized data lakes due to its scalability, high availability, and durability.

You can see an overview of the lake house architecture here:

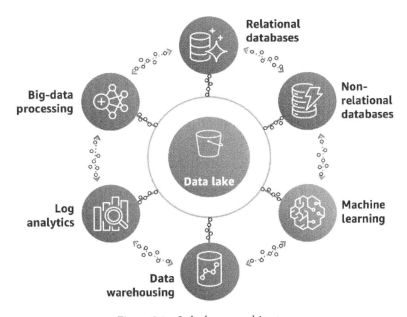

Figure 9.1 – Lake house architecture

Typical challenges and steps involved in building a data lake include the following:

- Identifying sources and defining the frequency with which the data lake needs to be hydrated

- Cleaning and cataloging the data

- Centralizing the configuration and application of security policies

- Integration of the data lake with analytical services that adhere to centralized security policies

Here is a representation of a lake house workflow moving data from raw format to analytics:

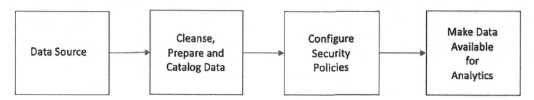

Figure 9.2 – Data workflow using the lake house architecture

The AWS Lake Formation service allows you to simplify the build, centralize management, and configure security policies. AWS Lake Formation leverages AWS Glue for cataloging, data ingestion, and data transformation.

In this recipe, you will learn how to use Lake Formation to hydrate the data lake from a relational database, catalog the data, and apply security policies.

Getting ready

To complete this recipe, you will need the following to be set up:

- An IAM user with access to Amazon RDS, Amazon S3, and AWS Lake Formation.

- An Amazon RDS MySQL database to create an RDS MySQL cluster (for more information, see https://aws.amazon.com/getting-started/hands-on/create-mysql-db/).

  In this recipe, the version of the **MySQL engine** is **5.7.31**.

- A command line to connect to RDS MySQL (for more information, see https://docs.aws.amazon.com/AmazonRDS/latest/UserGuide/USER_ConnectToInstance.html).

- This recipe is using an **AWS EC2 Linux** instance with a **MySQL command line**. Open the security group for the **RDS MySQL** database to allow connectivity from your client.

How to do it...

In this recipe, we will learn how to set up a data flow MySQL-based transactional database to be cataloged using a Lake Formation catalog and query it easily using Amazon Redshift:

1. Let's connect to the MySQLRDS database using the following command. Enter the password and it will connect you to the database:

   ```
   mysql -h [yourMySQLRDSEndPoint] -u admin -p
   ```

2. We will create an ods database on MySQL and create a parts table in the ods database:

   ```
   create database ods;
   CREATE TABLE ods.part
   (
       P_PARTKEY        BIGINT NOT NULL,
       P_NAME           VARCHAR(55),
       P_MFGR           VARCHAR(25),
       P_BRAND          VARCHAR(10),
       P_TYPE           VARCHAR(25),
       P_SIZE           INTEGER,
       P_CONTAINER      VARCHAR(10),
       P_RETAILPRICE    DECIMAL(18,4),
       P_COMMENT        VARCHAR(23)
   );
   ```

3. On your client server, download the part.tbl file from https://github.com/PacktPublishing/Amazon-Redshift-Cookbook/blob/master/Chapter09/part.tbl to your local disk.

4. Now, we will load this file into the ods.part table on the MySQL database. This will load 20000 records into the parts table:

   ```
   LOAD DATA LOCAL INFILE 'part.tbl'
       INTO TABLE ods.part
       FIELDS TERMINATED BY '|'
       LINES TERMINATED BY '\n';
   ```

5. Let's verify the record count loaded into the ods.part table:

```
MySQL [(none)]> select count(*) from ods.part;
+----------+
| count(*) |
+----------+
|    20000 |
+----------+
1 row in set (0.00 sec)
```

6. Navigate to **AWS Lake Formation** and click **Get started**:

Figure 9.3 – Navigating to Lake Formation

7. Now, let's set up the data lake location. Choose a register location:

Figure 9.4 – Data lake setup

8. Enter the location of the S3 bucket or folder in your account. If you do not have one, create a bucket on S3 in your account. Keep the default IAM role and click on **Register location**. With this, Lake Formation will manage the data lake location:

Register location

Amazon S3 location
Register an Amazon S3 path as the storage location for your data lake.

Amazon S3 path
Choose an Amazon S3 path for your data lake.

| s3://hsp-lake-formation | **Browse** |

Review location permissions - strongly recommended
Registering the selected location may result in your users gaining access to data already at that location. Before registering a location, we recommend that you review existing location permissions on resources in that location.

Review location permissions

IAM role
To add or update data, Lake Formation needs read/write access to the chosen Amazon S3 path. Choose a role that you know has permission to do this, or choose the **AWSServiceRoleForLakeFormationDataAccess** service-linked role. When you register the first Amazon S3 path, the service-linked role and a new inline policy are created on your behalf. Lake Formation adds the first path to the inline policy and attaches it to the service-linked role. When you register subsequent paths, Lake Formation adds the path to the existing policy.

| AWSServiceRoleForLakeFormationDataAccess   ▼ |

⚠ Do not select the service linked role if you plan to use EMR.

Figure 9.5 – Registering an Amazon S3 location in the data lake

9. Next, we will create a database that will serve as the catalog for the data in the data lake. Click on **Create database**, as shown here:

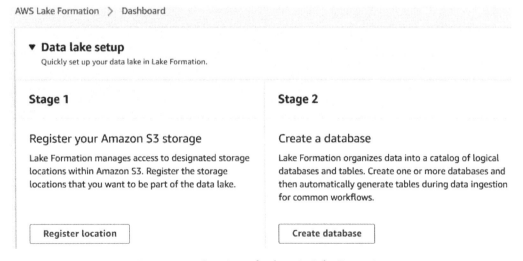

Figure 9.6 – Creating a database in Lake Formation

10. Use `cookbook-data-lake` as the database name. Select the `s3` path that you registered in AWS Lake Formation. Select the **Use only IAM access control for new tables in this database** checkbox. Click on **Create database**:

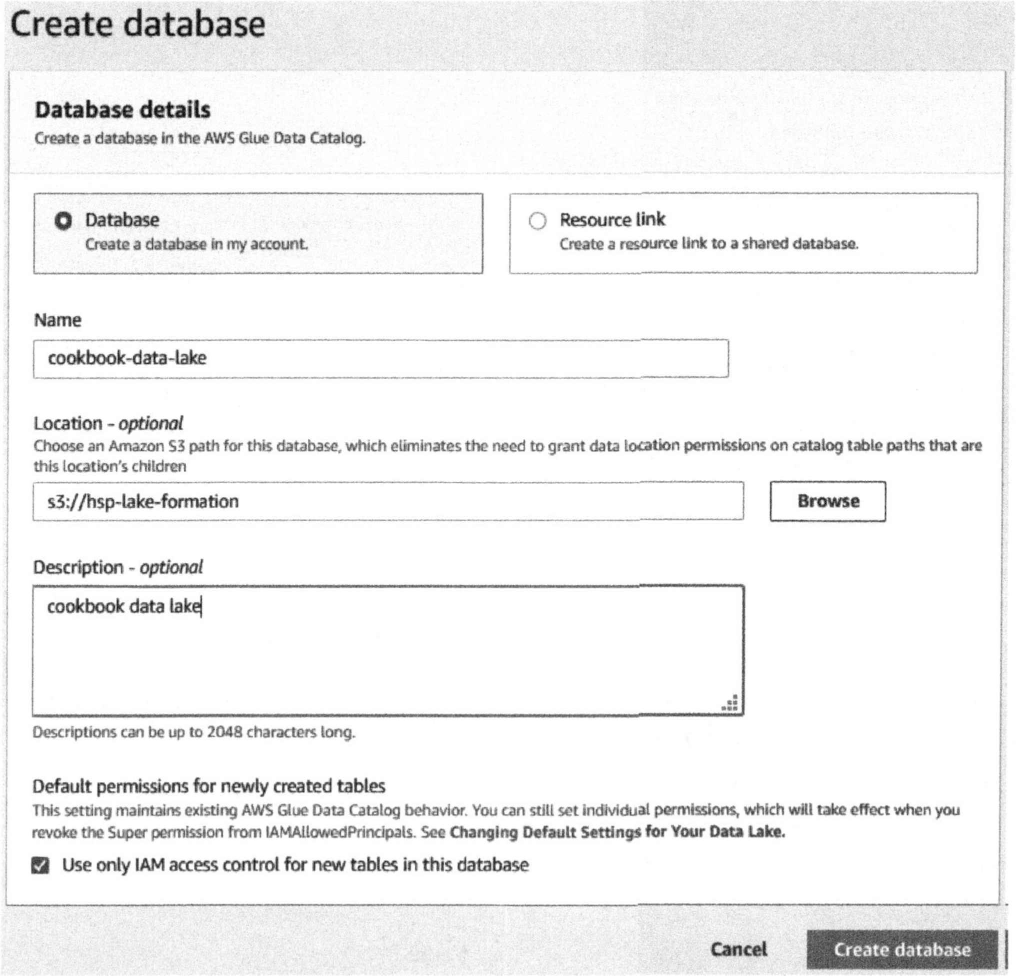

Create database

Database details
Create a database in the AWS Glue Data Catalog.

| ○ **Database**
 Create a database in my account. | ○ **Resource link**
 Create a resource link to a shared database. |

Name

> cookbook-data-lake

Location - optional
Choose an Amazon S3 path for this database, which eliminates the need to grant data location permissions on catalog table paths that are this location's children

> s3://hsp-lake-formation   **Browse**

Description - optional

> cookbook data lake

Descriptions can be up to 2048 characters long.

Default permissions for newly created tables
This setting maintains existing AWS Glue Data Catalog behavior. You can still set individual permissions, which will take effect when you revoke the Super permission from IAMAllowedPrincipals. See **Changing Default Settings for Your Data Lake.**

☑ Use only IAM access control for new tables in this database

Cancel   **Create database**

Figure 9.7 – Configuring the Lake Formation database

11. Now, we will hydrate the data lake from MySQL as the source. From the left menu, select **Blueprint**, and then click on **Create blueprint**.

12. Select **Database snapshot**, then right-click on **Create a connection in AWS Glue** to open a new tab:

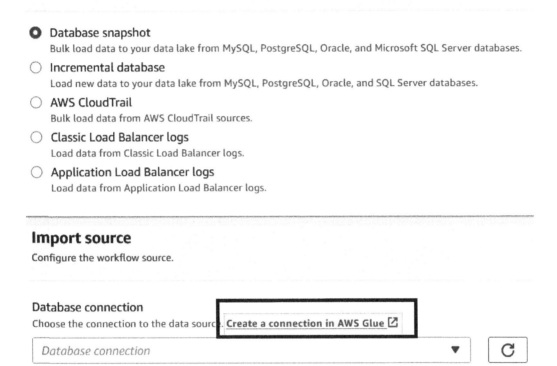

Blueprint type

Configure a blueprint to create a workflow.

⦿ Database snapshot
Bulk load data to your data lake from MySQL, PostgreSQL, Oracle, and Microsoft SQL Server databases.

○ Incremental database
Load new data to your data lake from MySQL, PostgreSQL, Oracle, and SQL Server databases.

○ AWS CloudTrail
Bulk load data from AWS CloudTrail sources.

○ Classic Load Balancer logs
Load data from Classic Load Balancer logs.

○ Application Load Balancer logs
Load data from Application Load Balancer logs.

Import source

Configure the workflow source.

Database connection
Choose the connection to the data source. **Create a connection in AWS Glue** ⧉

Database connection ▼   ↻

Figure 9.8 – Using a blueprint to create a database snapshot-based workflow

13. Set the following properties, as shown in *Figure 9.9*:

- **Connection name**—datalake-mysql
- **Connection type**—Amazon RDS
- **Database engine**—MySQL

14. Select **Next**:

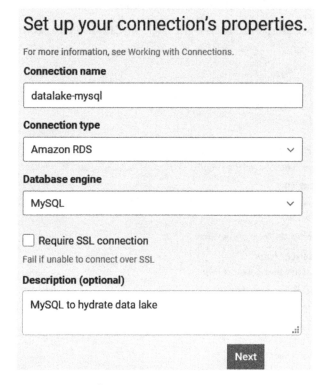

Figure 9.9 – Configuring Amazon RDS connection properties

15. Next, to set up access to your data store, set the following properties:

- Select an **Instance** name from the drop-down menu.

- **Database name**—ods.

- **Username**—admin.

- Enter the password you used to create the database.

16. Select **Next** and click **Finish**:

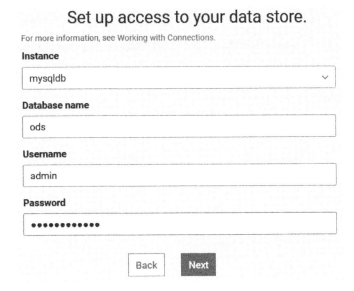

Figure 9.10 – Configuring the MySQL connection credentials

17. Select the `datalake-mysql` connection and select `TestConnection`. For the
    IAM role, use `AWSGlueServiceRole-cookbook`. Select `TestConnection`.
    This will take a few minutes. When it is successful, it will show a **connected
    successfully to your instance** message. If you run into issues with the connection
    setup, you can refer to the following **Uniform Resource Locator** (**URL**): `https://`
    `aws.amazon.com/premiumsupport/knowledge-center/glue-test-`
    `connection-failed/`.

    Once successfully connected, you will see a **connected successfully to your
    instance** message, as shown here:

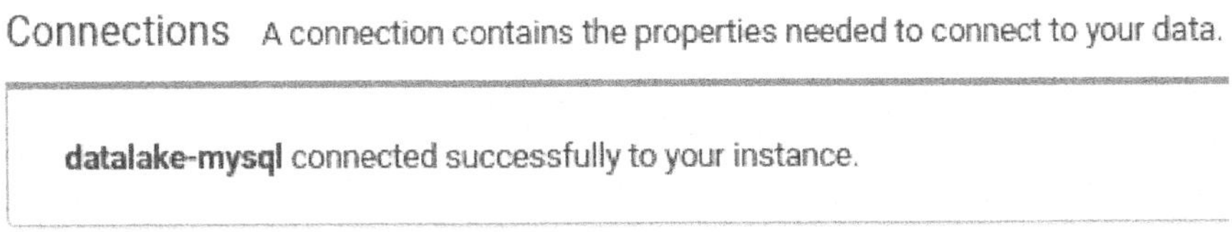

    Connections   A connection contains the properties needed to connect to your data.

    datalake-mysql connected successfully to your instance.

Figure 9.11 – Verifying a successful connection to the MySQL database

18. In AWS Lake Formation, set the following properties under **Create blueprint**:

a. For **Database connection**, from the drop-down menu select **datalake-mysql**.

b. For **Source data path**, enter ods/part:

Use a blueprint

Blueprint type
Configure a blueprint to create a workflow.

- ⦿ **Database snapshot**
  Bulk load data to your data lake from MySQL, PostgreSQL, Oracle, and Microsoft SQL Server databases.
- ○ **Incremental database**
  Load new data to your data lake from MySQL, PostgreSQL, Oracle, and SQL Server databases.
- ○ **AWS CloudTrail**
  Bulk load data from AWS CloudTrail sources.
- ○ **Classic Load Balancer logs**
  Load data from Classic Load Balancer logs.
- ○ **Application Load Balancer logs**
  Load data from Application Load Balancer logs.

Import source
Configure the workflow source.

Database connection
Choose the connection to the data source. **Create a connection in AWS Glue** [↗]

| datalake-mysql ▼ | C |

Source data path
Enter the path from which to ingest data. For JDBC databases with schema support, enter database/schema/table (case sensitive). Substitute the percent (%) wildcard for schema or table.

| ods/part |

Figure 9.12 – Using a blueprint to create a database snapshot-based workflow

19. For **Import target**, select **cookbook-data-lake** for the **Target database** field. For **Target location**, specify your bucket path with mysql as the folder. We will unload the data from MySQL in **Parquet** format:

Import target

Configure the target of the workflow.

Target database

Choose a database in the AWS Glue Data Catalog. **Create database** ⬀

| cookbook-data-lake ▼ | ⟳ |

Target storage location

Choose a data lake location or other Amazon S3 path.

| s3://hsp-lake-formation/mysql | Browse |

Data format

Choose the output data format.

| Parquet ▼ |

Figure 9.13 – Setting up the target for the data workflow

20. For **Import frequency**, select **Run on demand**:

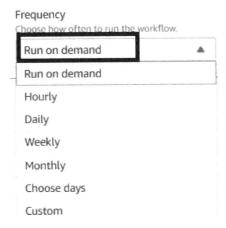

Import frequency

Schedule the workflow.

Frequency

Choose how often to run the workflow.

| Run on demand | ▲ |

Run on demand

Hourly

Daily

Weekly

Monthly

Choose days

Custom

Figure 9.14 – Configuring the import frequency for the workflow

21. For **Import options**, specify the name of the workflow as `hydrate-mysql`. Under **IAM role**, use `AWSGlueServiceRole-cookbook`. For **Table prefix**, use `mysql`. Select **Create**:

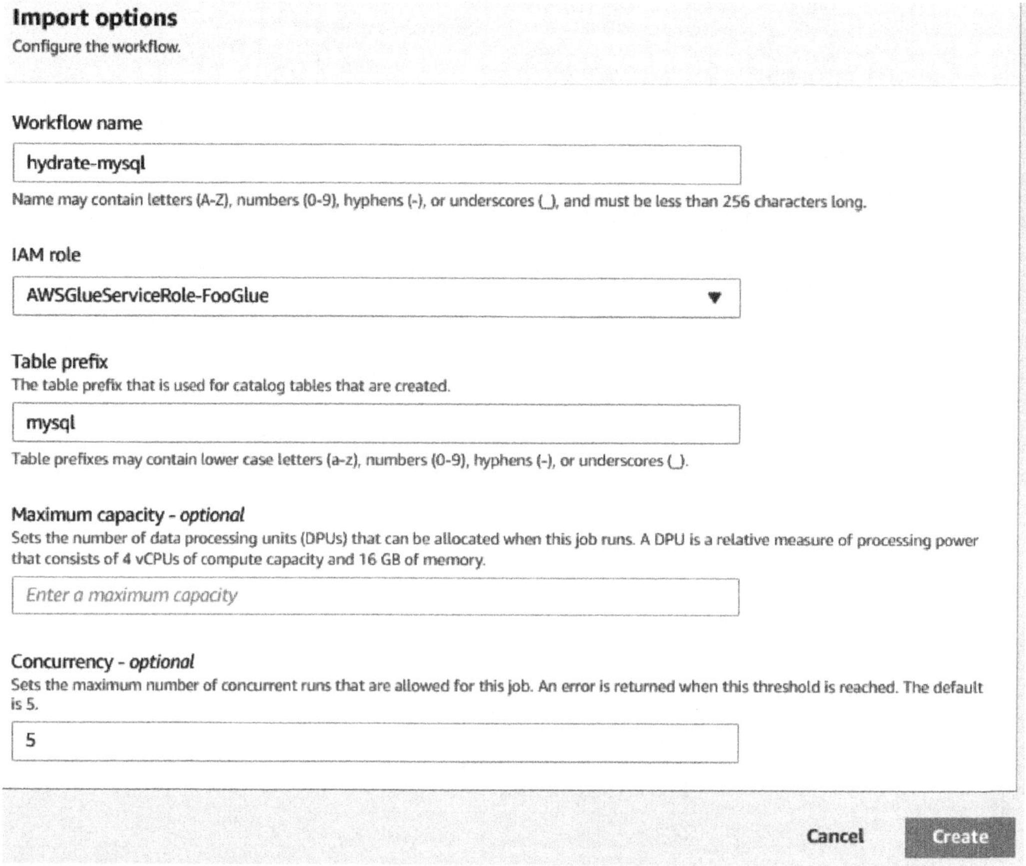

Import options
Configure the workflow.

Workflow name

hydrate-mysql

Name may contain letters (A-Z), numbers (0-9), hyphens (-), or underscores (_), and must be less than 256 characters long.

IAM role

AWSGlueServiceRole-FooGlue ▼

Table prefix
The table prefix that is used for catalog tables that are created.

mysql

Table prefixes may contain lower case letters (a-z), numbers (0-9), hyphens (-), or underscores (_).

Maximum capacity - *optional*
Sets the number of data processing units (DPUs) that can be allocated when this job runs. A DPU is a relative measure of processing power that consists of 4 vCPUs of compute capacity and 16 GB of memory.

Enter a maximum capacity

Concurrency - *optional*
Sets the maximum number of concurrent runs that are allowed for this job. An error is returned when this threshold is reached. The default is 5.

5

Cancel   Create

Figure 9.15 – Configuring import options for the workflow

22. When the workflow is created, select **Workflows**. Select **Actions** and start the workflow:

a. The workflow will crawl the `mysql` table metadata, which will catalog it in the `cookbook-data-lake` database.

b. It will then unload the data from the `mysql ods.part` table in Parquet format on the S3 location you provided.

c. Finally, it will crawl the Parquet data on S3 and create a table in the `cookbook-data-lake` database.

You can see an overview of this here:

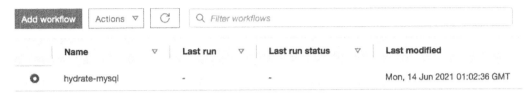

Figure 9.16 – Crawling the target S3 Parquet bucket

23. To view the status of the workflow, click on **Run Id**. Then, select **View graph**:

Figure 9.17 – Visualizing the data workflow

24. You can view the workflow steps and the corresponding status of the steps:

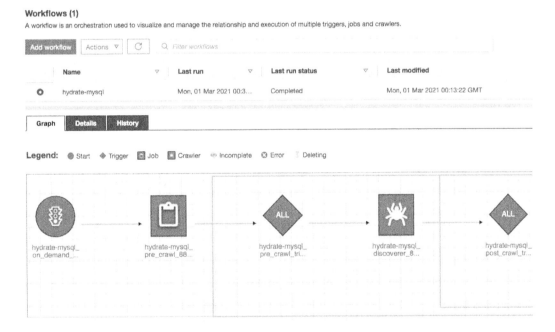

Figure 9.18 – Data workflow steps

25. On successful completion of the workflow, the **Last run status** field will be marked as **COMPLETED**:

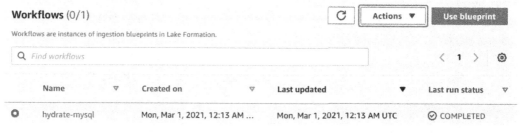

Figure 9.19 – Data workflow execution status

26. Let's now view the details of your first data lake. To view the tables created in your catalog, in the AWS Lake Formation console, from the left select **Databases**. Then, select `cookbook-data-lake`.

27. Select **View tables**:

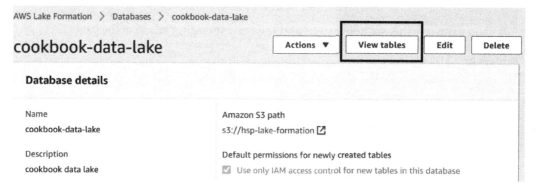

Figure 9.20 – Viewing tables created for the target

28. Let's verify the target dataset:

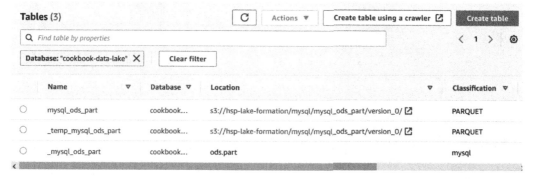

Figure 9.21 – Verifying the target dataset

29. To view the metadata of the Parquet unloaded data, select the `mysql_ods_part` table. This table is the metadata of the data. The crawler identified the column names and the corresponding data types:

Column #	Name ▽	Data type
1	p_container	string
2	p_mfgr	string
3	p_comment	string
4	p_size	int
5	p_partkey	bigint
6	p_retailprice	decimal(18,4)
7	p_name	string
8	p_type	string
9	p_brand	string

Figure 9.22 – Viewing metadata for the target

30. The classification is `PARQUET` and the table points to the location of `s3`, where the data resides:

Table details

Table name
mysql_ods_part

Description
-

Database
cookbook-data-lake

Classification
PARQUET

Location
s3://hsp-lake-formation/mysql/mysql_ods_part/version_0/

Figure 9.23 – Verifying the target table format

31. To view the unloaded files on S3, navigate to your S3 location:

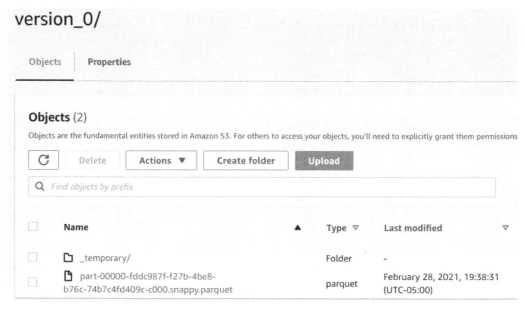

Figure 9.24 – Verifying the underlying Parquet files in Amazon S3

32. Going back to AWS Lake Formation, let's see how the permissions can be managed. In this step, we will use the mysql_ods_part table. Select the mysql_ods_part table, select **Actions**, and select **Grant**:

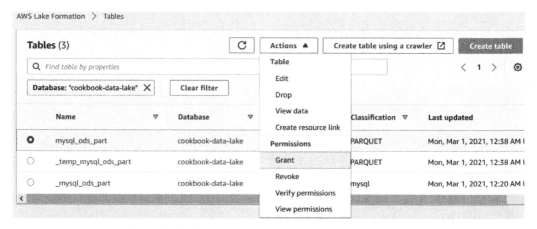

Figure 9.25 – Setting up permissions for the target dataset

33. AWS Lake Formation enables you to centralize the process of configuring access permissions to the IAM roles. Table-level and fine-grained access at column level can be granted and controlled from a centralized place:

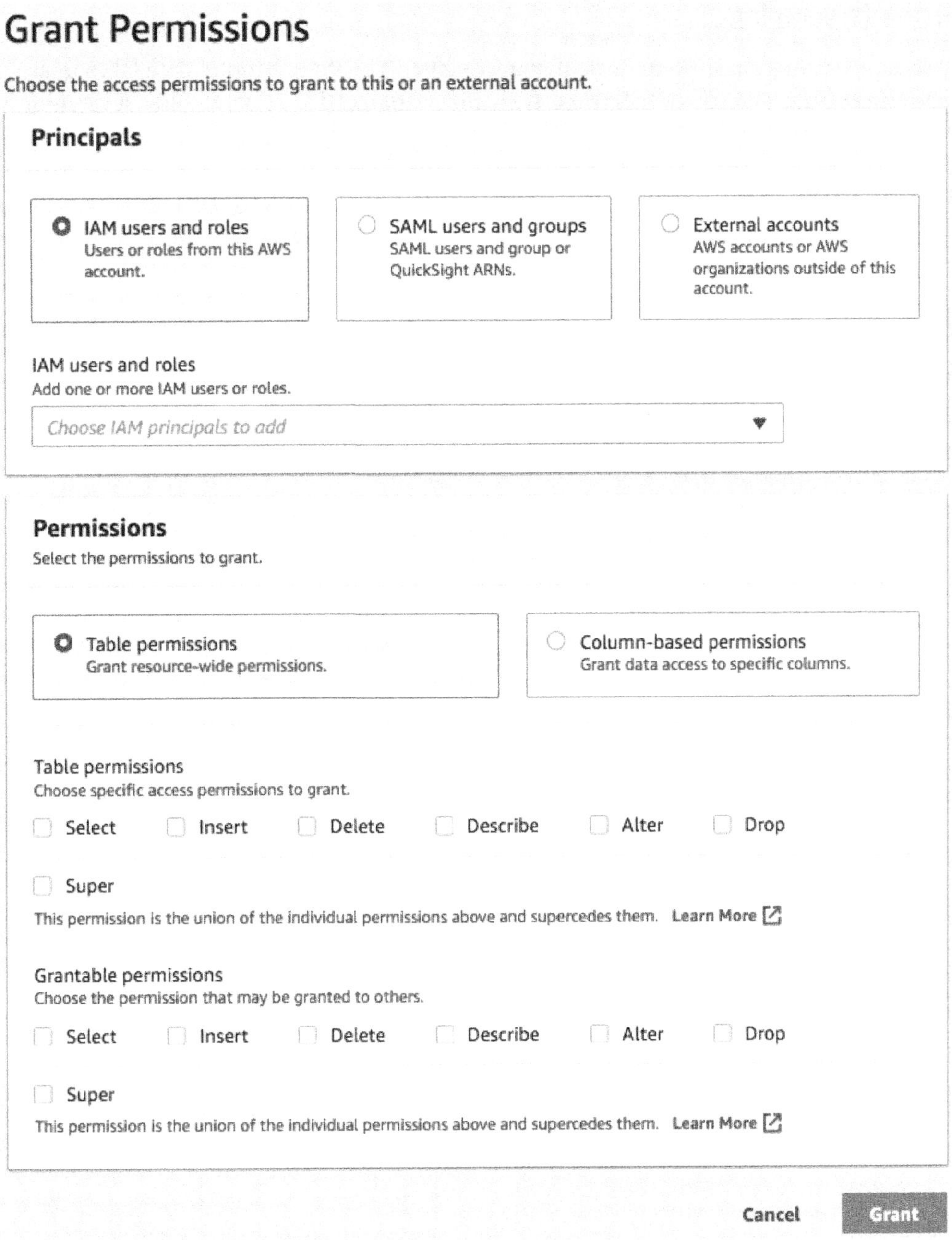

Grant Permissions

Choose the access permissions to grant to this or an external account.

Principals

○ **IAM users and roles**
Users or roles from this AWS account.

○ **SAML users and groups**
SAML users and group or QuickSight ARNs.

○ **External accounts**
AWS accounts or AWS organizations outside of this account.

IAM users and roles
Add one or more IAM users or roles.

Choose IAM principals to add ▼

Permissions

Select the permissions to grant.

○ **Table permissions**
Grant resource-wide permissions.

○ **Column-based permissions**
Grant data access to specific columns.

Table permissions
Choose specific access permissions to grant.

☐ Select   ☐ Insert   ☐ Delete   ☐ Describe   ☐ Alter   ☐ Drop

☐ Super
This permission is the union of the individual permissions above and supercedes them. **Learn More** [↗]

Grantable permissions
Choose the permission that may be granted to others.

☐ Select   ☐ Insert   ☐ Delete   ☐ Describe   ☐ Alter   ☐ Drop

☐ Super
This permission is the union of the individual permissions above and supercedes them. **Learn More** [↗]

Cancel   **Grant**

Figure 9.26 – Administering the Lake Formation catalog

Later in the chapter, using the *Extending a data warehouse using Amazon Redshift Spectrum* recipe, you will learn how to query this data using Amazon Redshift.

How it works...

AWS Lake Formation simplifies the management and configuration of data lakes in a centralized place. AWS Glue's **extract, transform, load** (**ETL**) functionality, leveraging Python and Spark Shell, ML transform enables you to customize workflows to meet your needs. The AWS Glue/Lake Formation catalog integrates with Amazon Redshift for your data warehousing, Amazon Athena for ad hoc analysis, Amazon SageMaker for predictive analysis, and Amazon **Elastic MapReduce** (**EMR**) for big data processing.

Exporting a data lake from Amazon Redshift

Amazon Redshift empowers a lake house architecture, allowing you to query data within the data warehouse and data lake using Amazon Redshift Spectrum and also to export your data back to the data lake on Amazon S3, to be used by other analytical and ML services. You can store data in open file formats in your Amazon S3 data lake when performing the data lake export to integrate with your existing data lake formats.

Getting ready

To complete this recipe, you will need the following to be set up:

- An IAM user with access to Amazon Redshift

- An Amazon Redshift cluster deployed in the eu-west-1 AWS Region with the retail dataset created from *Chapter 3, Loading and Unloading Data,* using the *Loading data from Amazon S3 using COPY* recipe

- Amazon Redshift cluster masteruser credentials

- Access to any SQL interface such as a SQL client or the Amazon Redshift Query Editor

- An AWS account number—we will refer to this in the recipes as [Your-AWS_Account_Id]

- An Amazon S3 bucket created in the eu-west-1 Region—we will refer to this in the recipes as [Your-Amazon_S3_Bucket]

- An IAM role attached to the Amazon Redshift cluster that can access Amazon S3—we will refer to this in the recipes as [Your-Redshift_Role]

How to do it...

In this recipe, we will use the sample dataset created from *Chapter 3, Loading and Unloading Data, t*o write the data back to the Amazon S3 data lake:

1. Connect to the Amazon Redshift cluster using a client tool such as MySQL Workbench.

2. Execute the following analytical query to verify the sample dataset:

```
SELECT c_mktsegment,
       COUNT(o_orderkey) AS orders_count,
       SUM(l_quantity) AS quantity,
       COUNT(DISTINCT P_PARTKEY) AS parts_count,
       COUNT(DISTINCT L_SUPPKEY) AS supplier_count,
       COUNT(DISTINCT o_custkey) AS customer_count
FROM lineitem
  JOIN orders ON l_orderkey = o_orderkey
  JOIN customer c ON o_custkey = c_custkey
  JOIN dwdate
    ON d_date = l_commitdate
    AND d_year = 1992
  JOIN part ON P_PARTKEY = l_PARTKEY
  JOIN supplier ON L_SUPPKEY = S_SUPPKEY
GROUP BY c_mktsegment limit 5;
```

Here's the expected sample output:

```
c_mktsegment | orders_count |    quantity   | parts_count
| supplier_count | customer_count
--------------+--------------+---------------+------------
-+----------------+----------------
  MACHINERY   |        82647 | 2107972.0000 |       75046
|          72439 |       67404
  AUTOMOBILE  |        82692 | 2109248.0000 |       75039
|          72345 |       67306
  HOUSEHOLD   |        82521 | 2112594.0000 |       74879
|          72322 |       67035
  BUILDING    |        83140 | 2115677.0000 |       75357
|          72740 |       67411
  FURNITURE   |        83405 | 2129150.0000 |       75759
|          73048 |       67876
```

3. Create a schema to point to the data lake using the following command, by replacing the [Your-AWS_Account_Id] and [Your-Redshift_Role] values:

```
CREATE external SCHEMA datalake_ext_schema
FROM data catalog DATABASE 'datalake_ext_schema'
iam_role 'arn:aws:iam::[Your-AWS_Account_Id]:role/[Your-Redshift_Role] '
CREATE external DATABASE if not exists;
```

4. Create an external table that will be used to export the dataset:

```
CREATE external TABLE datalake_ext_schema.order_summary
  (c_mktsegment VARCHAR(10),
   orders_count BIGINT,
   quantity numeric(38,4),
   parts_count BIGINT,
   supplier_count BIGINT,
   customer_count BIGINT
   )
STORED
AS
PARQUET LOCATION
's3://[Your-Amazon_S3_Bucket]/order_summary/';
```

> **Note**
>
> You are able to specify the output data format as PARQUET. You can use any of the supported data formats—see https://docs.aws.amazon.com/redshift/latest/dg/c-spectrum-data-files.html for more information.

5. Use the results of the preceding analytical query to export the data into the external table that will be stored in Parquet format in Amazon S3 using the following command:

```
INSERT INTO datalake_ext_schema.order_summary
SELECT c_mktsegment,
       COUNT(o_orderkey) AS orders_count,
```

```
        SUM(l_quantity) AS quantity,
        COUNT(DISTINCT P_PARTKEY) AS parts_count,
        COUNT(DISTINCT L_SUPPKEY) AS supplier_count,
        COUNT(DISTINCT o_custkey) AS customer_count
  FROM lineitem
    JOIN orders ON l_orderkey = o_orderkey
    JOIN customer c ON o_custkey = c_custkey
    JOIN dwdate
      ON d_date = l_commitdate
     AND d_year = 1992
    JOIN part ON P_PARTKEY = l_PARTKEY
    JOIN supplier ON L_SUPPKEY = S_SUPPKEY
  GROUP BY c_mktsegment;
```

6. You can now verify the results of the export using the following command:

```
select * from datalake_ext_schema.order_summary limit 5;
```

Here's the expected sample output:

```
  c_mktsegment | orders_count |    quantity    | parts_count
  | supplier_count | customer_count
  --------------+--------------+---------------+------------
  -+----------------+----------------
  HOUSEHOLD    |        82521 | 2112594.0000 |      74879
  |         72322 |         67035
  MACHINERY    |        82647 | 2107972.0000 |      75046
  |         72439 |         67404
  FURNITURE    |        83405 | 2129150.0000 |      75759
  |         73048 |         67876
  BUILDING     |        83140 | 2115677.0000 |      75357
  |         72740 |         67411
  AUTOMOBILE   |        82692 | 2109248.0000 |      75039
  |         72345 |         67306
```

7. In addition, you are also able to inspect the s3://[Your-Amazon_S3_
    Bucket]/order_summary/ Amazon S3 location for the presence of Parquet
    files, as shown here:

```
$ aws s3 ls s3://[Your-Amazon_S3_Bucket]/order_summary/
```

Here is the expected output:

```
2021-03-02 00:00:11          1588 20210302_000002_331241_258
60550_0002_part_00.parquet
2021-03-02 00:00:11          1628 20210302_000002_331241_258
60550_0013_part_00.parquet
2021-03-02 00:00:11          1581 20210302_000002_331241_258
60550_0016_part_00.parquet
2021-03-02 00:00:11          1581 20210302_000002_331241_258
60550_0020_part_00.parquet
```

The preceding sample output shows a list of all the Parquet files underlying the external table.

Extending a data warehouse using Amazon Redshift Spectrum

Amazon Redshift Spectrum allows Amazon Redshift customers to query data directly from an Amazon S3 data lake. This allows us to combine data warehouse data with data lake data, which makes use of open source file formats such as Parquet, **comma-separated values (CSV)**, Sequence, Avro, and so on. Amazon Redshift Spectrum is a serverless solution, so customers don't have to provision or manage it. It allows customers to perform unified analytics on data in an Amazon Redshift cluster and data in an Amazon S3 data lake, and easily create insights from disparate datasets.

Getting ready

To complete this recipe, you will need the following to be set up:

- An IAM user with access to Amazon Redshift
- An Amazon Redshift cluster deployed in the eu-west-1 AWS Region with the retail dataset created from *Chapter 3, Loading and Unloading Data,* using the *Loading data from Amazon S3 using COPY* recipe
- Amazon Redshift cluster masteruser credentials
- Access to any SQL interface such as a SQL client or the Amazon Redshift Query Editor

- An AWS account number—we will refer to this in the recipes as [Your-AWS_ Account_Id]

- An Amazon S3 bucket created in the eu-west-1 Region—we will refer to this in the recipes as [Your-Amazon_S3_Bucket]

- An IAM role attached to the Amazon Redshift cluster that can access Amazon S3 and AWS Glue—we will refer to this in the recipes as [Your-Redshift_Role]

How to do it...

In this recipe, we will create external table in an external schema, and query data directly from Amazon S3 using Amazon Redshift:

1. Connect to the Amazon Redshift cluster using a client tool such as MySQL Workbench.

2. Execute the following query to create an external schema, by replacing the [Your-AWS_Account_Id] and [Your-Redshift_Role] values:

```
create external schema packt_spectrum
from data catalog
database 'packtspectrumdb'
iam_role 'arn:aws:iam::[Your-AWS_Account_Id]:role/[Your-
Redshift_Role]'
create external database if not exists;
```

3. Execute the following command to copy data from the Packt S3 bucket to your S3 bucket using the following command, by replacing [Your-Amazon_S3_ Bucket]:

```
aws cp s3://packt-redshift-cookbook/spectrum/sales s3://
[Your-Amazon_S3_Bucket]/spectrum/sales --recursive
```

4. Execute the following query to create an external table, by replacing [Your-Amazon_S3_Bucket]:

```
create external table packt_spectrum.sales(
salesid integer,
listid integer,
sellerid integer,
buyerid integer,
eventid integer,
```

```
dateid smallint,
qtysold smallint,
pricepaid decimal(8,2),
commission decimal(8,2),
saletime timestamp)
row format delimited
fields terminated by '\t'
stored as textfile
location 's3://[Your-Amazon_S3_Bucket]/spectrum/sales/'
table properties ('numRows'='172000');
```

5. Execute the following command to query data in S3 directly from Amazon Redshift:

```
select count(*) from packt_spectrum.sales; --
expected sample output -
count
------
172462
```

6. Execute the following command to create a table locally in Amazon Redshift:

```
create table packt_event(
eventid integer not null distkey,
venueid smallint not null,
catid smallint not null,
dateid smallint not null sortkey,
eventname varchar(200),
starttime timestamp);
```

7. Execute the following command to load data in the event table, by replacing the
    [Your-AWS_Account_Id] and [Your-Redshift_Role] values:

```
copy packt_event from 's3://packt-redshift-cookbook/
spectrum/event/allevents_pipe.txt'
iam_role 'arn:aws:iam::[Your-AWS_Account_Id]:role/[Your-
Redshift_Role]
delimiter '|' timeformat 'YYYY-MM-DD HH:MI:SS' Region
'us-east-1';
```

8. Execute the following query to join the data across the Redshift local table and the Spectrum table:

```
SELECT top 10 packt_spectrum.sales.eventid,
       SUM(packt_spectrum.sales.pricepaid)
FROM packt_spectrum.sales,
     packt_event
WHERE packt_spectrum.sales.eventid = packt_event.eventid
AND   packt_spectrum.sales.pricepaid > 30
GROUP BY packt_spectrum.sales.eventid
ORDER BY 2 DESC;
```

Here's the expected output:

```
eventid | sum
--------+---------
    289 | 51846.00
   7895 | 51049.00
   1602 | 50301.00
    851 | 49956.00
   7315 | 49823.00
   6471 | 47997.00
   2118 | 47863.00
    984 | 46780.00
   7851 | 46661.00
   5638 | 46280.00
```

Now, Amazon Redshift is able to join the external and local tables to produce the desired results.

Data sharing across multiple Amazon Redshift clusters

Amazon Redshift RA3 clusters decouple storage and compute, and provide the ability to scale either of them independently. The decoupled storage allows for data to be read by different consumer clusters that allow workload isolation. The data producer cluster controls access to the data that is shared. This feature opens up the possibility to set up a flexible multi-tenant system—for example, within an organization, data produced by a business unit can be shared with any of the different teams such as marketing, finance, data science, and so on that can be independently consumed using their own Amazon Redshift clusters.

Getting ready

To complete this recipe, you will need the following:

- An IAM user with access to Amazon Redshift

- Two separate two-node Amazon Redshift `ra3.xlplus` clusters deployed in the eu-west-1 AWS Region:

    a. The first cluster should be deployed with the retail sample dataset from *Chapter 3, Loading and Unloading Data*. This cluster will be called the Producer Amazon Redshift cluster, where data will be shared from (outbound). Note down the namespace of this cluster—this can be found by running a `SELECT current_namespace` command. Let's say this cluster namespace value is `[Your_Redshift_Producer_Namespace]`.

    b. The second cluster can be an empty cluster. This cluster will be called the Consumer Amazon Redshift cluster, where data will be consumed (inbound). Note down the namespace of this cluster—this can be found by running a `SELECT current_namespace` command. Let's say this cluster namespace value is `[Your_Redshift_Consumer_Namespace]`.

- Access to any SQL interface such as a SQL client or the Amazon Redshift Query Editor

How to do it...

In the recipe, we will use the Producer Amazon Redshift RA3 cluster, with the sample dataset to be shared with the consumer cluster:

1. Connect to the Producer Amazon Redshift cluster using a client tool such as MySQL Workbench.

2. Execute the following analytical query to verify the sample dataset:

```
SELECT DATE_TRUNC('month',l_shipdate),
       SUM(l_quantity) AS quantity
FROM lineitem
WHERE l_shipdate BETWEEN '1992-01-01' AND '1992-06-30'
GROUP BY DATE_TRUNC('month',l_shipdate);


--Sample output dataset
    date_trunc        |      quantity
----------------------+-----------------
 1992-05-01 00:00:00  | 196639390.0000
 1992-06-01 00:00:00  | 190360957.0000
 1992-03-01 00:00:00  | 122122161.0000
 1992-02-01 00:00:00  |  68482319.0000
 1992-04-01 00:00:00  | 166017166.0000
 1992-01-01 00:00:00  |  24426745.0000
```

3. Create a datashare and add the `lineitem` table so that it can be shared with the consumer cluster using the following command, replacing [Your_Redshift_Consumer_Namespace] with `consume cluster namespace`:

```
CREATE DATASHARE SSBDataShare;
ALTER DATASHARE SSBDataShare ADD TABLE lineitem;
GRANT USAGE ON DATASHARE SSBDataShare TO NAMESPACE '
[Your_Redshift_Consumer_Namespace]';
```

4. Execute the following command to verify that data sharing is available:

```
SHOW DATASHARES;
```

Here's the expected output:

```
owner_account,owner_namespace,sharename,shareowner,share_
type,createdate,publicaccess
```

```
123456789012,redshift-cluster-data-share-
1,ssbdatashare,100,outbound,2021-02-26 19:03:16.0,false
```

5. Connect to the Amazon Redshift Consumer cluster using a client tool such as MySQL Workbench. Execute the following command:

```
DESC DATASHARE ssbdatashare OF NAMESPACE [Your_Redshift_
Producer_Namespace];
```

Here's the expected output:

```
producer_account  |           producer_namespace
 | share_type | share_name | object_type |
object_name
-------------------+----------------------------------
-+-----------+-----------+------------+---------------
------------------
 123456789012        | [Your_Redshift_Producer_Namespace]|
INBOUND    | ssbdatashare | table        | public.lineitem
```

6. Create local databases that reference the datashares using the following command:

```
CREATE DATABASE ssb_db FROM DATASHARE ssbdatashare OF
NAMESPACE [Your_Redshift_Producer_Namespace];
```

7. Create an external schema that references the ssb_db datashare database by executing the following command:

```
CREATE EXTERNAL SCHEMA ssb_schema FROM REDSHIFT DATABASE
'ssb_db' SCHEMA 'public';
```

8. Verify the datashare access to the linetime table using a full qualification, as follows:

```
SELECT DATE_TRUNC('month',l_shipdate),
       SUM(l_quantity) AS quantity
FROM ssb_db.public.lineitem
WHERE l_shipdate BETWEEN '1992-01-01' AND '1992-06-30'
GROUP BY DATE_TRUNC('month',l_shipdate);
```

Here's the sample dataset:

```
       date_trunc        |     quantity
-------------------------+-----------------
  1992-05-01 00:00:00    | 196639390.0000
  1992-06-01 00:00:00    | 190360957.0000
  1992-03-01 00:00:00    | 122122161.0000
  1992-02-01 00:00:00    |  68482319.0000
  1992-04-01 00:00:00    | 166017166.0000
  1992-01-01 00:00:00    |  24426745.0000
```

As you can see from the preceding code snippet, the data that is shared by the producer cluster is now is available for querying in the consumer cluster.

How it works...

With Amazon Redshift, you can share data at different levels. These levels include databases, schemas, tables, views (including regular, late-binding, and materialized views), and SQL **user-defined functions** (**UDFs**). You can create multiple datashares for a given database. A datashare can contain objects from multiple schemas in the database on which sharing is created.

By having this flexibility in sharing data, you get fine-grained access control. You can tailor this control for different users and businesses that need access to Amazon Redshift data. Amazon Redshift provides transactional consistency on all producer and consumer clusters and shares up-to-date and consistent views of the data with all consumers. You can also use SVV_DATASHARES, SVV_DATASHARE_CONSUMERS, and SVV_DATASHARE_OBJECTS to view datashares, the objects within the datashares, and the datashare consumers.

Querying operational sources using Federated Query

Amazon Redshift Federated Query enables unified analytics across databases, data warehouses, and data lakes. With the Federated Query feature in Amazon Redshift, you can query live data across from Amazon RDS and Aurora PostgreSQL databases. For example, you might have an up-to-date customer address data that you might want to join with historical order data to enrich your reports—this can be easily joined up using the Federated Query feature.

Getting ready

To complete this recipe, you will need the following:

- An IAM user with access to Amazon Redshift, AWS Secrets Manager, and Amazon RDS.

- An Amazon Redshift cluster deployed in the eu-west-1 AWS Region with the retail sample dataset from *Chapter 3, Loading and Unloading Data*.

- An Amazon Aurora serverless PostgreSQL database. Create an RDS PostgreSQL cluster (see `https://aws.amazon.com/getting-started/hands-on/building-serverless-applications-with-amazon-aurora-serverless/` for more information on this). Launch this in the same **virtual private cloud** (**VPC**) as your Amazon Redshift cluster.

- Access to any SQL interface such as a SQL client or the Amazon Redshift Query Editor.

- An IAM role attached to the Amazon Redshift cluster that can access Amazon RDS—we will refer to this in the recipes as `[Your-Redshift_Role]`.

- An AWS account number—we will refer to this in the recipes as `[Your-AWS_Account_Id]`.

How to do it...

In this recipe, we will use an Amazon Aurora serverless PostgreSQL database as the operational data store to federate with Amazon Redshift:

1. Let's connect to the Aurora PostgreSQL database using a Query Editor. Navigate to the Amazon RDS landing page and choose **Query Editor**.

2. Choose an instance from the **RDS instance** dropdown. Enter a username and a password. For the **Database** field, enter `postgres`, and then select **Connect to database**:

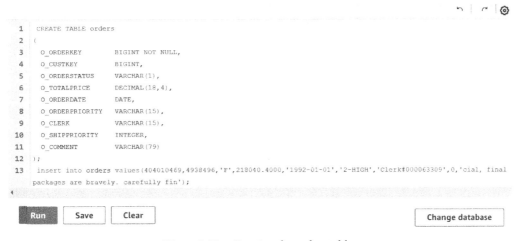

Connect to database   ✕

You need to choose a database and enter the database credentials to use the query editor. We will be storing your credentials and the connection in the AWS Secrets Manager service. Learn more 🗗

Database instance or cluster

rds-2ee55abd   ▼

Database username

postgres   ▼   Delete

Database password

•••••••••

Enter the name of the database

postgres

Cancel   **Connect to database**

Figure 9.27 – Configuring the Amazon Aurora PostgreSQL database

3. Copy and paste the SQL script available at `https://github.com/PacktPublishing/Amazon-Redshift-Cookbook/blob/master/Chapter09/aurora_postgresql_orders_insert.sql` into the editor. Select **Run**:

```
 1   CREATE TABLE orders
 2   (
 3     O_ORDERKEY        BIGINT NOT NULL,
 4     O_CUSTKEY         BIGINT,
 5     O_ORDERSTATUS     VARCHAR(1),
 6     O_TOTALPRICE      DECIMAL(18,4),
 7     O_ORDERDATE       DATE,
 8     O_ORDERPRIORITY   VARCHAR(15),
 9     O_CLERK           VARCHAR(15),
10     O_SHIPPRIORITY    INTEGER,
11     O_COMMENT         VARCHAR(79)
12   );
13   insert into orders values(404010469,4938496,'F',218040.4000,'1992-01-01','2-HIGH','Clerk#000063309',0,'cial, final
     packages are bravely. carefully fin');
```

Run   Save   Clear   Change database

Figure 9.28 – Creating the orders tables

4. We will now create an Aurora PostgreSQL database secret using AWS Secrets Manager to store the user ID and password.

5. Navigate to the AWS Secrets Manager console. Choose **Store a new secret**.

6. Select **Credentials for RDS database**, then enter the username and password. Select your database instance and click **Next**:

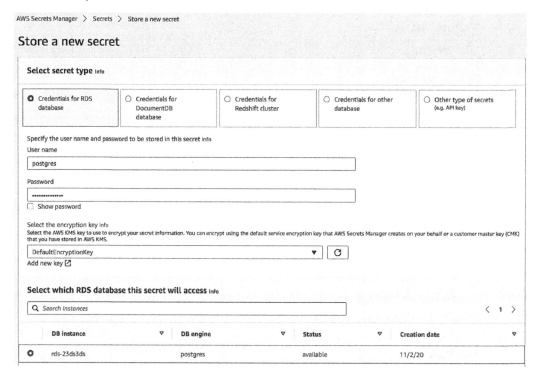

Figure 9.29 – Setting up credentials for RDS

7. Enter the the name of aurora-pg/RedshiftCookbook for the secret. Click **Next**:

Store a new secret

Secret name and description Info

Secret name
Give the secret a name that enables you to find and manage it easily.

> aurora-pg/RedshiftCookbook

Secret name must contain only alphanumeric characters and the characters /_+=.@-

Description - *optional*

> aurora-pg/RedshiftCookbook

Maximum 250 characters

Figure 9.30 – Creating an Aurora PostgreSQL secret

8. Click **Next**, keep the defaults, and choose **Store**.

9. Select the newly created secret and copy the **Amazon Resource Name (ARN)** of the secret:

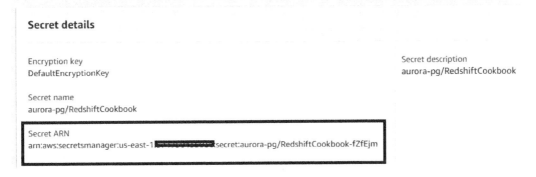

aurora-pg/RedshiftCookbook

Secret details

Encryption key
DefaultEncryptionKey

Secret name
aurora-pg/RedshiftCookbook

Secret ARN
arn:aws:secretsmanager:us-east-1▮▮▮▮▮▮▮▮▮▮secret:aurora-pg/RedshiftCookbook-fZfEjm

Secret description
aurora-pg/RedshiftCookbook

Figure 9.31 – Copying the Secret ARN value for the secret

10. To configure Amazon Redshift to federate with the Aurora PostgreSQL database, we need to attach an inline policy to the IAM role attached to your Amazon Redshift cluster to provide access to the secret created in the preceding steps. For this, navigate to the IAM console and select **Roles**.

11. Search for the correct role. Add the following inline policy. Replace [Your-AWS_Account_Id] with your AWS account number:

```
{
    "Version": "2012-10-17",
    "Statement": [
        {
            "Sid": "AccessSecret",
            "Effect": "Allow",
            "Action": [
                "secretsmanager:GetResourcePolicy",
                "secretsmanager:GetSecretValue",
                "secretsmanager:DescribeSecret",
                "secretsmanager:ListSecretVersionIds"
            ],
            "Resource": "arn:aws:secretsmanager:us-east-1:[Your-AWS_Account_Id]:secret:aurora-pg/RedshiftCookbook"
        },
        {
            "Sid": "VisualEditor1",
            "Effect": "Allow",
            "Action": [
                "secretsmanager:GetRandomPassword",
                "secretsmanager:ListSecrets"
            ],
            "Resource": "*"
        }
    ]
}
```

12. Let's set up Amazon Redshift to federate to the Aurora PostgreSQL database to query the orders' operational data. For this, connect to your Amazon Redshift cluster using an SQL client or the Query Editor from Amazon Redshift console.

13. Create an `ext_postgres` external schema on Amazon Redshift. Replace `[AuroraClusterEndpoint]` with the endpoint of the instance from your account for the Aurora PostgreSQL database. Replace the `[Your-AWS_Account_Id]` and `[Your-Redshift-Role]` values from your account. Also, replace `[AuroraPostgreSQLSecretsManagerARN]` with the value of the secret ARN from *Step 9*:

```
DROP SCHEMA IF EXISTS ext_postgres;
CREATE EXTERNAL SCHEMA ext_postgres
FROM POSTGRES
DATABASE 'postgres'
URI '[AuroraClusterEndpoint]'
IAM_ROLE 'arn:aws:iam::[Your-AWS_Account_Id]:role/[Your-Redshift-Role]'
SECRET_ARN '[AuroraPostgreSQLSecretsManagerARN]';
```

14. To list the external schemas, execute the following query:

```
select *
from svv_external_schemas;
```

15. To list the external schema tables, execute the following query:

```
select *
from svv_external_tables
where schemaname = 'ext_postgres';
```

16. To validate the configuration and setup of Federated Query from Amazon Redshift, let's execute a `count` query for the `orders` table in the Aurora PostgreSQL database:

```
select count(*) from ext_postgres.orders;
```

Here's the expected output:

```
1000
```

17. With Federated Query, you can join the external table with the Amazon Redshift local table:

```
SELECT O_ORDERSTATUS,
       COUNT(o_orderkey) AS orders_count
FROM ext_postgres.orders
  JOIN dwdate
   ON d_date = O_ORDERDATE
  AND d_year = 1992
GROUP BY O_ORDERSTATUS;
```

Here's the expected output:

```
o_orderstatus    orders_count
F                   1000
```

18. You can also create a materialized view using Federated Query. A materialized view will be physicalized on Amazon Redshift. You can refresh the materialized view to get fresher data from your **operational data store** (**ODS**):

```
create materialized view public.live_orders as
SELECT O_ORDERSTATUS,
       COUNT(o_orderkey) AS orders_count
FROM ext_postgres.orders
  JOIN dwdate
   ON d_date = O_ORDERDATE
  AND d_year = 1992
GROUP BY O_ORDERSTATUS;
```

As observed, the materialized view can federate between the Aurora PostgreSQL and Amazon Redshift databases.

10
Extending Redshift's Capabilities

Amazon Redshift allows you to analyze all your data using standard SQL, using your existing business intelligence tools. Organizations are looking for more ways to extract valuable insights from the data, such as big data analytics, **machine learning (ML)** applications, and a range of analytical tools to drive new use cases and business processes. Building an entire solution by sourcing data, transforming data, reporting data, and ML can easily be accomplished by taking advantage of the capabilities provided by AWS' analytical services. With native integrations between the analytical services already built in, you don't have to write any additional code while using these capabilities.

The following recipes will be covered in this chapter:

- Managing Amazon Redshift ML
- Visualizing data using QuickSight
- AppFlow for ingesting SaaS data in Redshift
- Data wrangling using Databrew
- Utilizing ElastiCache for sub-second latency
- Subscribing to third-party data using AWS Data Exchange

Technical requirements

You will need the following technical requirements to complete the recipes in this chapter:

- Access to the AWS Console.

- An AWS Administrator should create an IAM user by following *Recipe 1 – Creating an IAM user*, in the *Appendix*. This IAM user will be used in some of the recipes in this chapter.

- An AWS Administrator should create an IAM role by following *Recipe 3 – Creating an IAM role for an AWS service*, in the *Appendix*. This IAM role will be used in some of the recipes in this chapter.

- An AWS Administrator should deploy the AWS CloudFormation template (`https://github.com/PacktPublishing/Amazon-Redshift-Cookbook/blob/master/Chapter10/chapter_10_CFN.yaml`) and create two IAM policies:

  a. An IAM policy attached to the IAM user, which will give them access to Amazon Redshift, Amazon S3, AWS Glue, AWS Glue DataBrew, AWS IAM, Amazon QuickSight, Amazon SageMaker, AWS Secrets Manager, Amazon CloudWatch, Amazon CloudWatch Logs, AWS CloudFormation, AWS KMS, AWS CloudTrail, Amazon AppFlow, Amazon AppFlow, Amazon ElastiCache, and AWS Data Exchange.

  b. An IAM policy attached to the IAM role, which will allow the Amazon Redshift cluster to access Amazon S3, AWS Glue, and Amazon SageMaker.

- Attach an IAM role to the Amazon Redshift cluster by following *Recipe 4 – Attaching an IAM Role to the Amazon Redshift cluster* in the *Appendix*. Take note of the IAM role's name; we will reference it in the recipes as `[Your-Redshift_Role]`.

- An Amazon Redshift cluster deployed in AWS region eu-west-1.

- Amazon Redshift cluster master user credentials.

- Access to any SQL interface, such as a SQL client or the Amazon Redshift Query Editor.

- An AWS account number. We will reference it in the recipes as `[Your-AWS_Account_Id]`.

- An Amazon S3 bucket created in eu-west-1. We will reference it in the recipes as `[Your-Amazon_S3_Bucket]`.

- The code files that will be used in this chapter can be found in this book's GitHub repository: `https://github.com/PacktPublishing/Amazon-Redshift-Cookbook/tree/master/Chapter10`.

Managing Amazon Redshift ML

Amazon Redshift ML enables Amazon Redshift users to create, deploy, and execute ML models using familiar SQL commands. Amazon Redshift has built-in integration with Amazon SageMaker Autopilot, which chooses the best ML algorithm based on your data using its automatic algorithm selection capabilities. It enables users to run ML algorithms without the need for expert knowledge of ML. On the other hand, ML experts such as data scientists have the flexibility to select algorithms such as XGBoost and specify the hyperparameters and preprocessors. Once the ML model has been deployed in Amazon Redshift, you can run the prediction using SQL at scale. This integration completely simplifies the pipeline, which is required to create, train, and deploy the model for prediction. Amazon Redshift ML allows you to create, deploy, and predict using the data in the data warehouse, as follows:

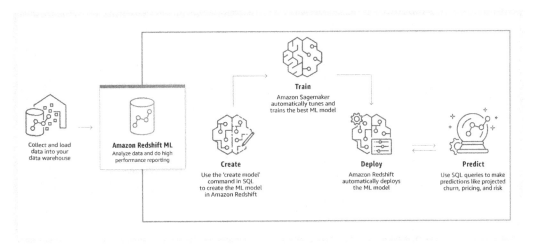

Figure 10.1 – Amazon Redshift ML capabilities

Getting ready

To complete this recipe, you will need the following:

- An IAM user with access to Amazon Redshift, Amazon S3, and Amazon SageMaker.

- An Amazon Redshift cluster deployed in AWS region eu-west-1 with the retail dataset from *Chapter 3, Loading and Unloading Data*.

- Amazon Redshift cluster master user credentials.

- Access to any SQL interface, such as a SQL client or the Amazon Redshift Query Editor.

- An IAM role attached to an Amazon Redshift cluster that can access Amazon S3 and Amazon SageMaker. We will reference it in this recipe as [Your-Redshift_ Role].

- An Amazon S3 bucket created in eu-west-1. We will reference it in this recipe as [Your-Amazon_S3_Bucket].

How to do it...

In this recipe, we will use the product reviews data that we set up in *Chapter 3*, the *Loading and Unloading Data* recipe. We will build the model to predict the star_ rating property of the products table. Let's get started:

1. Open any SQL client tool and execute the following query. This will create the training data to train the model. We will do this by using 50000 records from the apparel product category:

```
create table product_reviews.amazon_reviews
_train as
SELECT  *
FROM product_reviews
    where product_category = 'Apparel'
    limit 50000;
```

2. To create the model, execute the following query. This will use Autopilot to determine the problem type, with a max runtime of 900 seconds. This model will predict our `star_rating`. The CREATE MODEL SQL will run asynchronously. Here, Amazon Redshift will unload the data to the S3 bucket, and AutoPilot will use that dataset to train the model. Once the mode has been trained, the code will be compiled using Amazon SageMaker Neo and will be deployed to the Amazon Redshift cluster. The model can then be accessed using the user-defined `func_product_rating` function:

```
CREATE MODEL product_rating
FROM (
SELECT marketplace
        , customer_id
        , review_id
        , product_id
        , product_parent
        , product_title
        , product_category
        , star_rating
        , helpful_votes
        , total_votes
        , vine
        , verified_purchase
        , review_headline
        , review_body

  FROM product_reviews.amazon_reviews_train
     ) TARGET star_rating
FUNCTION func_product_rating
IAM_ROLE '[Your-Redshift_Role]'
SETTINGS(S3_BUCKET '[Your-Amazon_S3_Bucket]', MAX_RUNTIME
1800, S3_GARBAGE_COLLECT OFF);
```

3. To check the status of the model's creation process, execute the following query. Check if the model's state is **Ready**. When the model's state is **Ready**, it will show a problem type of **MulticlassClassificiation** and an accuracy of **0.62940**:

```
show model product_rating;
```

The preceding query will return an output similar to the following:

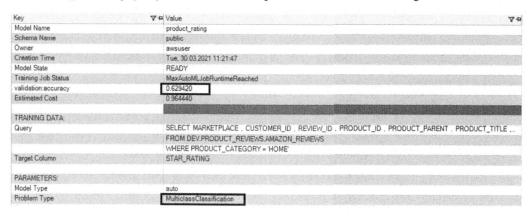

Key	Value
Model Name	product_rating
Schema Name	public
Owner	awsuser
Creation Time	Tue, 30.03.2021 11:21:47
Model State	READY
Training Job Status	MaxAutoMLJobRuntimeReached
validation:accuracy	0.629420
Estimated Cost	0.964440
TRAINING DATA:	
Query	SELECT MARKETPLACE , CUSTOMER_ID , REVIEW_ID , PRODUCT_ID , PRODUCT_PARENT , PRODUCT_TITLE ...
	FROM DEV.PRODUCT_REVIEWS.AMAZON_REVIEWS
	WHERE PRODUCT_CATEGORY = 'HOME'
Target Column	STAR_RATING
PARAMETERS:	
Model Type	auto
Problem Type	MulticlassClassification

Figure 10.2 – Output of the preceding query

4. To predict `start_ratings`, execute the following query to validate the accuracy of the ML model. The user-defined `func_product_rating` function predicts `stars_rating`. Here, we are comparing it to the actual value to determine the accuracy of the model:

```
WITH infer_data
AS (
        SELECT star_rating AS actual
        ,func_product_rating(marketplace
        , customer_id
        , review_id
        , product_id
        , product_parent
        , product_title
        , product_category
        , helpful_votes
        , total_votes
        , vine
        , verified_purchase
```

```
        , review_headline
        , review_body) AS predicted
  ,CASE
  WHEN star_rating = predicted
        THEN 1::INT
  ELSE 0::INT
  END AS correct
        FROM product_reviews.amazon_reviews
        where product_category = 'Home'
          )
          ,aggr_data
  AS (
        SELECT SUM(correct) AS num_correct
                    ,COUNT(*) AS total
        FROM infer_data
          )
  SELECT (num_correct::FLOAT / total::FLOAT) AS accuracy
  FROM aggr_data;
```

The preceding query will return the following output:

```
accuracy
0.627847778989157
```

How it works...

Amazon Redshift simplifies the pipeline to create the models and use the model for prediction using SQL. With Amazon Redshift, you can build models for different use cases, such as the following:

- Customer churn prediction
- Predicting if a sales lead will close
- Fraud detection

Here is an illustration of how Amazon Redshift integrates with Amazon SageMaker:

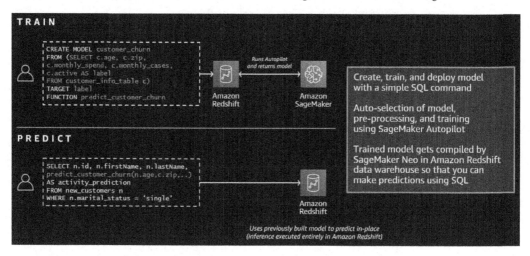

Figure 10.3 – Amazon Redshift and SageMaker integration

In the preceding illustration, the `customer_chrun` prediction model was created using SQL, and Amazon Redshift is communicating with SageMaker to create, train, and deploy the model. Once the model is ready, users can use a SQL query to make predictions for new datasets.

Visualizing data using Amazon QuickSight

Amazon QuickSight is a scalable, serverless, and embeddable ML powered **business intelligence (BI)** service built for the cloud. Visualizing the data warehouse data so that you can use BI tools such as Amazon QuickSight enables users such as business analysts, executive leaders, and more to make data-driven decisions faster. QuickSight dashboards can be accessed from any device and seamlessly embedded into your applications, portals, and websites.

Getting ready

To complete this recipe, you will need to do the following:

- Create an IAM user with access to Amazon Redshift and Amazon QuickSight.

- Create an Amazon Redshift cluster deployed in AWS region eu-west-1 with the retail sample dataset we set up in *Chapter 3*, *Loading and Unloading Data*.

- Create Amazon Redshift cluster master user credentials.

- Sign up for Amazon QuickSight Standard Edition using the instructions at `https://docs.aws.amazon.com/quicksight/latest/user/signing-up.html`.

How to do it...

In this recipe, we will use the product reviews data that we set up in *Chapter 3, Loading and Unloading Data*, and visualize it using Amazon QuickSight. Let's get started:

1. Navigate to QuickSight by going to `https://quicksight.aws.amazon.com/sn/start`. Then, from the menu, choose **Datasets** and click on **New dataset**, as follows:

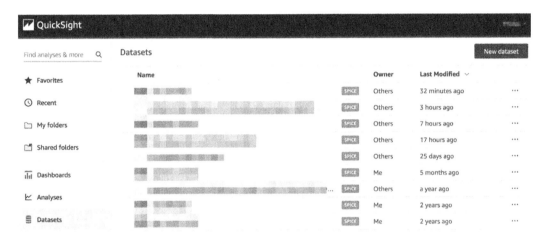

Figure 10.4 – Creating a new dataset source for Amazon QuickSight

2. Choose the **Redshift** (**manual connect**) option from the list of data sources available, as follows:

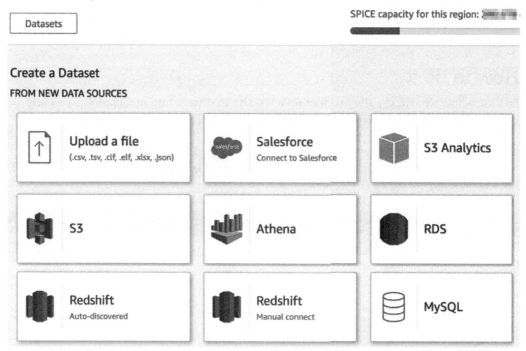

Figure 10.5 – Selecting an Amazon Redshift data source

3. In the New Redshift data source, provide a name such as **Redshift-Visualization** and provide the connection details shown in the following screenshot. Then, connect it to your Amazon Redshift cluster:

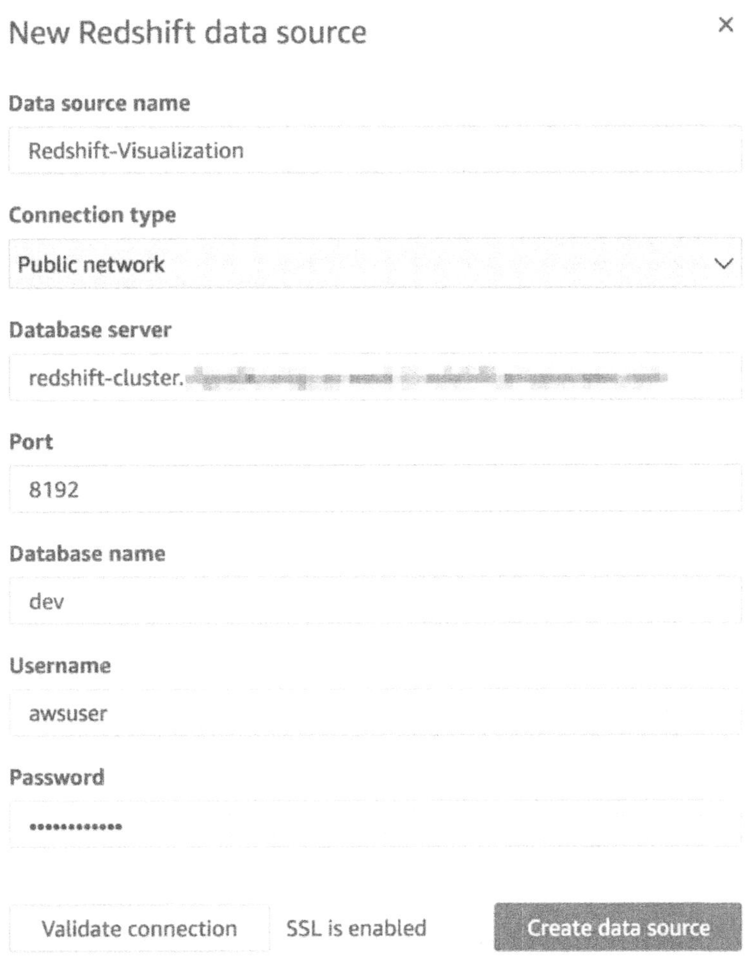

New Redshift data source   ✕

Data source name

Redshift-Visualization

Connection type

Public network   ⌄

Database server

redshift-cluster.

Port

8192

Database name

dev

Username

awsuser

Password

••••••••••••

Validate connection   SSL is enabled   **Create data source**

Figure 10.6 – Setting up an Amazon Redshift data source's connection details

4. Select the schema and pick the `product_reviews` table from the list. Then, press select to create the dataset, as follows:

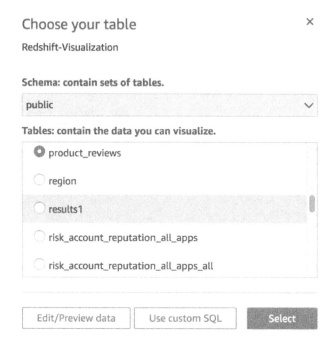

Figure 10.7 – Selecting the table for QuickSight analysis

5. From the QuickSight menu, choose **Analyses** and click on **New analysis**, as shown in the following screenshot. Then, select **Redshift-Visualization**:

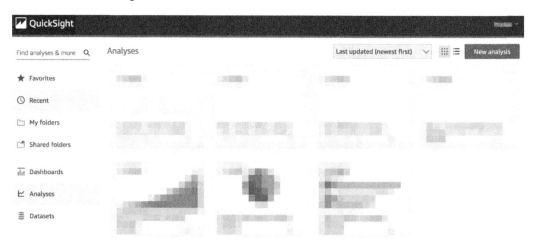

Figure 10.8 – Creating a New analysis using Quicksight

6. QuickSight will import the data and create the visualization, as follows:

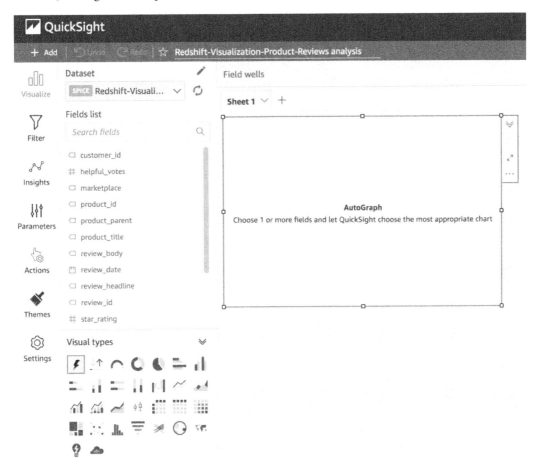

Figure 10.9 – QuickSight visualization creation

7. Click on the **review_date** and **total_votes** columns to create a trend showing the total number of votes on different days, as follows:

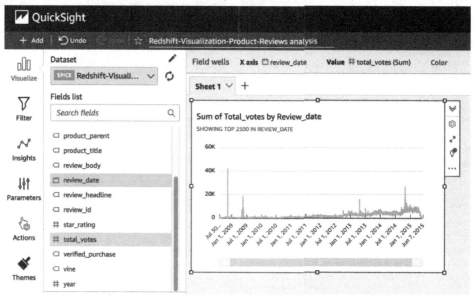

Figure 10.10 – QuickSight visualization using Autograph

How it works...

Amazon QuickSight lets you perform data analysis across several different data sources, such as text and Excel files, SaaS applications such as Salesforce, on-premises databases such as SQL Server, MySQL, and PostgreSQL, and AWS data sources such as Amazon Redshift, Amazon RDS, Amazon Aurora, Amazon Athena, and Amazon S3. QuickSight allows organizations to scale their business analytics capabilities to hundreds of thousands of users, and delivers fast and responsive query performance by using a robust in-memory engine known as **Super-fast Parallel In-memory Calculation Engine** (**SPICE**). You can use several analysis samples, all of which can be found at `https://docs.aws.amazon.com/quicksight/latest/user/getting-started.html`.

AppFlow for ingesting SaaS data in Redshift

Amazon AppFlow provides flexible ways to ingest data from different **Software-as-a-Service** (**SaaS**) applications, such as Salesforce, Zendesk, Slack, ServiceNow, and so on, into AWS services such as Amazon S3 and Amazon Redshift. This fully managed integration service allows you to set up data flows without writing any code. The data workflows also allow you to perform data transformations, such as mapping and filtering, and can be automated using a schedule/event.

Getting ready

To complete this recipe, you will need to do the following:

- Create an IAM user with access to Amazon Redshift and Amazon AppFlow.

- Create an Amazon Redshift cluster deployed in AWS region eu-west-1.

- Create Amazon Redshift cluster master user credentials.

- Gain access to any SQL interface, such as a SQL client or the Amazon Redshift Query Editor.

- Create an IAM role attached to an Amazon Redshift cluster that can access Amazon S3. We will reference it in this recipe as [Your-Redshift_Role].

- An Amazon S3 bucket created in eu-west-1. We will reference it in this recipe as [Your-Amazon_S3_Bucket].

- Create a free Salesforce developer account at https://developer. salesforce.com/form/signup/freetrial.jsp. Take note of the sign in information.

How to do it...

In this recipe, we will set up data ingestion from Salesforce to Amazon Redshift using Amazon AppFlow. Let's get started:

1. Open any SQL client tool and execute the following query to create a table where the salesforce data will be ingested:

```
CREATE SCHEMA salesforce;

CREATE TABLE IF NOT EXISTS salesforce.account
(
id VARCHAR(16383) ENCODE lzo
,isdeleted BOOLEAN ENCODE RAW
,masterrecordid VARCHAR(16383) ENCODE lzo
,name VARCHAR(16383) ENCODE lzo
,"type" VARCHAR(16383) ENCODE lzo
,parentid VARCHAR(16383) ENCODE lzo
,billingstreet VARCHAR(16383) ENCODE lzo
,billingcity VARCHAR(16383) ENCODE lzo
,billingstate VARCHAR(16383) ENCODE lzo
```

```
,billingpostalcode VARCHAR(16383) ENCODE lzo
,billingcountry VARCHAR(16383) ENCODE lzo
,billinglatitude VARCHAR(16383) ENCODE lzo
,billinglongitude VARCHAR(16383) ENCODE lzo
,billinggeocodeaccuracy VARCHAR(16383) ENCODE lzo
,shippingstreet VARCHAR(16383) ENCODE lzo
,shippingcity VARCHAR(16383) ENCODE lzo
,shippingstate VARCHAR(16383) ENCODE lzo
,shippingpostalcode VARCHAR(16383) ENCODE lzo
,shippingcountry VARCHAR(16383) ENCODE lzo
,shippinglatitude VARCHAR(16383) ENCODE lzo
,shippinglongitude VARCHAR(16383) ENCODE lzo
,shippinggeocodeaccuracy VARCHAR(16383) ENCODE lzo
,phone VARCHAR(16383) ENCODE lzo
,fax VARCHAR(16383) ENCODE lzo
,website VARCHAR(16383) ENCODE lzo
,photourl VARCHAR(16383) ENCODE lzo
,industry VARCHAR(16383) ENCODE lzo
,annualrevenue DOUBLE PRECISION ENCODE RAW
,numberofemployees INTEGER ENCODE az64
,description VARCHAR(16383) ENCODE lzo
,ownerid VARCHAR(16383) ENCODE lzo
,createddate VARCHAR(16383) ENCODE lzo
,createdbyid VARCHAR(16383) ENCODE lzo
,lastmodifieddate VARCHAR(16383) ENCODE lzo
,lastmodifiedbyid VARCHAR(16383) ENCODE lzo
,systemmodstamp VARCHAR(16383) ENCODE lzo
,lastactivitydate VARCHAR(16383) ENCODE lzo
,lastvieweddate VARCHAR(16383) ENCODE lzo
,lastreferenceddate VARCHAR(16383) ENCODE lzo
,jigsaw VARCHAR(16383) ENCODE lzo
,jigsawcompanyid VARCHAR(16383) ENCODE lzo
,accountsource VARCHAR(16383) ENCODE lzo
,sicdesc VARCHAR(16383) ENCODE lzo
,partition_0 VARCHAR(16383) ENCODE lzo
)
```

```
DISTSTYLE EVEN
;
```

2. Navigate to the AWS Console and pick the **Amazon AppFlow** service. Then, click **Create flow**, as shown in the following screenshot:

Figure 10.11 – Amazon AppFlow – Create flow

3. Set **Flow name** to `appflow_salesforce_to_redshift` and provide any (optional) **Flow description**, as follows. Then, click **Next**:

Figure 10.12 – Setting up the Flow details for the new flow

4.   For **Source details**, set the source name to **Salesforce** and provide the following details to set up the connection. Provide the necessary SalesForce credentials after clicking **Continue**:

- **Salesforce environment**: **Production**

- **Connection name**: `salesforce-source`:

Figure 10.13 – Setting up the Salesforce connection

5. Choose the **Salesforce objects** option and then **Account** from the **Choose Sales object** dropdown. This will be the source data to be ingested into Amazon Redshift:

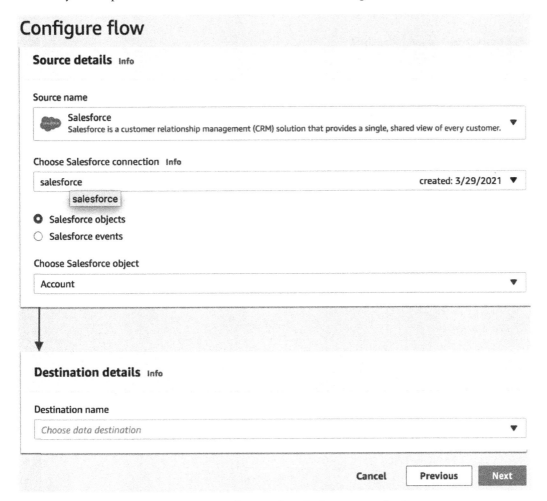

Figure 10.14 – Configuring the Salesforce source details

6. For **Destination details**, select **Amazon Redshift** and click on **Choose Amazon Redshift connection**. Then, select **Create new connection** and provide the following details. Once you've done that, click on **Connect**:

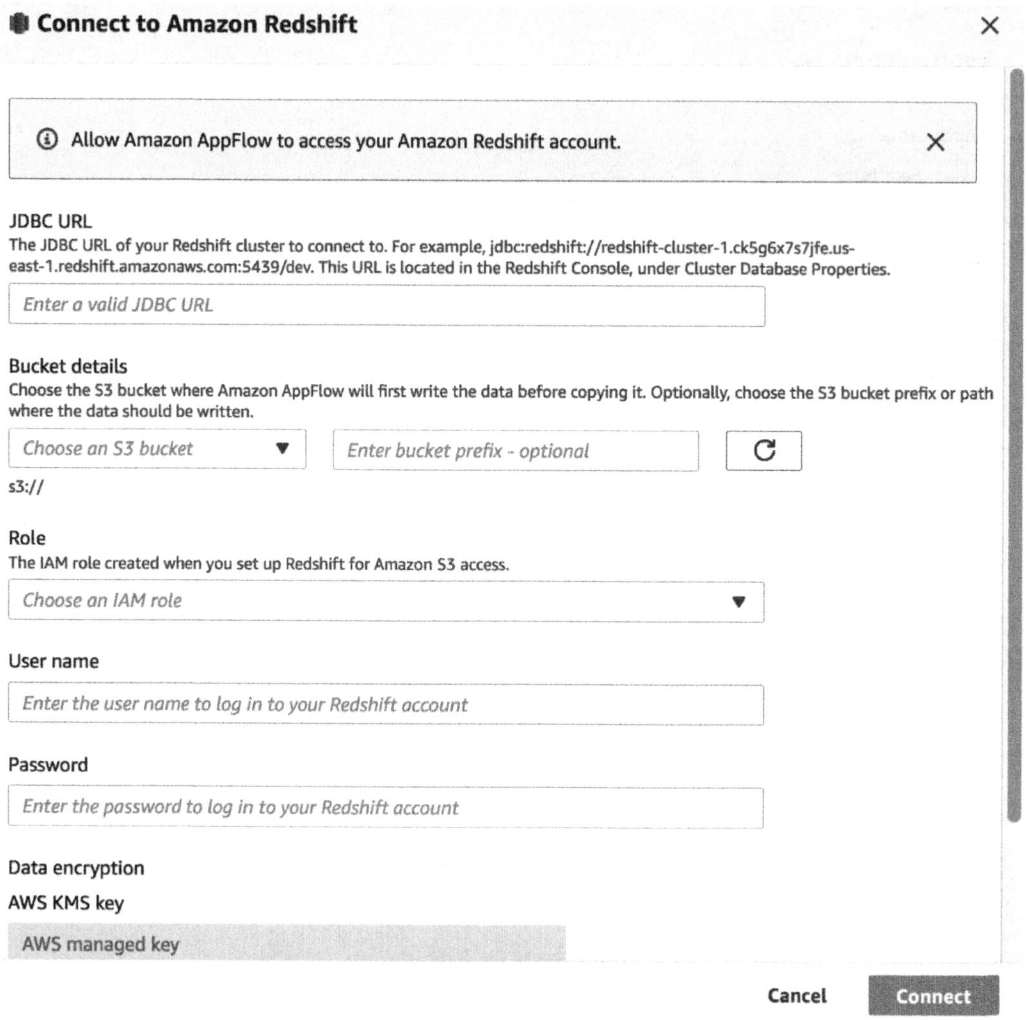

🔋 Connect to Amazon Redshift   ✕

> ⓘ Allow Amazon AppFlow to access your Amazon Redshift account.   ✕

JDBC URL
The JDBC URL of your Redshift cluster to connect to. For example, jdbc:redshift://redshift-cluster-1.ck5g6x7s7jfe.us-east-1.redshift.amazonaws.com:5439/dev. This URL is located in the Redshift Console, under Cluster Database Properties.

> Enter a valid JDBC URL

Bucket details
Choose the S3 bucket where Amazon AppFlow will first write the data before copying it. Optionally, choose the S3 bucket prefix or path where the data should be written.

> Choose an S3 bucket   ▼ | Enter bucket prefix - optional | C

s3://

Role
The IAM role created when you set up Redshift for Amazon S3 access.

> Choose an IAM role   ▼

User name

> Enter the user name to log in to your Redshift account

Password

> Enter the password to log in to your Redshift account

Data encryption

AWS KMS key

> AWS managed key

                                                            Cancel   **Connect**

Figure 10.15 – Setting up the destination as Amazon Redshift

Here are the details of the preceding screenshot:

- **JDBC URL**: Provide the JDBC URL in the format `jdbc:redshift://[RedshiftClusterEndpoint]:[RedshiftClusterPort]/[RedshiftClusterDatabase]`.

- **Bucket Details**: `[Your-Amazon_S3_Bucket]`.

- **Role**: `[Your-Redshift_Role]`.

- **Username**: Redshift username.

- **Password**: Redshift cluster password.

7. In the **Choose Amazon Redshift object** section, select **salesforce**; then, for the **Choose Redshift table** section, select **account**, as follows:

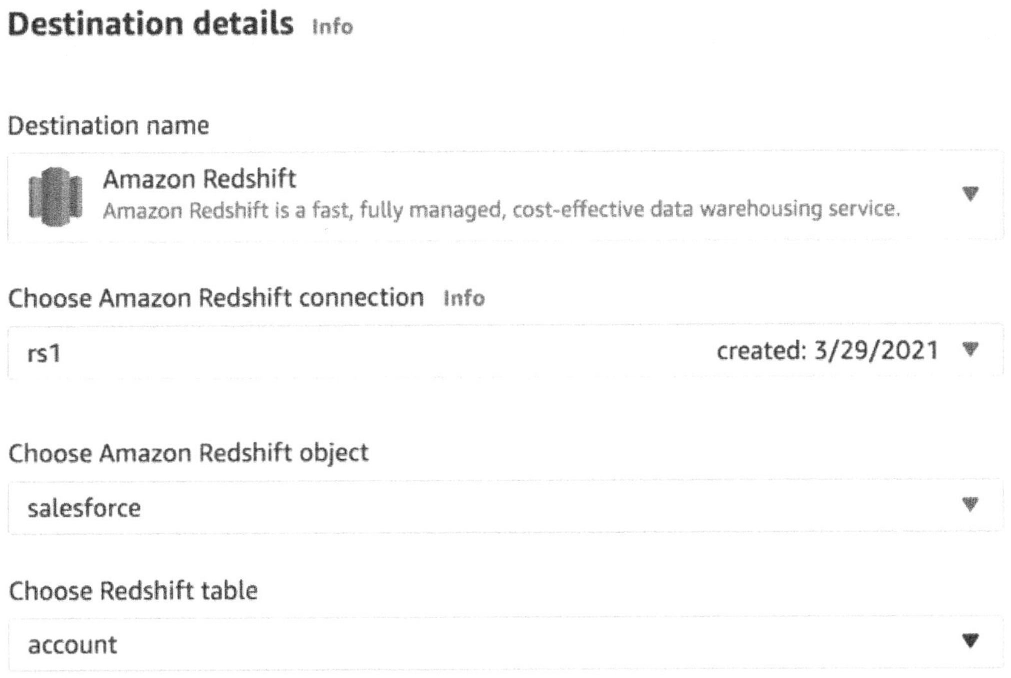

Destination details Info

Destination name

Amazon Redshift
Amazon Redshift is a fast, fully managed, cost-effective data warehousing service. ▼

Choose Amazon Redshift connection   Info

rs1   created: 3/29/2021 ▼

Choose Amazon Redshift object

salesforce   ▼

Choose Redshift table

account   ▼

Figure 10.16 – Setting up the destination as Amazon Redshift

8. Finish creating the workflow by setting **Error handling** to **Stop the current flow run** and **Flow trigger** to **Run on demand**. Then, click **Next**:

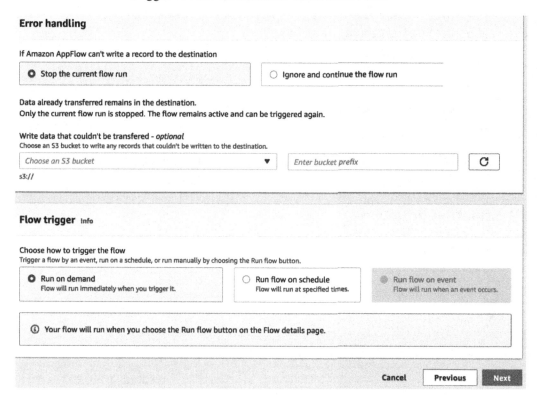

Figure 10.17 – Setting up the flow's error handling and trigger

9. In the **Mapping method** section, choose **Upload a .csv file with mapped fields**. Once you've done that, download the app_flow_mapping.csv file and upload it by clicking **Choose file**. Then, click **Next**:

Figure 10.18 – Setting up the mapping between the source and target

10. Continue with the defaults and review the options you've selected. Then, click **Create flow**. Once the **appflow_salesforce_to_redshift** AppFlow has been created, click on **Run flow**, as follows:

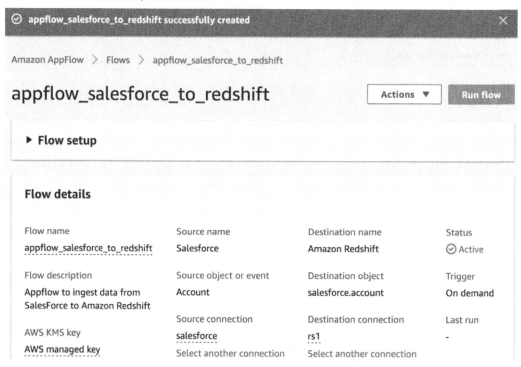

Figure 10.19 – Completing the setup for AppFlow

11. Once the data ingestion process has completed, you will get a notification stating **appflow_salesforce_to_redshift finished running successfully**, as follows:

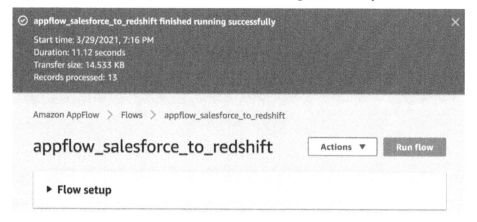

Figure 10.20 – Verifying the completion of AppFlow

12. Open any SQL client tool and execute the following query to verify that the data ingestion process worked:

```
SELECT id,
       TYPE,
       industry,
       annualrevenue,
       createddate,
       phone,
       billingstreet,
       shippingstreet
FROM salesforce.account LIMIT 3;
```

13. Here is the expected output:

```
id,type,industry,annualrevenue,createddate,
phone,billingstreet,shippingstreet
0015Y00002buihLQAQ     2021-03-12T20:47:50.000+0000
0015Y00002dKileQAC     Customer - Channel
Biotechnology     3.0E7   2021-03-12T20:45:57.000+0000
    (650) 867-3450     345 Shoreline Park
Mountain View,  CA 94043
USA     345 Shoreline Park
Mountain View, CA 94043
USA
0015Y00002dKilXQAS    Customer - Channel     Consulting
5.0E7    2021-03-12T20:45:57.000+0000
(785) 241-6200     1301 Hoch Drive
1301 Hoch Drive
```

As you can see, Amazon Redshift is successfully able to query the data from Salesforce using AppFlow.

How it works...

You can use AppFlow to set up secure data flows in minutes, without managing complex connectors or writing code. Here is an overview of how the architecture works. It allows you to easily set up workflows from SaaS applications:

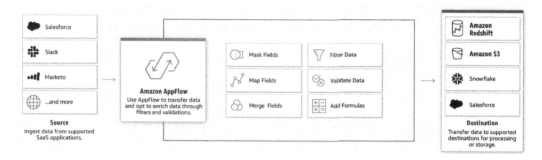

Figure 10.21 – Integrating AppFlow with Amazon Redshift

As shown in the preceding diagram, you can easily integrate data from third-party providers into Amazon Redshift using AppFlow and use SQL to query it conveniently.

Data wrangling using DataBrew

Amazon Redshift data warehouses allow your end users to get new insights from all your data easily. Ensuring data quality remains one of the core tenants for any data warehouse for building trust with your business analysts, data scientists, and more. Further, the decisions that are made due to these datasets are accurate for the intended business outcome. AWS Glue DataBrew is a data preparation tool that makes it easy to clean and normalize data before publishing it to Amazon Redshift.

You can choose from over 250 pre-built transformations to automate data preparation tasks, without the need to write any code. For example, you can de-dupe the dimensional tables using a DataBrew job before loading it into Amazon Redshift; this will ensure data integrity. DataBrew comes with out of the box integration with Amazon Redshift, and data can be prepared with just a few clicks using its visual interface.

Getting ready

To complete this recipe, you will need the following:

- IAM User with access to Amazon Redshift, AWS IAM, and AWS Glue DataBrew.

- An Amazon Redshift cluster deployed in AWS region eu-west-1.

- Amazon Redshift cluster master user credentials.

- Access to any SQL interface, such as a SQL client or the Amazon Redshift Query Editor.

- An IAM role attached to an Amazon Redshift cluster that can access Amazon S3. We will reference it in this recipe as [Your-Redshift_Role].

- An Amazon S3 bucket created in eu-west-1. We will reference it in this recipe as [Your-Amazon_S3_Bucket].

How to do it...

In this recipe, will use the Amazon.com customer product reviews dataset to demonstrate data cleansing and normalization. Please refer to *Chapter 7*, *Performance Optimization*, to learn how to set up the reviews_ext_schema.amazon_product_reviews_parquet table. Let's get started:

1. Open any SQL client tool and execute the following query to verify the presence of the reviews_ext_schema.amazon_product_reviews_parquet table:

```
SELECT verified_purchase,
       SUM(total_votes) total_votes,
       avg(helpful_votes) avg_helpful_votes,
       count(customer_id) total_customers
FROM reviews_ext_schema.amazon_product_reviews_parquet
WHERE review_headline = 'Y'
GROUP BY verified_purchase;
```

Here is the expected output:

```
verified_purchase | total_votes | avg_helpful_votes |
total_customers
-------------------+-------------+-------------------+---
-------------
 Y                 |           5 |                 0 |
4
(1 row)
```

2. Navigate to **AWS Glue DataBrew service** from **AWS Console** and click on **Create project CleanseNormalizeProductReviews**, as follows:

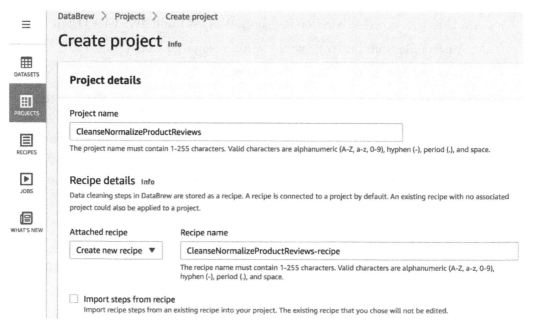

Figure 10.22 – Creating a new DataBrew project

3. Scroll down to **Create project** and click on **New dataset** in the **Select a dataset option** section. Set **Dataset name** to `ProductReviewsCleanse`:

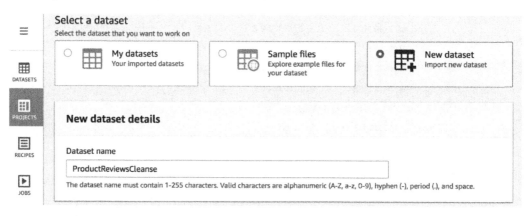

Figure 10.23 – Selecting a new dataset

4. On the **Connect to new dataset** page, locate the `reviews_ext_schema.`
   `amazon_product_reviews_parquet` table in the **All AWS Glue tables**
   section, as follows:

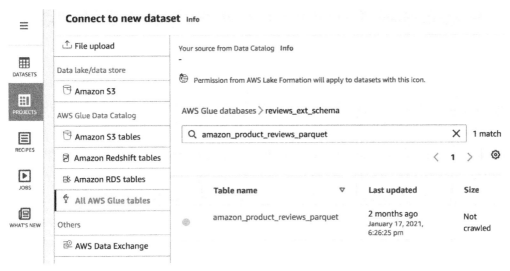

Figure 10.24 – Selecting the product reviews dataset

5. Choose **Create new IAM role** and pick a new IAM role suffix, such as **databrew**.
   Then, click on **Create Project**, as follows:

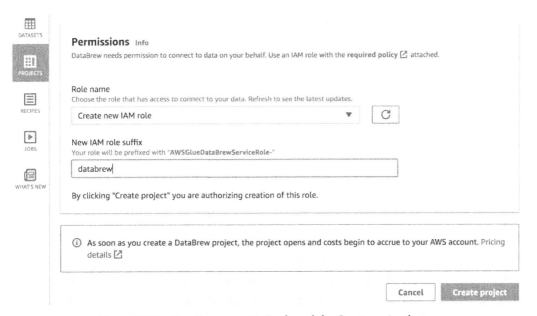

Figure 10.25 – Creating a new IAM role and the Create project button

6. DataBrew will sample the data and provision resources to process the data visually. When it's ready, you will notice a message stating **Created project CleanseNormalizeProductReviews**, as shown in the following screenshot:

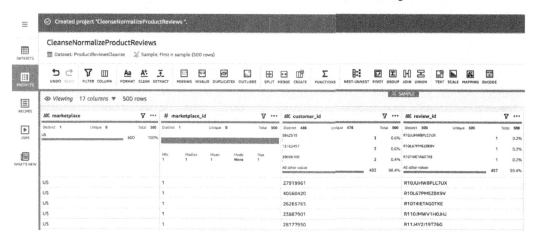

Figure 10.26 – CleanseNormalizeProductReviews is ready for processing

7. Highlight the `review_id` column and click on the **Duplicates** option. Then, set the source column to `review_id` and click on **Apply**, as follows:

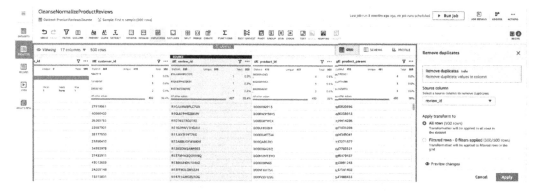

Figure 10.27 – Eliminating duplicates from the dataset

DataBrew will use the `review_id` column to eliminate any duplicates in the data.

8. Highlight the **marketplace** column and click on the **More** option. Pick a mapping for this column with an autogenerated numerical value, as follows:

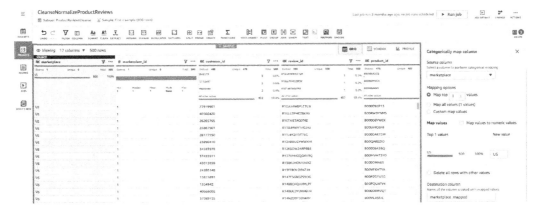

Figure 10.28 – Mapping the marketplace column to an autogenerated ID

9. You can now view a summary of the changes that were made to the data and click on **Create job**:

Figure 10.29 – Verifying the summary of changes that were made to the dataset

10. Set the job name to `CleanseNormalizeReviewDatasetJob`, with the job output file type set to **parquet**, and specify the S3 location (for example, `s3://[Your-Amazon_S3_Bucket]/data/reviews_parquet_databrew`) as the output. Then, click **Create and run job**:

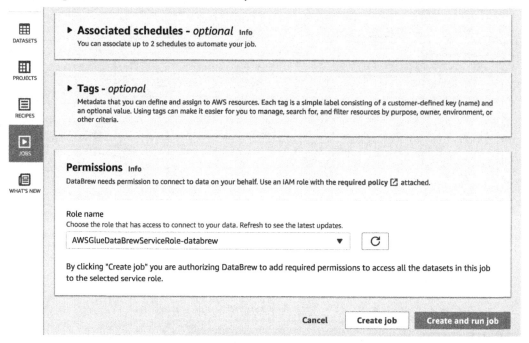

Figure 10.30 – Creating and running a DataBrew job

11. Open any SQL client tool and connect to Amazon Redshift. Then, create an external table using the preceding normalized and cleansed dataset by using the following command:

```
CREATE external TABLE reviews_ext_schema.amazon_product_
reviews_parquet_databrew(
    marketplace varchar(2),
    marketplace_id int,
    customer_id varchar(32),
    review_id varchar(24),
    product_id varchar(24),
    product_parent varchar(32),
    product_title varchar(512),
    star_rating int,
```

```
   helpful_votes int,
   total_votes int,
   vine char(1),
   verified_purchase char(1),
   review_headline varchar(256),
   review_body varchar(max),
   review_date date,
   year int)
stored as parquet
location 's3://[YOUR_S3_LOCATION]/data/reviews_parquet_
databrew';
```

Now, a new, cleaned, and normalized table of the `amazon_product_reviews_parquet_databrew` reviews table is available to your users.

How it works...

DataBrew has over 250 built-in transformations, all of which can be used to combine, pivot, and transpose the data without the need to write any code. AWS Glue DataBrew also automatically recommends transformations such as filtering anomalies; correcting invalid, incorrectly classified, or duplicate data; normalizing data to standard date and time values; and generating aggregates for analyses. DataBrew supports most of the open data formats, such **comma-separated values (.csv)**, JSON and nested JSON, Apache Parquet and nested Apache Parquet, and Excel sheets. With its out-of-the-box data integration, DataBrew can be used to prepare data with an interactive interface. Once you have defined the data transformation, you can create a job using DataBrew that can be executed on a schedule to pre-process the data with a defined frequency. This can then be integrated with your existing **extract, transform, and load** (ETL) pipelines.

Utilizing ElastiCache for sub-second latency

Amazon ElastiCache is a fully managed service that supports both Redis and Memcached in-memory databases. In-memory databases and caches allow you to build near-real-time applications that require sub-millisecond latency. ElastiCache allows you to scale both your write and read capacity for near-real-time applications. In this recipe, we will explore how ElasticCache can serve as a database cache.

Getting ready

To complete this recipe, you will need the following:

- An IAM user with access to Amazon Redshift and Amazon ElastiCache.

- An Amazon Redshift cluster deployed in AWS region eu-west-1 with the retail sample dataset we set up in *Chapter 3, Loading and Unloading Data.*

- Amazon Redshift cluster master user credentials.

- An EC2 Linux instance. Launch this in the same VPC as Amazon Redshift with a security group by providing access to your Amazon Redshift cluster by following the instructions at https://docs.aws.amazon.com/AWSEC2/latest/UserGuide/EC2_GetStarted.html. After creating, the cluster, run the setup and install script provided in this book's GitHub repository. It will be named chapter10.

How to do it...

In this recipe, will use the Amazon.com customer product reviews dataset to demonstrate data caching. Let's get started:

1. Navigate to the Amazon **ElastiCache** dashboard from the AWS console. Select **Subnet Groups** and then **choose Create subnet group**:

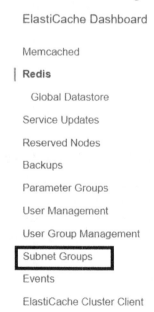

Figure 10.31 – Creating subnet groups in ElastiCache

2. Name the subnet group `cookbook-elc-subgroup`. Select the VPC where you have the Redshift cluster and EC2 instance. Select the subnets from the dropdown and choose **Add**. Then, click **Create**:

Create Subnet Group

To create a new Subnet Group give it a name, description, and select an existing VPC below. Once you select an existing VPC, you will be able to add subnets related to that VPC.

Name*	cookbook-elc-subgroup
Description*	cookbook-elc-subgroup
VPC ID	vpc-0a7fb491598256857

Add Subnet(s) to this Subnet Group. You may add subnets one at a time below or **add all the subnets** related to this VPC. You may make additions/edits after this group is created.

Availability Zone or Outpost Subnet ID	Availability Zone	Subnet ID	CIDR Block	Action
us-east-1a				
subnet-05a3fca6b5	us-east-1a	subnet-05a3fca6b51c0b943	10.0.16.0/20	Remove

Add

Cancel   Create

Figure 10.32 – Configuring the Subnet Group

3. Navigate to the Amazon **ElasticCache** dashboard from the AWS Console. Click on **Redis** and select **Create**:

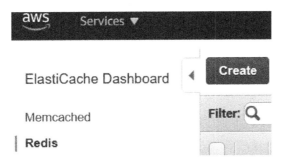

Figure 10.33 – Creating a Redis cluster

4.   For **Cluster engine**, choose **Redis**. For **Location**, choose **Amazon Cloud**:

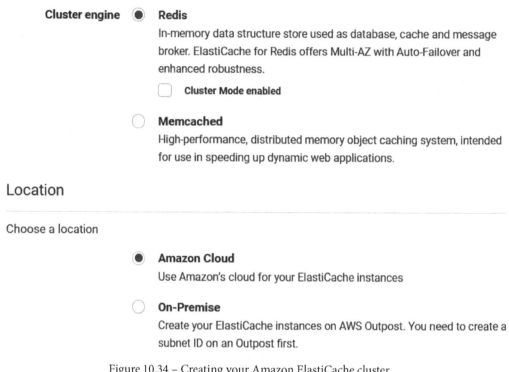

Create your Amazon ElastiCache cluster

Cluster engine ⦿ **Redis**

In-memory data structure store used as database, cache and message broker. ElastiCache for Redis offers Multi-AZ with Auto-Failover and enhanced robustness.

☐ **Cluster Mode enabled**

○ **Memcached**

High-performance, distributed memory object caching system, intended for use in speeding up dynamic web applications.

Location

Choose a location

⦿ **Amazon Cloud**

Use Amazon's cloud for your ElastiCache instances

○ **On-Premise**

Create your ElastiCache instances on AWS Outpost. You need to create a subnet ID on an Outpost first.

Figure 10.34 – Creating your Amazon ElastiCache cluster

5.   Enter `cookbook-elcache` as the name of the cluster. For the description, enter `elastic cache`. For the node type, select **cache.t3.micro**. Deselect **Multi-AZ** and keep the rest of the parameters as-is:

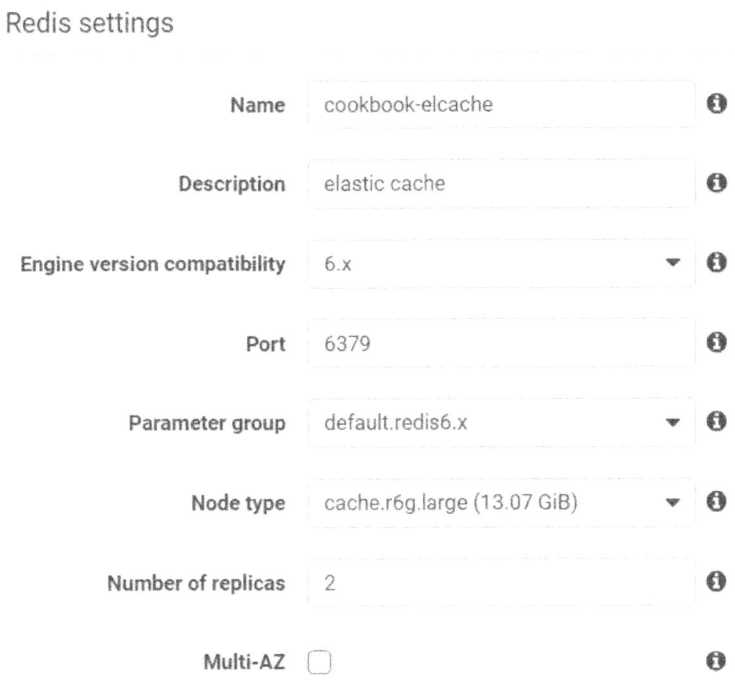

Redis settings

Name	cookbook-elcache
Description	elastic cache
Engine version compatibility	6.x
Port	6379
Parameter group	default.redis6.x
Node type	cache.r6g.large (13.07 GiB)
Number of replicas	2
Multi-AZ	☐

Figure 10.35 – Configuring the Redis settings

6. For **Subnet group**, select the subnet group we created in *step 1*:

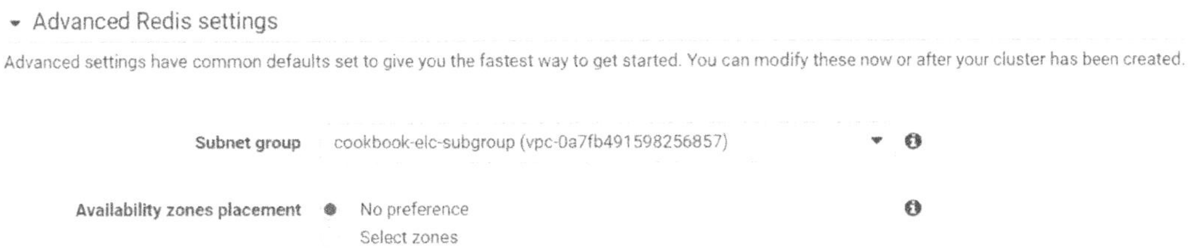

▾ Advanced Redis settings

Advanced settings have common defaults set to give you the fastest way to get started. You can modify these now or after your cluster has been created.

Subnet group	cookbook-elc-subgroup (vpc-0a7fb491598256857)
Availability zones placement	● No preference Select zones

Figure 10.36 – Configuring the subnet groups for the Redis cluster

7. Select a security group, which will allow EC2 to access the Redis cluster:

Figure 10.37 – Configuring EC2 access for the Redis cluster

8. Keep the default settings for the rest of the setup and choose **Create**.

9. Once the cluster has been created, its status will be set to **Read**:

Figure 10.37 – Creating the Redis cache cluster

10. Click on the checkbox next to the cluster's name. This will provide you with details about the cluster. Make a note of the primary endpoint. This endpoint will be used to access the ElasticCache cluster from EC2:

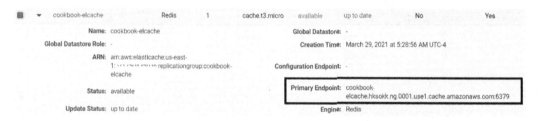

Figure 10.38 – Taking note of the primary endpoint for the Redis cluster

11. Log into your EC2 instance. Execute the following code to change the directory path where you downloaded the cookbook code from GitHub. Locate the `source.dat` file and execute the following:

```
cat source.dat
export REDIS_URL=redis://[redist-cluster-name]:6379/
export DB_HOST=[your-redshift-cluster-endpoint]
export DB_PORT=[redshift-port]
export DB_USER=[redshift-user]
export DB_PASS=[redshift-password]
export DB_NAME=[redshift-database]
```

12. Update the `source.dat` file with the values you captured for the `redis` cluster primary endpoint and the details of the Amazon Redshift cluster noted in the previous step.

13. To validate the connection with the Amazon Redshift cluster, execute the following code and, when prompted, enter your Redshift cluster password:

```
psql -h [your-redshift-cluster-endpoint] -U [redshift-
user] -d [redshift-database] -p [redshift-port]
----------------------on successful connection to Amazon
Redshift you will be brought to the prompt---
psql (9.2.24, server 8.0.2)
WARNING: psql version 9.2, server version 8.0.
         Some psql features might not work.
SSL connection (cipher: ECDHE-RSA-AES256-GCM-SHA384,
bits: 256)
Type "help" for help.
dev=#
```

14. To validate the connection to the `redis` cluster, navigate to the `redis-stable` directory. Execute the following code. After successfully connecting, you will be brought to the prompt:

```
src/redis-cli -c -h [redist-cluster-name] -p 6379
```

15. Navigate to the directory where you downloaded the cookbook source code from GitHub. Review the Python code in `elasticcache_redshift.py`. The script will use the environment variables to connect to Amazon Redshift and the Amazon **ElasticCache** cluster. On executing this code, the first execution of `fetch(sql)` verifies whether the key exists in the cache. If it does not exist, it executes the query against the Amazon Redshift cluster. The result is then stored in the cache as a value that corresponds to the hash key of the SQL. During the second execution of `fetch(sql)`, the result will be returned from the cache for the same SQL:

```python
def fetch(sql):
    """Retrieve records from the cache, or else from
the database."""
    key = hashlib.sha224(sql).hexdigest()
    res = Cache.get(key)

    print(key)
    if res:
        print('returning from cache')
        return json.loads(res)

    res = Database.query(sql)
    print('setting key in the cache')
    Cache.setex(key, TTL, json.dumps(res))
    Database.closecur()
    print('testing the existence of key in cache')
    test(key)
    return res
def test(key):
    print(' ')
    print('--------------------from cache-------------')
    return (Cache.get(key))
```

16. Execute the following code:

```
source source.dat
python elasticcache_redshift.py
401cc7ccb1a2b85f08166e35906b1fa9e312d8c04f7746dd3c3b01b5
setting key in the cache
testing the existence of key in cache
--------------------from cache-------------
[('THREE WOLF MOON SHIRT ADULT SIZE M', 61869L),
('Delicious PhD Darling Costume', 59309L),
('The Mountain Kids 100% Cotton Three Wolf Moon T-Shirt',
42144L), ('The Mountain Three Wolf Moon Short Sleeve
Tee', 26107L), ("Squeem 'Perfect Waist' Contouring
Cincher", 14665L), ("Ann Chery Women's Faja Clasica Waist
Cincher", 9536L), ("Ann Chery Women's Faja Deportiva
Workout Waist Cincher", 8497L), ('F500 American Flag
Pants by Best Form', 7378L), ("MUXXN Women's 1950s Retro
Vintage Cap Sleeve Party Swing Dress", 6728L),
("Levi's Men's 501 Original-Fit Jean", 6619L)]
401cc7ccb1a2b85f08166e35906b1fa9e312d8c04f7746dd3c3b01b5
returning from cache
[[u'THREE WOLF MOON SHIRT ADULT SIZE M', 61869],
[u'Delicious PhD Darling Costume', 59309],
[u'The Mountain Kids 100% Cotton Three Wolf Moon
T-Shirt', 42144], [u'The Mountain Three Wolf Moon Short
Sleeve Tee', 26107], [u"Squeem 'Perfect Waist' Contouring
Cincher", 14665], [u"Ann Chery Women's Faja Clasica Waist
Cincher", 9536], [u"Ann Chery Women's Faja Deportiva
Workout Waist Cincher", 8497], [u'F500 American Flag
Pants by Best Form', 7378], [u"MUXXN Women's 1950s
Retro Vintage Cap Sleeve Party Swing Dress", 6728],
[u"Levi's Men's 501 Original-Fit Jean", 6619]]
```

How it works...

The Amazon ElasticCache Redis cluster caches the `resultset` properties that were returned from Amazon Redshift. On cache miss, the query will be executed from Amazon Redshift; otherwise, it will be served from the cache. This significantly reduces the roundtrips to the Amazon Redshift cluster. The cache in **ElastiCache** will become stale based on the **time to live (TTL)** value:

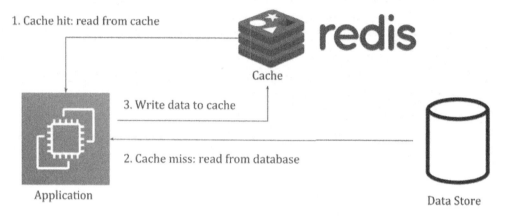

Figure 10.39 – Amazon Redshift integration with the Redis cluster

As we mentioned previously, Amazon Redshift utilizes the Redis-based cache to repeat queries.

Subscribing to third-party data using AWS Data Exchange

AWS Data Exchange makes it easy to find, subscribe to, and use third-party data in the cloud. Once you've subscribed to the data product, AWS Data Exchange can publish data into your own Amazon S3 bucket. You can then use this data for analysis with AWS analytics services, including Amazon Redshift. For example, suppliers, wholesalers, marketers, and data companies can obtain unique codes for every store in the retail trade market to target their products. Qualified data providers include category-leading and up-and-coming brands such as Reuters, Foursquare, TransUnion, Change Healthcare, Virtusa, Pitney Bowes, TP ICAP, Vortexa, IMDb, Epsilon, Enigma, TruFactor, ADP, Dun & Bradstreet, Compagnie Financière Tradition, Verisk, Crux Informatics, TSX Inc., Acxiom, Rearc, and many more.

Getting ready

To complete this recipe, you will need the following:

- An IAM user with access to Amazon Redshift and AWS Data Exchange.

- An Amazon Redshift cluster deployed in AWS region eu-west-1.

- Amazon Redshift cluster master user credentials.

- Access to any SQL interface, such as a SQL client or the Amazon Redshift Query Editor.

- An IAM role attached to an Amazon Redshift cluster that can access Amazon S3. We will reference it in this recipe as [Your-Redshift_Role].

- An Amazon S3 bucket created in eu-west-1. We will reference it in this recipe as [Your-Amazon_S3_Bucket].

For this recipe, we will subscribe to the free trial dataset Coronavirus (COVID-19) Data Hub from Amazon Data Exchange.

How to do it...

In this recipe, we will subscribe to the free trial **Coronavirus (COVID-19)** Data Hub from Amazon Data Exchange and access it through Amazon Redshift for analytics. Let's get started:

1. Navigate to AWS Data Exchange through the AWS Console and click on **Explore available data products**. Then, search for **Coronavirus (COVID-19) Data Hub** and subscribe to the $0 for the 1 month option:

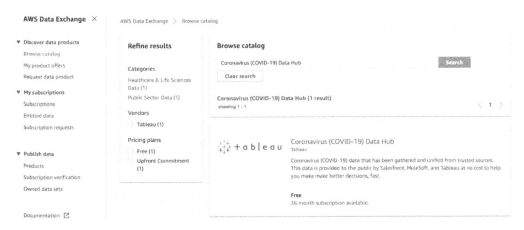

Figure 10.40 – AWS Data Exchange – browsing the published datasets

2. Navigate to **My subscriptions** and click on **Entitled data**. Then, select the latest version of the data:

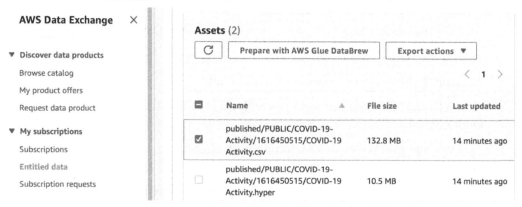

Figure 10.41 – Selecting .csv entitled data from the AWS Data Exchange

3. Click on **Export actions**. Select the `Amazon S3 bucket` folder and pick `s3://[Your-Amazon_S3_Bucket]/data/covid/ location`, as follows:

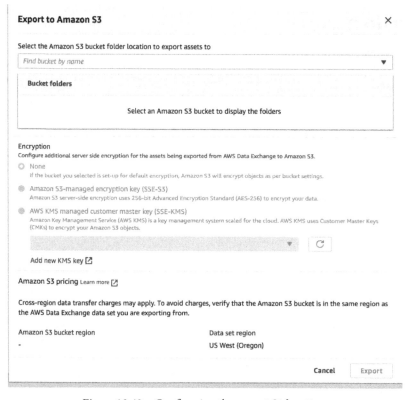

Figure 10.42 – Configuring the export S3 location

4. AWS Data Exchange will be published in `[Your-Amazon_S3_Bucket]`. You can verify this by navigating to the AWS S3 console, as follows:

Figure 10.43 – Selecting the AWS Data Exchange data for analysis

5. Open any SQL client tool and execute the following query to create an external table that will point to the Data Exchange COVID-19 dataset:

```
CREATE EXTERNAL TABLE reviews_ext_schema.covid_data(
   people_positive_cases_count bigint
,  county_name varchar
,  province_state_name varchar
,  report_date varchar
,  continent_name varchar
,  data_source_name varchar
,  people_death_new_count bigint
,  county_fips_number bigint
,  country_alpha_3_code varchar
,  country_short_name varchar
,  country_alpha_2_code varchar
,  people_positive_new_cases_count bigint
,  people_death_count bigint
)
ROW FORMAT SERDE 'org.apache.hadoop.hive.serde2.lazy.
LazySimpleSerDe'
WITH SERDEPROPERTIES ( 'field.delim'=',')
```

```
STORED AS INPUTFORMAT 'org.apache.hadoop.mapred.
TextInputFormat'
```

```
OUTPUTFORMAT 'org.apache.hadoop.hive.ql.io.
HiveIgnoreKeyTextOutputFormat'
```

```
LOCATION 's3://[Your-Amazon_S3_Bucket]/published/PUBLIC/
COVID-19-Activity/1616436115/COVID-19 Activity.csv'
```

```
;
```

6. Execute the following query to access the published COVID-19 dataset to verify it:

```
select people_positive_cases_count,county_
name,province_state_name,report_date from demo_bigdata.
covidanalyzepublished1 limit 10;
```

Here's the expected output:

```
people_positive_cases_count | county_name | province_
state_name | report_date

-------------------------------+-------------+--------------
---------+----

                          72 | King George | Virginia
   | 2020-06-05

                          88 | King George | Virginia
   | 2020-06-15

                           0 | King George | Virginia
   | 2020-03-13

                         829 | King George | Virginia
   | 2021-01-10

                         749 | King George | Virginia
   | 2021-01-01

                         736 | King George | Virginia
   | 2020-12-31

                         227 | King George | Virginia
   | 2020-09-22

                         225 | King George | Virginia
   | 2020-09-16

                         257 | King George | Virginia
   | 2020-10-15
```

As you can see, you can query third-party provided data using Amazon Redshift easily.

How it works...

AWS Data Exchange allows data subscribers to easily browse the vast catalog of published datasets and subscribe to them. This allows subscribers to access datasets and export them to Amazon S3. They can be then loaded into services such as Amazon Redshift for analysis.

Appendix

Recipe 1 – Creating an IAM user

You can use the following steps to create an IAM user:

1. Navigate to the IAM console.

2. Select **Users** and then choose **Add user**.

3. Type a username for the new user. IAM usernames need to be unique in a single AWS account. This username will be used by the user to sign in to the AWS console.

4. For the access type, select both **Programmatic access** and **AWS Management Console access**:

   - **Programmatic access** grants users access through the API, AWS CLI, or tools for Windows PowerShell. An access key and secret key are created for the user and are available to download on the final page.

   - **AWS Management Console access** grants users access through the AWS Management Console. A password is created for the user and is available to download on the final page.

5. For **Console password**, choose one of the following:

   - **Autogenerated password**: This will randomly generate a password for the user that meets the account password policy in effect.

   - **Custom password**: You can type a password that satisfies the account password policy in effect.

   - (Optional) You can select **Require password reset** to ensure that users are forced to change their password when they log in for the first time.

6. Select **Next: Permissions**.

7. Skip the **Set permissions** page and select **Next: Tags**.

8. Select **Next:Review**, and then select **Create user**.

9. This will generate the user's access keys (access key IDs and secret access keys) and password. Download the generated credentials by selecting **Download .csv** and then save the file to a safe location.

10. Share the credentials with users who need to access AWS services. This is an empty IAM user with no access to any AWS services. The AWS administrator will need to execute the CloudFormation template based on the relevant chapter to allow the appropriate access.

Recipe 2 – Storing database credentials using Amazon Secrets Manager

You can use the following steps to create an IAM user:

1. To create the secrets, navigate to the AWS Secrets Manager dashboard at `https://console.aws.amazon.com/secretsmanager/`.

2. Choose **Store a new secret**.

3. Then, choose **Credentials for Redshift Cluster**.

4. Specify the username and password.

5. Set the encryption key to `DefaultEncryptionKey`.

6. Select the Redshift cluster from the list that this secret will access, and click **Next**.

7. Specify the name for the secrets, keep the defaults, and click **Next**.

8. Keep the defaults for the **configure automatic rotation**, and click **Next**.

9. Review and choose **Store**.

10. Capture the secret store ARN.

Recipe 3 – Creating an IAM role for an AWS service

You can use the following steps to create an IAM user:

1. Navigate to the IAM console.

2. Select **Roles**, and then choose **Create role**.

3. For **Select type of trusted entity**, choose **AWS service**.

4. For **Choose a use case**, select **Redshift**.

5. For **Select your use case**, choose **Redshift – Customizable** (allows a Redshift cluster to call AWS services on your behalf). Click **Next: Permissions**.

6. Skip **Create Policy**, click **Next: Tags**, then click **Next: Review**.

7. Provide a role name and click **Create role**. Note the role name to attach it to the Amazon Redshift cluster.

Recipe 4 – Attaching an IAM role to the Amazon Redshift cluster

You can use the following steps to attach the IAM role to the Amazon Redshift cluster:

1. Navigate to the Redshift console.

2. Select **CLUSTERS** in the left navigation pane.

3. Select the checkbox beside the Amazon Redshift cluster and select **Actions**. From the dropdown, select **Manage IAM roles** under **Permissions**:

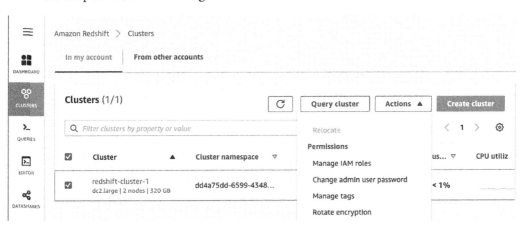

Figure A.1 – Managing the IAM role for the Amazon Redshift cluster

4. In the **Manage IAM roles** section, select the correct IAM role from the dropdown and click on **Associate IAM role**. Click on **Save changes**.

Packt.com

Subscribe to our online digital library for full access to over 7,000 books and videos, as well as industry leading tools to help you plan your personal development and advance your career. For more information, please visit our website.

Why subscribe?

- Spend less time learning and more time coding with practical eBooks and Videos from over 4,000 industry professionals

- Improve your learning with Skill Plans built especially for you

- Get a free eBook or video every month

- Fully searchable for easy access to vital information

- Copy and paste, print, and bookmark content

Did you know that Packt offers eBook versions of every book published, with PDF and ePub files available? You can upgrade to the eBook version at packt.com and as a print book customer, you are entitled to a discount on the eBook copy. Get in touch with us at customercare@packtpub.com for more details.

At www.packt.com, you can also read a collection of free technical articles, sign up for a range of free newsletters, and receive exclusive discounts and offers on Packt books and eBooks.

Other Books You May Enjoy

If you enjoyed this book, you may be interested in these other books by Packt:

Azure Data Factory Cookbook

Dmitry Anoshin, Dmitry Foshin, Roman Storchak, Xenia Ireton

ISBN: 978-1-80056-529-6

- Create an orchestration and transformation job in ADF

- Develop, execute, and monitor data flows using Azure Synapse

- Create big data pipelines using Azure Data Lake and ADF

- Build a machine learning app with Apache Spark and ADF

- Migrate on-premises SSIS jobs to ADF

- Integrate ADF with commonly used Azure services such as Azure ML, Azure Logic Apps, and Azure Functions

- Run big data compute jobs within HDInsight and Azure Databricks

Snowflake Cookbook

Hamid Qureshi, Hammad Sharif

ISBN: 978-1-80056-061-1

- Get to grips with data warehousing techniques aligned with Snowflake's cloud architecture
- Broaden your skills as a data warehouse designer to cover the Snowflake ecosystem
- Transfer skills from on-premise data warehousing to the Snowflake cloud analytics platform
- Optimize performance and costs associated with a Snowflake solution
- Stage data on object stores and load it into Snowflake
- Secure data and share it efficiently for access

Packt is searching for authors like you

If you're interested in becoming an author for Packt, please visit `authors.packtpub.com` and apply today. We have worked with thousands of developers and tech professionals, just like you, to help them share their insight with the global tech community. You can make a general application, apply for a specific hot topic that we are recruiting an author for, or submit your own idea.

Share Your Thoughts

Now you've finished *Amazon Redshift Cookbook*, we'd love to hear your thoughts! Scan the QR code below to go straight to the Amazon review page for this book and share your feedback or leave a review on the site that you purchased it from.

https://packt.link/r/1800569688

Your review is important to us and the tech community and will help us make sure we're delivering excellent quality content.

Index

C

U

V

W

Made in the USA
Monee, IL
25 October 2021